G000022153

CURRICULUM

DISTRICT STORIES OF
A PATH TO IMPROVED ACHIEVEMENT

EDUCATION IN A COMPETITIVE AND GLOBALIZING WORLD

Additional books in this series can be found on Nova's website
under the Series tab.

Additional e-books in this series can be found on Nova's website
under the e-book tab.

CURRICULUM

DISTRICT STORIES OF
A PATH TO IMPROVED ACHIEVEMENT

DAVID A. SQUIRES
EDITOR

n**o**va
publishers
New York

Copyright © 2014 by Nova Science Publishers, Inc.

All rights reserved. No part of this book may be reproduced, stored in a retrieval system or transmitted in any form or by any means: electronic, electrostatic, magnetic, tape, mechanical photocopying, recording or otherwise without the written permission of the Publisher.

For permission to use material from this book please contact us:
Telephone 631-231-7269; Fax 631-231-8175
Web Site: http://www.novapublishers.com

NOTICE TO THE READER

The Publisher has taken reasonable care in the preparation of this book, but makes no expressed or implied warranty of any kind and assumes no responsibility for any errors or omissions. No liability is assumed for incidental or consequential damages in connection with or arising out of information contained in this book. The Publisher shall not be liable for any special, consequential, or exemplary damages resulting, in whole or in part, from the readers' use of, or reliance upon, this material. Any parts of this book based on government reports are so indicated and copyright is claimed for those parts to the extent applicable to compilations of such works.

Independent verification should be sought for any data, advice or recommendations contained in this book. In addition, no responsibility is assumed by the publisher for any injury and/or damage to persons or property arising from any methods, products, instructions, ideas or otherwise contained in this publication.

This publication is designed to provide accurate and authoritative information with regard to the subject matter covered herein. It is sold with the clear understanding that the Publisher is not engaged in rendering legal or any other professional services. If legal or any other expert assistance is required, the services of a competent person should be sought. FROM A DECLARATION OF PARTICIPANTS JOINTLY ADOPTED BY A COMMITTEE OF THE AMERICAN BAR ASSOCIATION AND A COMMITTEE OF PUBLISHERS.

Additional color graphics may be available in the e-book version of this book.

Library of Congress Cataloging-in-Publication Data

Curriculum : district stories of a path to improved achievement / David A. Squires, editor.
      pages cm.
   Includes index.
   ISBN 978-1-62948-673-4 (hardcover)
   1. Curriculum planning--United States--Case studies. 2. Education--Standards--United States--Case studies. 3. Teacher participation in curriculum planning--United States--Case studies. 4. School districts--United States--Case studies. 5. Educational accountability--United States--Case studies. I. Squires, David A.
   LB2806.15C838 2014
   375'.001--dc23
                              2013045171

Published by Nova Science Publishers, Inc. † New York

CONTENTS

ACKNOWLEDGMENTS

A book's author stands on many shoulders.

Many thanks are due the teachers and administrators from the many districts who implemented the Balanced Curriculum process and saw achievement gains. Their skill in developing the curriculum and ensuring implementation shows that a curriculum that accounts for alignment improves achievement.

To the many authors whose work is cited in this book, thanks for your efforts in helping to develop a chorus of studies that show the power of curriculum to affect achievement.

To my wife, Maureen, and daughter, Allison, for their many hours of work in reading and commenting on the manuscript. Your love has seen me through this and many other projects.

To two dear friends who also critiqued early versions: Dr. Jim McConnell and Dr. David Champagne. Your care and your comments inspired further work on my part.

INTRODUCTION TO PART ONE: CHAPTERS 1 AND 2

In Part I, readers are introduced to the books central concepts, represented by the acronym "ASIA": alignment, structure of the curriculum, implementation and assessment. These themes emerged from the Districts who used curriculum as the central framework for district improvement and improved student achievement. In the second chapter the Balanced Curriculum, one curriculum model that produces improved achievement, is described and then used to illustrate the ASIA components.

In: Curriculum
Editor: David A. Squires

ISBN: 978-1-62948-673-4
© 2014 Nova Science Publishers, Inc.

Chapter 1

INTRODUCTION AND BOOK SUMMARY

INTRODUCTION

This chapter introduces curriculum as a framework for increasing scores in district school
s and introduces the contents of the book. Curriculum conjures up moldy three ring binders,
filled with ignored suggestions to teachers about how and what to teach. Often these binders
have been produced in the distant past by well-meaning teachers, but because no one is
accountable for the curriculum, the curriculum quickly fell into "a black hole" where teachers
store important documents they never use. Newer national standards and assessment
specifications haven't been incorporated into the curriculum because the district has faced a
tough and continuing financial crisis, so monies for curriculum development have been
severely curtailed. Besides, our students are doing fairly well on the current state tests, so
what's the big deal? There are new national standards which will become the framework for
new national tests. But, the tests are years off; no use paying attention to them now. I am a
busy person and don't have time to pay attention to things that don't matter. Talk to most
school people and they will give you a similar answer.

THE ASIA FRAMEWORK – AN OVERVIEW

Curriculum can be a road to school and district improvement. This book sets out to
debunk the myth that curriculum doesn't make a difference in student achievement. We
present data from at least fifteen districts across the country that has used curriculum
development as a central focus of their improvement schemes. But their curriculum
development has four important components, common across the districts and schools in our
sample and represented by the acronym ASIA, for Alignment, Structure of the Curriculum
and Stability, Implementation and Infrastructure, and Assessment. Curriculum developed with
these four areas in mind, can, and have, improved student achievement.

- Alignment – These districts have aligned their curriculum to current state
  standards and assessment specifications. They have taken seriously the

assistance from states to help define what all students should know and be able
do to.

- Structure of the Curriculum – The curriculum's structure spells out clearly what
  needs to be taught and puts limits on teachers to decide what and how to teach,
  while ensuring consistent outcomes across teachers. Stability – In districts where
  curriculum was a framework for improving student achievement, the
  superintendents of this district were in power for over four years, at a minimum.
- Implementation and Infrastructure – These school s and districts have
  coordinated efforts across their districts to put infrastructure in place to insure
  the curriculum is taught by all teachers. There are management systems in place
  so that building administrators know who is implementing the curriculum and
  who isn't.
- Assessment – Assessment is a powerful tool to know whether the curriculum is
  being taught by relying on assessment data on student performance, not teacher's
  impressions. This involves more than looking at the yearly tests, although that is
  important. It means that each curriculum is assessed in a consistent fashion
  during the year and the results are given back to teachers so they can modify
  their instruction to fully meet students' needs.

Take the first letter of each of these categories to make the acronym "ASIA ". The
problem is as big as ASIA. But the problem of student achievement can be solved, as
demonstrated by the districts highlighted in this book, by paying attention to curriculum
incorporating the ASIA framework. Districts highlighted in this book that have done so have
reliably increased their student achievement more than the state averages.

QUICK CRITIQUES OF
EXISTING CURRICULUM DEVELOPMENT MODELS

As most readers have never experienced a curriculum that could make such a difference
in student achievement, we understand your skepticism. Indeed, popular curriculum
development systems don't contain many of the ASIA specifications. Understanding by
Design (UBD) (Wiggins and McTigh, 2005) doesn't have a management system, and doesn't
deal with alignment; UBD does do a good job with assessment, the cornerstone of the system,
but has little research to show its effectiveness in improving achievement.

Lynn Erickson's "Concept-Based Curriculum" (Erickson, L., 2001) also does not deal
with alignment or have a management system. The assessment structure is weaker than UBD.
And there is little evidence that the system can improve achievement.

Curriculum Mapping, (Jacobs, H.H., 2004) also lacks alignment and a management
system. Generally, teachers are asked to summarize the curriculum that they teach by months.
This is easily done, which may account for Curriculum Mapping's popularity, but the hard
work occurs after this when districts, or teacher committees, are supposed to integrate the
maps into one map that everyone will follow. Districts have a hard time completing this step,
perhaps because teachers become more invested in their "curriculum structure" because it is

now written down, and are not able to compromise, usually because the district doesn't have the infrastructure in place to push the compromise. So the easy first steps rarely produce a final curriculum product. Like the other systems, it lacks alignment, the infrastructure of a management system, and assessments.

The Parallel Curriculum (Tomlinson et al., 2002) proposes four ways of looking a curriculum: 1). The Core of Basic Curriculum, 2). The Curriculum of Connections, 3). The Curriculum of Practice, and 4). The Curriculum of Identity. Districts are to construct their curriculum by establishing the Core Curriculum and modifying it as needed with the other three types of curriculum. While sophisticated in concept, details of alignment, the management system and assessments are not treated in-depth, so there is little guidance for districts to use. Further, there is no outcome data given with this curriculum system, so we don't know whether people who have adopted the approach have gotten improved achievement.

This book seeks to break with the past curriculum development strategies that have not produced improved achievement. We looked for districts that have used curriculum as a means of improving achievement, and figured out the commonalities between them as one way to solve the problem of improving student achievement. The above curriculum development systems currently lack components that are important in these improving districts; mainly, alignment, the infrastructure of management systems, and to some extent, assessment (with the exception of UBD). We believe that curriculum development needs to enter a new age where systems take into account user experience in the field and produces improved achievement. The systems that have done that have in common the ASIA frameworks: Alignment, Structure of the Curriculum and Stability, Implementation and Infrastructure and Assessment. If you are interested in how successful school s approached curriculum and have gotten improved achievement, then this book is for you.

STRUCTURE OF THE BOOK

The book is divided into four parts. The first part includes the first two chapters; the first chapter summarizes the book's focus and introduces the ASIA framework. The second chapter is about the Balanced Curriculum, a curriculum development model that has produced improved achievement in every district that followed its curriculum development guidelines and assured implementation over the last fifteen years. The second chapter also applies the ASIA framework to the Balanced Curriculum model: Alignment, Structure of the Curriculum and Stability, Implementation and Infrastructure, and Assessment, which were also held in common by the districts reported in this book.

The second part of the book (5 chapters) describes the research base for each of the four components of the ASIA framework: Alignment, Structure of the Curriculum and Stability, Implementation and Infrastructure, and Assessment. An additional chapter describes one model for making plans for improvement or curricular implementation in a district. With the assessment section, stories of two school districts – Philadelphia, PA and Cumberland, PA,- who have extensive experience implementing sophisticated assessment systems.

The third part of the book describes six other districts that have used curriculum as a framework for improving student achievement. The first chapter in this section describes three urban districts that won the Booker Prize: Aldine, TX; Garden Grove Unified School District, CA; and Norfolk Public Schools, VA; and used curriculum as a way to improve student achievement. Then four separate chapters are offered, by Superintendents and Assistant Superintendents of districts in Connecticut serving three different levels of Socio-Economic status: high – Farmington Public Schools, Ct, medium – Bristol Public Schools, CT and low – Norwalk Public Schools, CT (Two chapters). The four chapters tell the stories of how the district leadership organized their successful achievement gains on state tests, through emphasizing curriculum which incorporated the ASIA framework.

The last section of the book has three chapters: the first chapter (13) delineates the commonalities of the districts who used curriculum to improve student achievement. Chapter 14 examines other popular improvement strategies through the ASIA framework. Chapter 15 suggests steps in planning to implement the ASIA framework with your schools and district.

The book is written with a wide range of professionals in mind. Certainly Superintendents and Central Office administrators charged with improving student achievement will find the book useful. Principals and other school leaders will find suggestions about improving their roles to make a difference in student achievement. Teachers can come to understand what is needed and necessary in helping to improve student achievement through implementing a curriculum. School Board members will find the stories of successful change efforts a good conversation starter for their work in governance. University professors can more fully understand what is needed from school and district leadership to improve student achievement and use the ASIA framework as one way to structure their presentation of improving achievement.

The ASIA framework is not the only way student achievement can be improved. Other approaches have been successfully applied, as in the two other winners of the Booker Prize that did not emphasize curriculum development, demonstrated (*Zavadsky, 2009*). We do believe however, that curriculum development that incorporates the ASIA framework provides powerful strategies to improve student achievement that are available to all school districts.

The next chapter describes the Balanced Curriculum, a web -based curriculum development tool that districts use to create, align and assess their curriculum authored by the district's teachers. The Balanced Curriculum has produced improved achievement in every district that wrote the curriculum with fidelity and paid attention to implementation (Squires, 2012)

REFERENCES

Erickson, H.L. (2001). *Stirring the head, heart, and soul: Redefining curriculum and instruction.* (Second Edition). Thousand Oaks, CA: Corwin Press.

Jacobs, H.H. (Ed.) (2004). *Getting results with curriculum mapping.* Alexandria, VA: Association of Curriculum and Supervision.

Tomlinson, C.A., Kaplan, S.N., Renzulli, J.S., Purcell, J., Leppien, J., Burns, D. (2002). *The parallel curriculum: A design to develop high potential and challenge high-ability learners.* Thousand Oaks, CA.: Corwin Press.

Squires, D.A. (2012). Curriculum alignment research suggests that alignment can improve student achievement. The Clearing House: A Journal of Educational Strategies, Issues and Ideas, 85:4, 129-135.

Squires, D.A. (2013). The balanced curriculum model: Description and results. SAGE Open, January-March 2013; vol. 3, 1:2158244013478012, first published on February 27, 2013.

Wiggins, G. & McTighe, J. (2005). *Understanding by Design.* (2nd Edition). Alexandria, VA: Association of Curriculum and Supervision.

Zavadsky, H (2009). Bringing School Reform to Scale: Five Award-winning Urban Districts. Harvard Education Press, Cambridge, MA. http://www.hepg.org/hep/book/ 110/ BringingSchoolReformToScale.

In: Curriculum
Editor: David A. Squires

ISBN: 978-1-62948-673-4
© 2014 Nova Science Publishers, Inc.

Chapter 2

THE BALANCED CURRICULUM MODEL

David A. Squires, Ph.D.

Southern Connecticut State University, New Haven, CT, US

INTRODUCTION TO THE BALANCED CURRICULUM MODEL

The Balanced Curriculum has produced improved achievement in every district that has written their curriculum according to this design and done a credible job of implementing the curriculum (Squires, 2005, 2013). In this chapter we explain the Balanced Curriculum's framework and how it addresses ASIA (Alignment, Structure and Stability, Implementation and Infra-structure, and Assessment) and the implications for teachers, principals, and central office administrators. We also reference the categories of the ASIA framework listed in Appendix A. These categories were developed from the research mentioned in Chapters 3-7 and will also be applied to the curriculum descriptions in Chapters 8-12. Chapter 13 uses these categories as a way to comment on the district descriptions as a whole. We recommend that you read this chapter, only glancing at the categories, as they will become self-explanatory after reading chapters 3-7.

The components of the on-line Balanced Curriculum are:

- Courses
- Time-Bound Units
- Significant Tasks (or assured activities)
- Alignment of Significant Tasks to Standards and Assessment Specifications
- Curriculum-embedded Assessment Aligned to State Standards and Assessment Specifications
- A Management System for Tracking a Class's Progress
- A Record of Teacher Comments to Guide Staff Development Planning
- Yearly Curriculum Revision Process

A description of each component follows.

1. Courses, Units and Significant Tasks Guide Time, Content and Process Dimensions of the Curriculum

The curriculum is written by the district's teachers /authors to guide instruction (*I-1-Curriculum Focus*). Courses are divided into time bound units so teachers know the pace of instruction (*Str-2-Time Parameters*). This ensures that everyone will complete the course's curriculum and students do not get left behind. Within the unit, significant tasks or assured activities described by district teachers/authors in a paragraph specify what district teachers should teach (an objective) and the instructional processes to use (*Str-3-Instructional Process, Str-1-Content*). The significant tasks take longer to complete than a daily lesson plan and generally encompass two days to two weeks of activities. The unit's significant tasks take approximately 70/% of the unit's time. The other 30% is spent however the teacher decides to meet class needs, through remediation or enrichment or both. This allows teachers to manage the creative aspects of instruction.

Forty to sixty significant tasks usually make up a course. The significant tasks are the teacher's promise that most students will be ready for the following course or grade level because all of accomplished the significant tasks. Below is a sample significant task for a High School English Course.

Students will set up an in class debate to examine the controversial issues in TO KILL A MOCKINGBIRD. They will have to take a stand on an issue and develop arguments to defend their positions. They will spend time examining the text and providing quotes as evidence to support their claims. They will be able to use their arguments in a structured debate format and setting. Students will give each other feedback on their debates using class generated rubrics. [1]

Figure 2.1. Sample Significant Task for High School English.

2. Align Significant Tasks to Standards and High-Stakes Assessment Specifications

Alignment of curriculum to standards and high stakes testing provides a powerful predictor of the curriculum's impact, as demonstrated by the many research studies (e.g., Squires, 2009, Wishnick, 1989; Schmidt et al., 2001; Porter & Smithson, 2001) (*Str-4 – Alignment, AL-1-Included, AL-3-State Standards, AL-4-Assessment Specs*). The significant tasks are aligned by the curriculum authors (*I-2-Teacher Involvement*) to state standards and high-stakes assessment specifications. The vocabulary from the standards is explicitly incorporated in the significant tasks by the district's curriculum authors. Then the authors use the web site to generate a report showing the author designated alignments for each significant task. Figure 2.2 illustrates how a significant task about a "Portfolio Project" is aligned to Connecticut standards and state test blueprints. [2]

---

[1] Other examples of significant tasks can be found by going to www.balancedcurriculum.com using the User Name: SCSU Student, Password: 1234. There are over 300 courses there that have significant tasks developed for a vast variety of courses. The work is taken from Southern CT State University students who participate in the Educational Leadership Program, that certifies them to become principals.

[2] The web site contains all state and national standards, as well as local standards or a district's power standards for all enrollees.

Portfolio Project

Students will create a portfolio based on the reading of the book, SPEAK. As they read, they will respond to different issues in different types of writing assignments, while discussing in their journals how they handle new vocabulary words. They will have to write creative letters that will explain the thoughts of certain characters, essays that analyze theme, and summaries that explain major happenings in the book. Editing groups will work on commas in a series, fragments, misplaced modifiers and proper nouns.

Standard	Code	Description
Bloom's Taxonomy	An	Analysis
	S	Synthesis
CAPT* Grade 10 – Response to Lit.	CAPT1.2	Does the student describe the thoughts, opinions and/or questions that arise as he or she reads the story?
	CAPT2.1	Does the student use clues or evidence from the story to make inferences, raw conclusions, predict events, infer motives and generalizations beyond the text?
	CAPT3.2	Does the student apply is or her understanding of people and life in general to make associations between the story and his or her view of the world?
	CAPT 4.4	Does the student examine the fit between the text of the story and his or her prior knowledge and life experience, and attempt to reconcile differences if appropriate?
CAPT Grade 10 – Editing and Revising	CAPT 1.1a	Commas in a series
	CAPT 1.5	Tone
	CAPT 2.1	Fragment
	CAPT 3.4	Misplaced Modifier
	CAPT 4.2	Proper Nouns
CT Language Arts Standards	912.01.02	Students will examine the fit between the text and prior knowledge by recording differences, extracting clues or evidence, making inferences, drawing conclusions, predicting events, inferring motives and generalizing beyond the text.
	912.01.08	Students will apply their understanding of textual features of each genre to their interpretation of that genre.
	912.01.09	Students use word recognition strategies to perfect reading fluency in ever more sophisticated words.
	912.02.01	Students will select from the complete variety of text structures (essay, short story, poetry, academic essay, report, research paper, response to literature, documentary, etc.) the appropriate organizational pattern for addressing audience, purpose and point of view

*CAPT = Connecticut Academic Performance Test

Figure 2.2. Alignment of the Significant Task to the Standards and the Assessment Specifications.

In Figure 2.2 the significant task is listed at the top. The first column lists the state standards and assessment specifications that the authors aligned to the significant tasks. For example, CAPT Grade 10 Response to Literature is the state assessment specifications for the part of the reading test for the state. The second column contains the state's "code" for this assessment specification. The third column lists what the state includes in that item. For example, in the area of "CAPT 10 – Editing and Revising," commas in a series, tone, misplaced modifiers and proper notes are all aligned to the significant task. The curriculum authors debated among themselves and came to a consensus about the most important areas for alignment with the significant task, as many alignments are possible (*I-2-Teacher Involvement, Str-4 –Alignment, AL-2-Standard Way*). Only the most important are aligned.

3. Balancing the Aligned Curriculum

Next, the alignments are summarized by course, so the teachers /authors can determine if the "balance" among the standards is appropriate for the course as a whole.

Alignment of CAPT* Specifications	
To Units and Significant Tasks	
CAPT Grade 10 – Response to Literature: Forming an Initial Understanding	
CAPT 1.1 = Topic Sentence	
Unit	*Significant Task Title*
Search for Self	Balanced Person
Survival	Physical/Mental Survival
Power	Power Structures
CAPT	CAPT Preparation
CAPT 1.2 = Supportive Detail	
Unit	*Significant Task Title*
Search for Self	Records of Daily Life
Short Story	Unified Effect
Betrayal	Poster Project
CAPT 1.5 = Tone	
Unit	*Significant Task Title*
Search for Self	Portfolio Project

*CAPT = Connecticut Academic Performance Test

Figure 2.3. Alignments of Connecticut Test Specifications to Significant Tasks.

Figure 2.3 shows that for the CAPT (Connecticut Academic Performance Test) four significant tasks in four different units were aligned to the "Topic Sentence" content area on the state test. For "Supportive Detail" there were three significant tasks in three different units. For "Tone" there was one significant task in one unit aligned to this area of the test.

From above, the teachers /authors may consider whether one significant task on tone (CAPT 1.5) provides sufficient emphasis for the 9th grade English, as only one significant task is aligned to the "Tone" standard. Curriculum teachers/authors use their professional judgments as well as item analysis of district test scores to support their decisions. For example, if students in the district didn't do well on the items testing "Tone" on the state test, then the teachers/curriculum authors may want to add more significant tasks in other units which address "Tone". On the other hand, if the test results on tone were satisfactory, they may decide not to change it, as one significant task has shown to be adequate. This helps maintain curriculum consistency while ensuring standards are met.

Another report (Figure 2.4) shows the number of significant tasks addressed by each standard and sub standards. For example, look at the second standard listed below as K4.02.02. In the first column, "3" indicates that there are three significant tasks aligned to this standard. The standard is given in the third column

Grade Two

Standard: **CT Language Arts 2003 K-4**

Aligned Significant Tasks: **Subtopics**

Students will produce written, oral and visual texts to express, develop and substantiate ideas and experiences.

	K4.02.01	Students will decide upon purpose, audience and point of view, then select from a group of text types, such as narrative, nonfiction and poetry, the most appropriate genre to convey their meaning.
3	K4.02.02	Students will speak, write or draw in a variety of modes (narratives, "all-about" nonfiction pieces, poetry) to tell stories that their audience understands
1	K4.02.03	Students will generate questions for gathering data from appropriate first-hand, visual and print sources, and categorize the data to produce a product.
5	K4.02.04	Students will compose a piece of writing based on ideas generated through any of a variety of ways (writing, drawing, talking, webbing, listing, brainstorming), revise and proofread it, and present it to an audience.
	K4.02.05	Students will collect and examine, individually or with classmates, an array of their own stories and drawings, discuss the features they like, and say what they might do differently the next time.

Figure 2.4. Report of Number of Significant Tasks for the Course Aligned to Significant Tasks.

The curriculum authors can use this report to ask questions about inadequate alignment and over-emphasized alignment.

Inadequate Alignment. After reviewing the last figure, the curriculum authors might ask why are there no significant tasks addressing the first standard and last standard in this section? Does the curriculum (via significant tasks) actually address these areas and they were not aligned because other alignments took priority? Was the alignment was miscoded? Or, did the curriculum (significant tasks) ignore these areas (usually inadvertently), and code others in its place? The teachers /curriculum authors may decide to add or modify significant tasks so these areas can be addressed.

Over-emphasized Alignment. The curriculum authors will need to decide whether the emphasis on K4.02.04 with alignment to five significant tasks is over-emphasized given that two other standards (K4.02.01 & K4.02.05) have not been addressed. The curriculum authors will need to decide if alignment to five standards is too many. They may reason that because of the emphasis in the state test, coverage is necessary for the five significant tasks. Conversely, they could reason that such emphasis is inappropriate given the unaligned standards. Significant tasks may need to be rewritten for appropriate alignment to take place. This assures that all the significant tasks address the standards and assessment specifications in ways that the district's curriculum authors know is appropriate.

4. Assessing the Curriculum

Each significant task provides an opportunity for assessment (*Str-4 –Alignment*). As the significant tasks are aligned to the standards, the assessment for each significant task automatically covers similar territory (*AL-5-Local Testing Aligned*). Teachers/authors construct a performance assessment for each significant task so students across the district have a standard way of demonstrating performance and teachers have a uniform way of giving and grading the performance (*A-1 –Uniform assessment*). The data from the assessments provides the district with comparable information about students' competence on the significant task and also indicates how well they performed on the aligned standards. The district will need to plan time for assessment and the use of assessment data in the instructional cycle (*A-2-Time in Schedule*). The district can use assessment reports aggregated by school, task or aligned standards (*Str-5 –Assessment*). Such data can be used in recommending improvements to the curriculum or in grade level professional development.

Another type of assessment required in the Balanced Curriculum, the Format Assessment, provides all students with the once-per-unit opportunity to practice using the same format as the high stakes state test. The format assessment is usually in the form of a quiz. As the format assessments usually occur at the end of units, extensive test preparation is no longer necessary before the high-stakes test. Spaced practice is a better way to learn to take tests than through massed practice, often anxiety provoking practice right before the state assessment.

5. Implementing the Curriculum

The district must plan strategies to ensure that the curriculum is actually implemented by the district's teachers, and that they are actually teaching the significant tasks. This helps address teacher accountability. As all teachers use the same significant tasks for a course, tracking a teacher's progress is a matter of determining if the significant tasks are taught. On the Balanced Curriculum web site where the curriculum is located, teachers can log in and check off their completion of a significant task, view their own completion record, but cannot view other's completion records. Principals can check the progress of all teachers in their buildings. District staff can access completion information across district school s, providing easily accessible information for managing student learning, without micro-managing the teacher's instruction (*Str-6-Managed*).

6. Modifying the Curriculum

The curriculum plan now generates data so the curriculum can be modified based on the data. In modifying the curriculum, teachers and administrators need to ask questions of the data (*A-3-Monitor and Evaluate, I-3—Resources*), as shown by the following questions shown in Figure (2.5):

Data Source	Questions data can help to answer
Alignment of Significant Task to Standards	Are all standard areas covered?
The Balance of the Curriculum	Does the existing balance of alignment with the standards promote increased achievement?
Significant Task Assessments	Do significant task assessments align with high-stakes assessment?
Format Assessments	Do format assessments align with high-stakes assessments?
Completion Information	Which significant tasks had low/high completion ratings? Did these correlate with test results?
High-stakes/Standardized Test Results	For areas of low results, should the district increase emphasis on that area through more significant tasks and/or more time devoted to the aligned units/significant tasks?

Figure 2.5. Using Data Generated by Curriculum Implementation.

RESULTS FROM SCHOOLS AND DISTRICTS IMPLEMENTING THE BALANCED CURRICULUM MODEL

By using and implementing the Balanced Curriculum approach, curriculum can be the key to improved achievement. Data from the many school s and districts across the country that have used the Balanced Curriculum process to design their own curriculum shows the process significantly improves achievement (Squires, 2005, pp. 295-307, 2013). As the figure 9.1 demonstrates, school districts that both designed *and implemented* the curriculum saw their scores improve significantly (http://www.balancedcurriculum.com/results.htm).

As the Balanced Curriculum operates from the web, with access determined by passwords, districts can save money through coordinated web-based review and revision of their own curricula, rather than via a paper-based process. Most districts can pay for the web site access by what they save in printing and publication costs.

HOW THE BALANCED CURRICULUM ADDRESSES THE ASIA FRAMEWORK

Next we demonstrate how the Balanced Curriculum addresses the ASIA framework: (Alignment, Structure of the Curriculum, Implementation and Infrastructure, and Assessments) and what the implications are for teachers, principal and central office administrators. We use the same organization to address the curriculum efforts in the three districts not using the Balanced Curriculum model, but improving achievement never the less.

Place and Date	Subject	Grades	School Demographics	Results
Red Bank, NJ 1978-92	R,LA, Math	K-8	800 approx 60% Blk 20% Hisp 20% White 60% Free/Reduced lunch	Student averages at all grade levels went from below grade level to above grade level in R, LA, and Math over a period of 7 years on a variety of standardized tests used by the district.
Richardson Elementary, Washington, DC 1993-94	Reading	1-6	360 approx. 96% Blk 100% Free/Reduced Lunch	Improvements pre implementation to post implementation. (Normal growth for a year's schooling is 1.0) Grade / Grade Equiv. Improvement 1-2 / .8 2-3 / 1.2 3-4 / -.6 4-5 / 1.2 5-6 / 1.1

Collection of New York City SURR Schools (Schools under Registration and Review i.e., declining scores for three years in a row) 1994 (Pre)-97(Post) — Reading and Writing — K-6 — 1000 (approx) students per school. Mostly high poverty high minority schools

School Grade	State Test Pre	% passing Post
PS 191		
Gr 3 Re	32.9	49.0
Gr 5 Wr	80.3	91.7
PS 165		
Gr 3 Re	35.3	54.8
Gr 5 Wr	54.1	47.1
Gr 6 Re	74.5	66.7
PS 156		
Gr 3 Re	26.9	72.2
Gr 5 Wr	47.1	77.6
PS 115		
Gr 3 Re	68.0	75.6
Gr 5 Wr	94.8	90.3
PS 43		
Gr 3 Re	48.8	54.7
Gr 5 Wr	75.6	90.0
Gr 6 Re	59.6	80.5
PS 15		
Gr 3 Re	72.7	79.3
Gr 5 Wr	76.7	89.8
Gr 6 Re	79.4	79.0
PS 27		
Gr 3 Re	34.9	57.4
Gr 5 W	89.6	78.9
Gr 6 Re	52.8	55.6
Yonkers Hostos/Micros		
Gr 3 Re	42	87
Gr 6 Re	36	62

Place and Date	Subject	Grades	School Demographics	Results
District 13 (Brooklyn, NY) 1997-2000	Reading	K-8	18 elementary 4 Middle 1000 Students per school (Total 20,000 students). Mostly Black and poor	**Implementing Schools** Gained 7% more students scoring above grade level on city tests in Reading from previous year **Non-Implementing Schools** Lost 6% of students who scored above grade level on city tests in Reading from previous year
Newburg, New York 1999-2002	Reading	K-8	6 elementary 2 middle Equal mix of White, Hispanic and Black El. Schools 350-800 MS 750-1200	Fall to Spring Gain of Scores on District Standardized Test (expected growth =.6) Reading / LA (in Grade Equivalents) 1.7 / 1.3 1.8 / 1.6 1.5 / 1.4 1.5 / 1.4 .8 / .8 .9 / .9

Place and Date	Subject	Grades	School Demographics	Results		
Passaic, NJ 2001-2003	Reading	K-8	8 Elementary Schools Mainly Hispanic and Black, primarily poor	Percent Proficient on Grade 4 State Test in Reading		
				School	Pre	Post
				No. 1	67.6	84.8
				No. 3	69.8	91.9
				No. 5	43.9	64.1
				No. 6	73.6	73.8
				No. 9	64.9	73.5
				No. 10	NA	57.1
				No. 11	54.3	78.2
				Learning Center	94.1	95.0
Englewood Cliffs, NJ 2001-2004	Reading	K-8	1 Elementary 1 Middle 400 Students in District Upper Middle Class – Large ESL population	On State Test: Level 1 = Below Proficient, Level 2 = Proficient Level 3 = Above Proficient		
				Grade 8 State Test		
				Pre 95% at Level 1 & 2 5% at Level 3 (highest)		Post 71% at Level 1 & 2 29% at Level 3 (highest)
				Grade 4 State Test		
				Pre 97% at Level 1 & 2 3% at Level 3 (highest)		Post 80% at Level 1 & 2 20% at Level 3 (highest)
Hertford County, NC 2001-2004	Reading	K-8	Rural 70% Black 30% White	**State Test** Level 3 & 4 (Proficient and Above)		
				Riverview Elementary	% at Level 3&4	
				Grades 3 to Grade 4 improvement	+30.98%	
				Grades 4 to Grade 5 improvement	+24.19%	
				Ahoskie Elementary		
				Grades 3 to Grade 4 improvement	-.71%	
				Grades 4 to Grade 5 improvement	24.13%	
				Hertford County Middle School		
				Grades 6 to Grade 7 improvement	+17.94%	
				Grades 7 to Grade 8 improvement	+22.23%	

Place and Date	Subject	Grades	School Demographics	Results for 3-5 Math				
Meriden Public Schools, CT 2005-2007 2006-2007 scores reported after first year of implementation	Math	K-5	8900 Total schl pop 8 Elementary Schools Black 15% Hispanic 41% White 42% Other 2% 56.5% Poverty (Only one school at one grade level declined; all other schools and grade levels increased)		Scores At or Above Proficient (3 or better on a 5 point scale)	Change	Scores At or Above Goal (4 or better on a 5 point scale)	Change
				District				
				G3 2006	54.8%		26.2%	
				Gr4 2007	66%		44.7%	
						11.2%		18.5%
				Gr 4 2006	60.4%		40.3%	
				Gr 5 2007	70.2%		49.2%	
						9.8%		8.9%

Figure 2.6. Results from Schools and Districts that have developed and implemented the Balanced Curriculum (Squires, 2005).

Alignment

A central feature of the Balanced Curriculum is the ability to align significant tasks (specifies the objective and the strategy for teaching the objective) to state standards and assessments (*Str-1-Content, Str-3-Instructional Process, AL-3-State Standards, AL-4-Assessment Specs.*) (Implications of assessments for teachers, principals and central office are covered in the last section of the ASIA framework.) Teachers then don't have to complete the alignment work as they progress through the curriculum; the curriculum authors align the significant tasks to the standards and assessment specifications during curriculum development, then adjust the significant tasks so there is a "balanced" emphasis on the standards, within the context of district needs. The alignment work is completed before the curriculum is implemented. Teachers, principals, and central office personnel don't have to worry about over- or under-emphasis of particular standards or test specifications because the curriculum authors have already balanced the curriculum for the district. The curriculum authors are essentially making a "bet" that their particular balance of the standards and assessment specifications is what will produce improved achievement. Since all students receive the same "balanced" curriculum, the district is assured on improved results (*AL-2-Standard Way*). This bet has become true in all districts where the curriculum has been implemented as student achievement has improved.

The assessments, created from the significant tasks, consequently are aligned to the assessment specifications and standards, because the significant task is aligned to the assessment specifications and standards (*AL-5-Local Testing Aligned*). This creates a unified system of curriculum and assessment that is well aligned.

Implications for Teachers

Teachers do not have to complete the tedious work of aligning the curriculum. Their job is to teach and test the curriculum, not design the curriculum and assessments. They can be confident in their district colleagues work in assuring that all standards and assessment specifications have been met during the curriculum design process. As long as they follow the units, the significant tasks and assess using the format and content assessments, they can be assured that all standards and assessment specifications have been addressed. One huge load off the teacher's plate!

Implications for Principals

Principals understand that by partially centralizing expectations for what is taught in the curriculum, they can be assured that coverage of the curriculum means that the standards and assessment specifications will be covered. They don't need to supplement the curriculum with other activities that might (by chance) improve test scores. Alignment makes the difference.

Principals also have a management system that takes little additional time (*Str-6-Managed*). Principals can know that their teachers are up to speed and covering appropriate content.

Implications for Central Office

The Central Office now doesn't have to worry about the differences in what is taught between school s; they know that if the curriculum gets taught, all the standards and assessment specifications will be met by all teachers. And they have the additional assurance that because local teachers created the curriculum, and decided how to "balance" the significant tasks, the curriculum was made to address the unique characteristics of the District and the schools within the district. The curriculum is uniquely matched to district needs because the district's teachers developed the curriculum and decided on the alignments.

Structure of the Curriculum and Stability

We outlined the structure of the Balanced Curriculum in this chapter. The structure addresses the

- Content to be taught
- The process by which the content is taught
- How the content and process are organized by time.

The content and process of what is taught is contained in a paragraph description of the significant task that takes 2-8 days to teach. Units are given begin dates and end dates, but teachers have the flexibility within the unit's time frame to spend as much or as little time on the significant tasks based on their teaching style and the characteristics of their class. Teachers therefore have a general time requirement that specifies that they need to complete all the unit's significant tasks within the time period specified by the unit. The curriculum structure allows all teachers to know the approximate time frame for teaching the content and process involved with the unit's significant tasks.

The significant tasks (contained in units and courses) taught by everyone in the course is the center piece in the Balanced Curriculum. The significant tasks ensure consistency in what is taught, and the important instructional processes to be included. The district will know what teachers are addressing for 70% of the units time (the rest is divided between re-teaching and enrichment activities, depending on the progress of the class and the class' mastery of prerequisite skills. Without some structure in the curriculum to assure coverage of important content and instructional processes, a curriculum will lack power to produce results. Time is also addressed flexibly by requiring that units be taught over a specific period of time, yet the time for teaching significant tasks can vary by teacher as the teacher responds to the needs to the class.

Stability of leadership was important as most superintendents had been in place for a few years when the process of developing the curriculum began. This provided a context of confidence that this wasn't just a new routine, but a change in the culture of the District or School (*Stab-1-Stability*).

Implications for Teachers

The structure of the curriculum provides teachers with a description of the significant tasks that all teachers will cover and assess in each unit, allowing teachers to focus on the immediate job of teaching, while understanding that the curriculum has been designed to cover all the standards and assessment specifications when looked at from a year's perspective, due to the alignment capability. As all teachers will teach the same significant tasks for 70% of the unit's time, there is enough consistency in the curriculum across teachers at the same grade level and school s to ensure that students are getting approximately the same instruction, yet the teacher has the freedom to cover the significant tasks in whatever ways are consistent with a teacher's style and the composition of the class.

Teachers also know that the district's curriculum authors (teachers themselves) created the curriculum to make sure the prerequisite skills for this year were addressed during the previous year. Teachers will not have to worry about uneven curriculum coverage by students who come to them from the previous grade-level or course.

Implications for Principals

Principals can be instructional leaders as they make sure all staff is following the curriculum through teaching each significant task and reporting this in their lesson plan s. Principals can easily review lesson plans that contain the significant tasks of the curriculum. Principals will not have to worry about the skills of students transferring in from other school s in the district because the same curriculum is taught in all schools, with consistency insured by a uniform time line across the district for teaching the units.

Implications for the Central Office

Central Office knows that having the curriculum organized by units and significant tasks gives teachers what needs to be covered and presents principals with ways to monitor if the units and significant tasks are being followed. The central office knows that the written curriculum (the units and significant tasks) has been aligned to the content and format assessment. The content and format assessments have been aligned to the state test specifications, and that all students will have practice in these domains. (More on this under the Assessment topic later in the chapter.) This also points to the importance of having Stability at the central office, so such a change can remain in place.

Implementation and Infrastructure

The Balanced Curriculum has the following build-in to assure that the curriculum can be implemented and changed: significant tasks and unit comments and a record of the completions of significant tasks. We recommend that changes be made once per year.

Comments

Comments can be recorded by anyone with an appropriate log on to the web site. Anyone with teacher access to the web site can make comments on any course (although generally teachers usually make comments on only the courses they are teaching.) The comments generally involve a suggestion of how to improve a significant task or unit, identification of a problem with the significant task or unit, or a comment about time constraints *I-6 Curriculum Revision, Str-6-Managed)*. The comments allow for direct teacher feedback to the curriculum, and the teachers/curriculum authors who will revise the curriculum. From the comments, it is relatively easy to discern themes for improvement. For example, if most of the comments involve questions of time, then the authors may want to consider revising the unit timeline. If there are good suggestions for improvement, authors can strengthen significant tasks and units using those suggestions, or incorporating changes of their own. As unit and significant task comments are placed on the web site right after teaching takes place, the comments are reflective of current conditions. They stay on the web site until they are removed after the curriculum has been revised (*I-5-Plan Written, I-6 Curriculum Revision*).

Completions

Completions are also logged onto the website by individual teachers, allowing school and/or district administrators to check teacher's progress in teaching the curriculum through a standard report from the web site. Completions are recorded for each teacher assigned to specific courses (*Str-6-Managed*). We have found that 99% of teachers are honest with their recording of completions; if they haven't completed a significant task, they won't enter a completion. Completions take one minute to record on the web site, as it is as simple as checking off tasks that have been completed. As the curriculum is designed so the significant tasks take up only 70% of the unit, and the curriculum was written by teachers in the district, it is assumed that everyone will complete the curriculum, thus assuring appropriate prerequisite skills for the next year's courses. Building and district administrators are strongly encouraged to get completion reports from the web site on a weekly basis and follow up with teachers who have fallen behind. District administrators can check on building administrators to make sure progress is being made and that the completions are being filled out by all teachers. One of the most important reasons for failure on State assessments is that the topics have not been covered, or covered too lightly. If the Balanced Curriculum is taught, and teachers record their progress with completions, then administrators are fulfilling their role as instructional leaders by assuring that the Balanced Curriculum is actually taught.

Yearly Curriculum Revisions

The curriculum can then be revised on a yearly basis to take into account comments, the teachers completion history, the current test results, and the results from the curriculum embedded assessments. We suggest that the most caring and knowledgeable teachers (2 to 3 per course) spend a day or two over the summer, revising the curriculum, based on the completions and comments on the web site (*I-6 Curriculum Revision, I-5-Plan Written, I-4-Group Support*).

During this one or two day period, the teachers would print out reports of all the comments that have been logged for the course for both units and significant tasks. They would look for patterns in the comments and make a list of changes to the units or the significant tasks that address the comments.

Next they would print out a preformatted report which would show the completion history for teachers who taught the course during the year. For example, if a majority of the teachers had a difficult time completing all the units or significant tasks, this may mean that there was too much curriculum for too little time. Adjustments would need to be made by the curriculum authors of revising the scope and sequence of units, and/or deleting or combining some significant tasks.

Once the authors completed the revisions, they would need to align the new parts of the curriculum and, from the reports available on the web site, determine whether standards were over or under emphasized. Further changes to units and significant tasks would need to be made and the new alignments recorded and validated for balance. Since the units and significant tasks changed, the authors would also have to review the content and format assessments to reflect the new units and significant tasks. The assessment alignments should also be rechecked to make sure they maintain the balance in the assessments.

Implications for Teachers

Teachers show that they are following the curriculum by recording completion of significant tasks on the web site (this process usually takes less than a minute per significant task.) Teachers can see their record of completions but cannot see other teacher's records (*Str-6-Managed*).

Teachers can also "talk back" to the curriculum by recording comments for either individual significant tasks or whole units which indicate problems that the teacher had in implementation, or suggestions for improving the unit or significant task. This ensures that a record of ways the curriculum might be improved is kept. Teachers can view all comments that they and others place on the web site. All teachers are therefore involved in the curriculum revision process through their completion and comments on the web site.

Implications for Principals

Principals know the importance of teachers recording their completions and comments (*Str-6-Managed*). The principal can get a report from the Balanced Curriculum web site which details how many significant tasks each teacher has completed. Principals regularly review their school's progress by getting and reviewing this report once a week, (after checking that teachers' lesson plan s address the significant tasks in the curriculum) and arrange to speak with those who appear to be behind. A wise principal will know that a week or two variations in the teacher's completion of significant tasks is not important; what is important is a teacher falling behind three or more weeks, as the principal knows that this means that the teacher will have to constrict the curriculum coverage for the year. This will guarantee that children have not completed the curriculum for the year, and will enter the next year with deficiencies. The principal may also want to attend grade level meetings or department meetings to work with teacher groups on completion information. Instructional specialists or coaches can also take on these duties as well. The goal of the principal is to ensure that by the end of the year all teachers have taught what is specified by the units and significant tasks of the curriculum. This insures that all students have the necessary prerequisite skills for next year's course.

Implications for Central Office

The central office's role is to make sure the school s and teachers have taught the units and the significant tasks. Administrators at the central office can log on to the web site and receive a completion report organized to show each school, and how many units the teachers at each grade level or course in the school have completed (*Str-6-Managed*). The central office needs to follow up with the principal about what they are doing with teachers who are significantly behind or are not logging their completions on the web site.

Likewise, the Central Office needs to monitor comments similar to the way they have monitored completions. Are school s recording their comments on the web site? The Central Office can follow up with school principals if this isn't taking place. The Central Office will recognize that having comments are a necessary component of revising the curriculum on a yearly basis, and the central office will need to organize and fund such revision activities.

Revision involves inspecting the current curriculum and comparing it to the yearly state test results, the format and content assessment results (if the district keeps these), the completions, the comments, and the alignment reports to determine if changes need to be made (*I-6 Curriculum Revision*). For example, if the test results indicate low scores in an area, and the content and format assessments also have low scores in that area, then the curriculum revisers need to revise the curriculum in that area. To do this, they call for an alignment report from the web site that shows the significant tasks that have been aligned with the test specification of the area that scored low. Obviously, because of the low scores, the significant tasks aligned to this test specification weren't strong enough to produce higher test scores. Of course, there needs to be a plan in place to make sure that this takes place.

Assessments

Next, the curriculum authors need to examine current state test results to see where the curriculum needs to be improved on a yearly basis (*A-3-Monitor and Evaluate, A-4-Course Teachers Work Together*). Good state assessments allow teachers and administrators to learn from item or strand analysis about the result's patterns. If a particular strand is weak. The curriculum authors can get alignment reports on the units and significant tasks, and also an alignment report of the assessments. If a particular strand's results demonstrate weakness, then the curriculum authors can examine the alignment reports from the web site to determine what emphasis is currently being given. For example, if there is a weakness from the state test on measurement, the alignment reports can take a look at the number of significant tasks that have been aligned to measurement. Curriculum authors can then examine the significant tasks indicated by the report, and judge whether the significant tasks contain enough information or practice to assure student mastery. If not, then the curriculum authors will have to revise the units or significant tasks, and make concurrent revisions to the alignments and the assessments.

A second component of the alignment is to align the curriculum embedded assessments to the format and content of the State assessments. This assures that all the State assessment specifications are addressed in the curriculum-embedded testing and is unusually specific in addressing whether state assessment specifications have been covered in the curriculum embedded assessments. Such a design insures that results from student assessments can be compared with the results from the state assessments, providing data for various levels of data teams that focuses on whether students have mastered the concepts in the curriculum. If not, significant tasks may need to be revised so that more powerful tasks can be substituted to get the desired results (*A-3-Monitor and Evaluate, A-1 –Uniform assessment*).

Implications for Teachers

Teachers can then be assured that the assessments that they are giving are aligned to the state assessments, and that if their students take the content and format assessments, they will be adequately prepared for the test (*Str-5 –Assessment, AL-5-Local Testing Aligned, AL-6-Other Categories*). (The format assessments are given once per unit and provide students with a quiz that resembles the state yearly assessment.) They don't have to construct any additional activities to ensure that their students are prepared for the state assessment. The teachers won't need to review for the state assessment, as this has been done once per unit throughout the year. Therefore, teachers will have more instructional time and less review time for the state test. And they can have confidence in the process because the curriculum embedded tests have been aligned with the state tests. It's always good news when there is less work for teachers.

Implications for Administrators

Administrators can also be confident that students who complete the format assessment will know the formats and how to answer them on the yearly state test. Administrators will want to check with their teachers that the teachers have used with students the format and content assessments. Perhaps in their yearly introduction of expectations for the school, they should state that use of the format and content assessments are required, as this will give students the needed and necessary practice on the content and format of the state test.

Implications for the Central Office

The Central Office also knows that if all students in the district have practice with the aligned format and content assessments that they don't need to schedule or require that teachers spend extra time during the school year or before the state tests in test preparation. They should insure that their principals don't schedule valuable instructional time in reviewing for the test, as this has been taken care of through practice on the aligned format and content assessments. The alignment process embedded in the curriculum development process insures that students and teachers are prepared for the state standardized test.

Assessments

Likewise, the curriculum authors can examine results from the assessments and compare them with the results from the state assessments. To continue our example, if the state assessments indicate a problem in measurement, then the curriculum authors will want to examine how measurement was assessed, and whether that assessment is consistent with the results from the state test. The curriculum authors may need to examine:

- Whether the level of difficulty of the state's assessment is at the same level as the way the curriculum embedded assessment is structured.
- Whether the content of the state assessment is mirrored in the curriculum embedded assessment.
- Whether the format of the state's assessment is replicated in the curriculum embedded assessment.

For example, let's suppose that the state's assessment item is a unique way of assessing student knowledge and was currently not included in the curriculum embedded assessment. The authors would then change the way that item was assessed.

The same process could be used for curriculum embedded assessments. For example, let's say that they state assessments on measurement didn't have positive results. We would expect that the results of the curriculum embedded assessments would not be stellar as well. If the curriculum embedded assessments indicated good results for measurement, then the curriculum authors would need to examine the curriculum embedded assessments to determine if they were difficult enough (and make sure they were similar to the state test). Conversely, if the state test results were good in measurement, but the curriculum embedded test results weren't, then the curriculum embedded items on measurement may need to be revised so that they became easier (*Str-5 –Assessment, A-4-Course Teachers Work Together*).

Implications for Teachers

Teachers do not have to construct assessments individually, as developing assessments is part of the curriculum development process. Teachers do not have to worry that the assessments are aligned to the standards and assessment specifications, as this is incorporated in the curriculum development process. The teacher's job is to teach, assessments have been constructed as part of the curriculum development process.

Implications for Principals

Principals need to make sure the assessments are being used. A few principals have required that teachers show the assessments when recording completion of their significant tasks. Others do spot checks, figuring that most staff are following the system requirements. Principals or their designees often meet with grade levels as the grade level debriefs how they did on the assessments and how they can comment on the web site to improve the assessment process for the unit for the next year.

Implications for the Central Office

The Central Office needs to devise a way to understand when the assessments aren't doing their job. An assessment can be too easy, or too difficult, or with good results from the assessment there could be poor results on the standardized test items that align with a significant task. This involves collecting data about the assessment from teachers and then using the data to make decisions about the tests that are part of the curriculum. Data needs to be collected from all school s, so that decisions are made given the scope of the testing information.

This is how the Balanced Curriculum reflects alignment, structure of the curriculum and stability, implementation and infrastructure, and assessment.

In Part II of the book, we examine the research behind each aspect of the ASIA framework (alignment, structure of the curriculum, implementation and infrastructure, and assessment.) The ASIA framework has been found in the Balanced Curriculum and also in the District stories of districts that concentrated on curriculum development as a strategy for improving student achievement.

REFERENCES

Porter, A. C., & Smithson J. L. (2001). *Defining, developing, and using curriculum indicators* (CPRE Research Report Series RR-048). Philadelphia: Consortium for Policy Research in Education, University of Pennsylvania.

Schmidt, W. H., McKnight, C. C., Houang, R. T., Wang, H. C., Wiley, D. E., Cogan, L. S., & Wolfe, R. G. (2001). *Why school s matter: A cross-national comparison of curriculum and learning*. San Francisco: Jossey-Bass.

Squires, D.A. (2005). *Aligning and balancing the standards-based curriculum*. Thousand Oaks, CA: Corwin Press.

Squires, D.A. (2009). *Curriculum alignment: Research-based strategies for increasing student achievement*. Thousand Oaks, CA: Corwin Press.

Squires, D.A. (2013). The balanced curriculum model: Description and results. SAGE Open, January-March 2013; vol. 3, 1: 2158244013478012, first published on February 27, 2013.

Wishnick, K. T. (1989). *Relative effects on achievements scores of SES, gender, teacher effect and instructional alignment: A study of alignment's power in mastery learning*. Unpublished doctoral dissertation, University of San Francisco, CA.

INTRODUCTION TO PART TWO: CHAPTERS 3, 4, 5, 6 AND 7

The second part of the book (5 chapters) describes the research base for each of the four components of the ASIA framework: Alignment, Structure of the Curriculum, Implementation and Infrastructure, and Assessment. Current research is given for each area so that readers can know the research that is behind using these four framework areas. An additional chapter describes one model for making plans for improvement in a district. We begin with a chapter on the research supporting the concept of alignment as a critical marker in curriculum development.

In: Curriculum
Editor: David A. Squires

ISBN: 978-1-62948-673-4
© 2014 Nova Science Publishers, Inc.

Chapter 3

THE ALIGNMENT RESEARCH

David A. Squires, Ph.D.
Southern Connecticut State University, New Haven, CT, US

INTRODUCTION TO ALIGNMENT

Alignment of the curriculum to state standards and assessment specifications is very important in districts for getting improved achievement. Alignment means that the curriculum is designed to make sure that assessments and standards coverage are addressed in the instruction process. The tested content of state tests needs to be covered in instruction, or students will not have the opportunity to understand the tested content. That seems easy, but few curriculum designs (Wiggins & McTigh, *Understanding by Design, (*2005)*;* Erickson's Concept-Based Curriculum in *Stirring the Head, Heart and Soul,* (2001); Tomlinson's *Parallel Curriculum (*2002); Posner and Rudnitsky's *Course Design,* (2006), and Jacobs' *Curriculum Mapping,* (2004)), actually incorporate alignment into a curriculum design that makes sure that what is tested gets taught. Equally important is aligning curriculum to state standards. A Balanced Curriculum and the district's stories show that curriculum can be the key to student achievement, if the curriculum includes alignment. The summary of alignment research presented below provides the research base to back up this assertion. Next a check list is proposed for people designing curriculum to assure that they have incorporated as many of the variables of the ASIA framework as possible.

In this chapter, we review the research which supports alignment to state standards and assessment specifications. In citing the research, we summarize the book Curriculum Alignment: Research-based Strategies for Increasing Student Achievement (Squires, 2009, 2012).

WHAT IS ALIGNMENT?

Alignment is an agreement or a match between two categories, such as state standards matching the content of a district curriculum. For example, if the state standards mention "number concepts" and the curriculum covers "number concepts" alignment between the standards and the curriculum occurs. The categories match. Of course the content incorporated by number concepts in both instances needs to match as well.

Curriculum can be aligned to standards acknowledging that standards are general, while curriculum is more specific. For example a writing standard states, "Write on self-selected topics in a variety of literary forms." The curriculum for a year contains a number of specific opportunities for student to write on self-selected topics using a variety of literary forms. Thus, each writing opportunity so specified, is aligned to the standard, even though the curriculum is more specific than the standard. Please note that the standard is more general than what is specified in the curriculum, and so the standard and the curriculum are in alignment. By ensuring alignment in the curriculum, students then will have many opportunities to learn and practice, "Writing on self-selected topics in a variety of literary forms."

One difficulty is that there are numerous standards and assessment specifications that can be provided for any curriculum. We wish national standards would align with state standards and state standards would align with state assessments. We wish national tests such as the NAEP (National Assessment of Educational Progress) would align with the SAT (Scholastic Aptitude Test) would align with the ACT test (American College Testing). We wish these tests would align to other commercial standardized tests, state assessments, and district and teacher assessment s. What we wish and what we know are different.

A second difficulty is that the subject area standards and/or assessment specifications can be numerous with some subject areas having over two hundred standard statements, making it impossible to have one discrete activity align to one standard, as there are just too many standards for 180 days of instruction. What districts need is a curriculum that specifies what students should know and be able to do that is aligned to all the standards and assessment specifications. This book addresses many models (from the districts highlighted in this book) that demonstrate how curriculum has been developed to ensure alignment with the standards. Let us first address the research around alignment and then see how alignment is integrated with the three other areas of the ASIA model: Structure of the Curriculum, Infrastructure and Implementation, and Assessments.

THE ALIGNMENT MATRIX

Fenwick English's three components of curriculum -- the written, the taught, and the tested (English, 1992) – provide an organization of examining the alignment research. The written curriculum is usually the curriculum document produced by the school district or the textbooks and/or standards. The taught curriculum comes from teachers enacting the written curriculum. This may take the form of lesson plan s, or records, such as videotaping, of actual classroom instruction. The tested curriculum consists of standardized or state tests, and curriculum embedded tests and may also include student written assignments.

Any of these categories can be aligned to any of the other categories with complete alignment shown in the diagram below. The research cited in the text is placed on the diagram below.

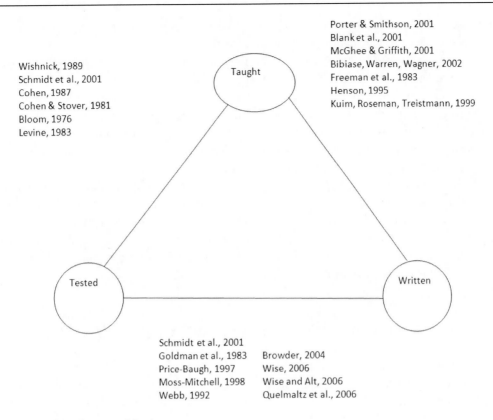

Porter & Smithson, 2001
Blank et al., 2001
McGhee & Griffith, 2001
Bibiase, Warren, Wagner, 2002
Freeman et al., 1983
Henson, 1995
Kuim, Roseman, Treistmann, 1999

Wishnick, 1989
Schmidt et al., 2001
Cohen, 1987
Cohen & Stover, 1981
Bloom, 1976
Levine, 1983

Schmidt et al., 2001
Goldman et al., 1983
Price-Baugh, 1997
Moss-Mitchell, 1998
Webb, 1992

Browder, 2004
Wise, 2006
Wise and Alt, 2006
Quelmaltz et al., 2006

Figure 3.1. The Alignment Matrix.

ALIGNMENT OF THE TAUGHT CURRICULUM TO THE WRITTEN AND TESTED CURRICULUM

Porter and Smithson (2001) developed a way to standardize descriptions of Science and Math content so comparisons could be made on daily teacher logs (taught curriculum), teacher survey instruments indicating what teachers taught (taught curriculum) and aligning what they taught to national Science and Math standards (written curriculum). The logs, surveys and standards were shown to be congruent. The data was gathered from a few states that had increased student requirements in Science and Mathematics.

"We were able to demonstrate a strong, positive and significant correlation (.49) between the content of instruction and student achievement gains. When we controlled for prior achievement, students' poverty level, and content of instruction (using an HLM [Hierarchical Linear Modeling] approach in our analysis), practically all variation in student learning gains among types of first year high school mathematics courses was explained (Porter et al., 1994, p.4)

Thus, instruction (taught curriculum) when aligned to standards (written curriculum) was linked to significantly increased student achievement.

Blank et al. (2001) found that alignment research is difficult to apply in urban settings because of central office indifference and teacher turnover. Where implementation was high in the experimental group, instruction was more closely aligned to state standards than in control school s. Thus, better alignment is possible between instruction (taught curriculum) and standards (written curriculum) even in urban settings.

McGhee and Griffith (2001) showed that improved achievement can be a result of staff development on aligning instruction (taught curriculum) to state standards (written curriculum), using released test items from the state test and spending time during staff development to align those released items to the state standards and then to the curriculum. During this process, the teachers discussed the implications for instruction and curriculum specification (taught curriculum). Thus, understanding and aligning curriculum with state assessment items can produce improved achievement.

DiBiase, Warren and Wagner (2002) examined an effort to align chemistry lab instruction to lectures and national standards. Students were randomly assigned to groups taking the old course (unaligned) and students studying the new course (aligned). Student achievement improved for those taking the newly aligned course over the achievement of those taking the old course. Thus, alignment of the taught and written curriculum showed benefits in improved achievement.

ALIGNMENT AND THE WRITTEN CURRICULUM – TEXTBOOKS

Where there isn't a strong influence from a written district curriculum, textbook content holds sway. Therefore, it is important to understand the research around the strengths and needs of textbooks so they can be a positive force in developing a solid curriculum. Alignment problems will be highlighted.

Freeman et al. (1983) demonstrated that textbooks are inadequately aligned to standardized tests by showing that one-half to two-thirds of the topics covered by the standardized test don't have twenty practice problems in the textbooks. Thus, textbooks (written curriculum) should be aligned with the testing (tested curriculum) because, if this isn't done, the test might contain content that isn't taught or practiced.

Howson (1995) concluded that U.S. textbooks cover over three hundred topics (written curriculum), too many to provide students with enough practice to understand the concepts and with little guidance for teachers as to which concepts should be emphasized the most. Thus, textbooks topic coverage may be too much for the time needed or allotted for instruction (taught curriculum).

Schmidt et al. (2001) showed that teachers use textbooks as one clue to determine what to emphasize. If the textbook covers the topic in depth, then teachers will gear their instruction on that topic to be in depth as well. Thus, textbooks (written curriculum) do provide clues that teachers use to determine levels of coverage in instruction (taught curriculum).

Studies of textbooks conducted by the American Association for the Advancement of Science (AAAS) showed the alignment between quality of instruction in the textbook (written curriculum) and teacher guidance provided by the textbooks in Math and Science for middle and high school to be of generally poor quality. Thus, relying on a textbook's scope and sequence may negatively affect the quality of teaching. Perhaps an aligned curriculum could do a better job.

Goodman et al., (1987) found elementary reading textbooks did not emphasize comprehension which filled only 2% of instructional content. There was misalignment between the content of instruction and the content of the testing. Thus, it would be important to examine the alignment between texts (written curriculum) and tests (tested curriculum).

Price-Baugh's study (1997) showed that the number of practice items (written curriculum) correlated to student scores on a state assessment (tested curriculum).

Moss-Mitchell (1998) studied one large school district where the district had aligned the textbook (written curriculum) and provided instructional material for teachers on topics not covered by the textbook, but included on the state tests(tested curriculum). Student achievement improved as a result. Thus, it appears that students do well on tested topics that are covered in the curriculum and also covered in instruction. Coverage of important topics is a critical indicator of student performance; if topics aren't covered, students don't fair as well on state tests that test those topics.

In summary, textbooks may not be well aligned to state tests and it would be important for school districts to identify the major gaps and provide teachers with material to cover those gaps such as Moss-Mitchell did in her study.

ALIGNMENT OF STATE TESTS TO STATE STANDARDS: THE WRITTEN – TESTED CONNECTION

Most research on alignment examines the relationship between state standards (written curriculum) and state tests (tested curriculum). For example, Webb (1997) demonstrated a way to validly and reliably align state tests to state standards. Based on his analysis of four unnamed states, alignment ranged from acceptable to unacceptable with data given from the states to back up the conclusion. Webb's work set the standard for reliably and validly judging alignment between standards and tests.

Browder et al. (2004), showed another way to determine alignment of standards to assessments and demonstrated that special education al tests (tested curriculum) were at times aligned to state standards (written curriculum).

Wise et al., (2006), and Wise and Alt, (2006) used standards from Delaware to show how to ensure vertical alignment of standards between grade levels. Results indicated where the vertical alignment of standards (written curriculum) in Delaware could be improved to cover the content of the state test (taught curriculum). Thus, alignment can be horizontal (test to standards) or vertical (examining the standards or the tests for patterns across grade levels).

Quellmalz et al., (2006), used an alignment process to refine the meaning of a standard on science inquiry and showed how an expanded definition of science inquiry (written curriculum) aligned with the items from three large-scale assessments (tested curriculum), pointing out how the assessments could be structured to better assess scientific inquiry. Thus, when examining the match between standard concepts and test items, both can be refined and improved.

Bowe and Kingsbury, (2007), and the National Center for Educational Statistics, (2007), demonstrate that state tests are not equivalent, making the requirement of No Child Left Behind for 100% of each state's student to pass state tests by 2014 problematic. Thus, alignment can also be used to compare tests across states to determine the differences (aligning the content of one test to the content of another test).

To summarize, the alignment between state assessments and state standards is problematic. State standards cover all the important concepts students should know and be able to do, while state tests only cover a fraction of the standards because they are constrained by the testing time where only a limited number of concepts can be assessed reliably and validly. There are now valid and reliable methods for determining the alignment between state assessments and state standards that can be used to improve this problematic condition.

ALIGNMENT IDEAS FROM AAAS (AMERICAN ASSOCIATION FOR THE ADVANCEMENT OF SCIENCE) OF PROJECT 2061

Project 2061, the date when Haley's comet will return near earth, outlines a number of useful strategies to address the issue of alignment, not based on research, but based on the logic inherent in the standards and assessments themselves. If a district is going into curriculum development, these strategies should be examined before the curriculum development starts, so the curriculum authors will have some strategies to deal with the standards. AAAS recommends (AAAS, 2001):

- Clarify benchmarks (standards)
- Unburden the curriculum
- Cut major topics
- Trim technical vocabulary
- Reduce wasteful repetition
- Learn to analyze curriculum material
- Align assessments to curriculum
- Relate instructional units to strand maps (provided by AAAS)
- Create strand maps for other subject areas

More detail on each of these strategies is provided by Squires, 2009 and resources found on the AAAS web site (http://www.aaas.org/). Given that the Third International Mathematics and Science Study (TIMSS) found that coverage in the United States for Mathematics was "a mile wide and an inch deep," strategies of cutting topics, reducing wasteful repetition and trimming technical vocabulary are very necessary and useful.

ALIGNMENT IDEAS FROM TIMSS (THIRD INTERNATIONAL MATHEMATICS AND SCIENCE STUDY)

The TIMSS compared results in Math and Science from over 40 countries by discerning the written curriculum through an analysis of textbooks, the taught curriculum from a random sample of teacher logs stating what teachers covered in the class, and the tested curriculum (The TIMSS tests given to students of all countries). Schmidt et al., (2001), demonstrated that the content of a country's curriculum (written curriculum) affects student achievement (on the tested curriculum). By developing a framework for describing curriculum, instruction and assessment results could be compared across countries. "The more curriculum of a topic area – no matter whether manifested as emphasis in content standard, as a proportion of textbook space, or as measured by either teacher implementation variable (coverage or instructional time) – is related to larger gains in that same topic area (Schmidt, et al., 2001, p.261." This means that the amount of coverage of topics in the textbook (written curriculum), for example, determined how well students did on the TIMSS test (tested curriculum). If there were many pages of coverage for perimeter, area, and volume, then students' results on the items for perimeter, are, and volume were higher than in countries with fewer pages in the textbook. This also holds true when measuring teacher time on a topic and the emphasis from the country's standards. What gets taught is related to gains in performance.

This finding was reinforced by a separate study of US students in Math by Schmidt et al., 2001. They found that "differences in learning among U.S. eighth-grade mathematics classrooms were related to concomitant differences in the amount of instructional time adjusted for difference among classrooms due to SES (Socio-economic Status) and prior learning (Schmidt et al., 2001, pp. 341-342)." Stated another way, the taught curriculum adjusted for differences in SES and student prior learning, affects the results from the tested curriculum.

For student learning, the extent of opportunities to learn curriculum means content coverage matters. The more time a teacher spends on a topic, the greater achievement score for that topic. Effect sizes, as measured by R^2, were between .4 and .6, thereby explaining a significant portion of the variance.

> "In other words, on average, for a classroom that spent about one week more on a topic than another classroom, where the two classroom were similar in SES composition and in terms of prior achievement, the former would have a predicted achievement score some 3 to 24 percentage point higher than that of the other class. Thus, it seems unsurprising that even a small amount of additional instruction (as little as a week for each) focused on these key topics would predict large increases in learning (around 20 percentile points). (Schmidt et al., 2001, p. 344)

Thus the taught curriculum impacts the tested curriculum. In order to get results, a district must control time and must control content covered in that time, if results are to improve. Controlling time and content is the function of curriculum. "Curriculum mattered to learning in mathematics and the sciences. In case after case, some significant relationship was found between achievement gains and curriculum; (Schmidt et al., 2001, p. 355.)" Making sure the curriculum is aligned to important content will result in improved achievement.

ALIGNMENT BETWEEN THE TESTED AND THE TAUGHT CURRICULUM

As the above quote from Schmidt et al., 2001, demonstrates, there is a connection between achievement and the alignment between the taught and the tested curriculum. Cohen (1987) found similar findings when he studied the connections between instruction and curriculum-embedded testing. Central to his ideas were, "Lack of excellence in American school s is not caused by ineffective teaching, but mostly by misaligning what teachers teach, what they intend to teach, and what they assess as having been taught" (Cohen, 1987, p. 18).

When instruction and assessment were aligned during sample lessons, both low- and high-aptitude, students scored well on curriculum embedded tests. Generally, alignment was more important for low aptitude students than high aptitude students, with low aptitude students making greater gains when alignment was present. When instruction aligns with assessment, large gains over a control group (instruction with no alignment) appeared across studies, with effect sizes ranging around 4 times what traditional instruction produced - effect sizes ranging for.25 to.50- or for instructionally aligned instruction and assessment, meaning that a student scoring at a 50 percentile would increase to between 84 and 98 percentile (Cohen & Stover (1981); Koczar, 1984; Tallarico, 1984; Fahey, 1986; Elia, 1986).This research promised better student results if instruction aligned practice with test items as well as the concepts the items tested, particularly for low-aptitude students.

Wishnick (1989) found that instruction provided in a mastery-learning setting and measured by a criterion–referenced test, predicted outcomes on the standardized test given at the end of the year. She also found that the power of instruction as measured by the CRTs (criterion-referenced tests) accounted for 40.32% of NRST (norm referenced standardized test) performance variance and the alignment effect accounted for 36.72% of NRST performance variance. Taken as whole, other variables, gender, teacher effect and SES accounted for 3% of NRST performance variance. This finding is at odds, with the general finding that SES, teacher and gender have a profound effect on student performance.

In addition, Wishnick found that SES is a potent factor in school performance when instruction is generated from a model of education that assumes a normal distribution of scholastic performance. But when the educational model assumes that all students can demonstrate mastery and when instruction is aligned to the standardized test, students perform well on competency tests, and SES loses its impact on school performance. Under competency-based criterion referenced instruction where instruction is aligned with the test content, alignment is more potent than SES. This demonstrates the power of aligning the taught curriculum to the tested curriculum.

What the Bloom (1976) model showed us is that when curriculum, instruction, and lesson plan ning are aligned with curriculum embedded tests (and there is a teach, test, re-teach, test model in place which define mastery learning), student results can improve dramatically in the laboratory and in school s and school districts that implement the model well (See for example Levine, D.U (1983) *Improving student achievement through Mastery Learning programs* or Gentile & Lalley, (2003), *Standards and Mastery Learning)*.

ALIGNMENT IN RELATION TO THE OTHER ASIA CRITERIA

In order to create alignment, a structure for the curriculum needs to be in place so that alignment can actually take place. For example, in the balanced curriculum, significant tasks are what are aligned to standards and assessments. Significant tasks specify in a paragraph what is to be taught in two days to two weeks time. A significant task is not a lesson plan, as it summarizes multiple lesson plans in a paragraph. Teachers also have the freedom to approach a significant task in ways that they think is best, once they have their eye on the assessment of the significant task. So the paragraph which describes the significant task is the "structure" used to facilitate alignment.

The curriculum authors, in Balanced Curriculum, know that they must write the significant task with vocabulary from the standards, so that the alignment process is in process while the significant tasks are being written. The significant tasks are written first, and then the alignment takes place. This "structure " in the curriculum writing process then allows the web site to generate an alignment report showing the number of significant tasks aligned to each standard.

There are usually about 40-60 tasks within a course, more for younger children, less for older students. Some standards for a specific grade level and subject area may contain 200 standard statements. So that all those standards can be covered, we allow multiple standards to be aligned with each significant task. A rough gauge we use is that if there are 50 significant tasks per course and the course has 200 standard statements, then we would ask the curriculum authors to align each significant task to five standards. (200 standards/50 significant tasks would be 4 standards if there were no repetitions. So we arbitrarily assign 5 alignments per task.)

The curriculum authors need to assign the alignments based on what is actually covered by the task. The authors have to decide on the most important standards for each task. So, if a task only "covers" one or two standards, maybe the significant task needs to be rewritten to cover more standards. Conversely, if a significant task covers many standards, it may be too general and need to be rewritten to be more specific. Thus, the alignment process provides another way to refine the curriculum through using the lens of the standards. Alignment is connected to the structure of the curriculum.

Alignment is also connected to the implementation of the curriculum. Again, for the Balanced Curriculum, the significant tasks provide all teachers with a paragraph description of what needs to be accomplished in the unit. The teacher must then develop lesson plan s which will put into place his/her interpretation of the significant task. Teachers can also work in teams to develop the lesson plans for implementing the significant tasks. The significant tasks are specific enough that teachers know what they have to do to implement. They are also assured that if they cover the significant tasks, they are covering the standards and assessment specifications for aligned with the significant tasks. Classroom teachers don't have to complete the alignment; they need only to implement the significant task.

Alignment is also connected with assessment. In the Balanced Curriculum, alignment of the significant tasks also means that the significant task assessment (content assessment) is aligned with the standards and assessment specifications as well. This can be accomplished by either aligning the significant task to the standards and assessment specifications or completing another alignment for the assessment only to the assessment specifications. Thus alignment insures that the assessments are in alignment also with the standards and assessment specifications.

Although the research is complex, the check list is simple for those considering the ASIA framework for designing and/or refining their curriculum.

A-1 Is alignment included as a piece of the curriculum design?
A-2 Has a standard way to construct alignment been designed? (For example, from balanced curriculum, are significant tasks aligned with standards and assessment specifications in a standard way?)
A-3 Does the alignment include aligning to state/ national standards?
A-4 Does the alignment include aligning to state/ national assessment specifications?
A-5 Is the local testing aligned with the state/ national assessment specifications?
A-6 Does the alignment include other categories such as Bloom's Taxonomy and/or national standards, or the recently constructed national standards for Reading, Math, Social Studies and Science?

Figure 3.2. Alignment's Contribution to Curriculum Criteria Alignment.

There is power in the alignment process because it is interconnected with structure of the curriculum; something in the curriculum's structure has to be aligned to the taught, tested and written curriculum. Alignment is connected to implementation and infrastructure as the alignment determines in part how the curriculum will be managed and changed. And alignment is connected to assessment; in the Balanced Curriculum the assessments are aligned to the standards and assessment specifications. Alignment does not stand alone.

The next chapter deals with the research around curriculum structure with a note on district stability.

REFERENCES

American Association for the Advancement of Science. (2001). *Designs for science literacy.* New York: Oxford University Press: Author.

Blank, R.K., Porter, A., Smithson, J. (2001). *New tools for analyzing teaching, curriculum and standards in Mathematics & Science: Results form survey of Enacted Curriculum Project.* Washington, DC: Council of Chief State School Officers.

Bowe, B.P. & Kingsbury, G.G. (2007, April). *Comparison of four state performance standard alignment methods.* Paper presented at the American Educational Research Association, Chicago, IL.

Browder, D., Flowers, C., Ahigrim-Deizell, L., Karvonen, M., Spooner, F., Algozzine, R. (2004). The alignment of alternate assessment content with academic and functional curricula, *Journal of Special Education, 30*(4), 211-223.

DiBiase, W.J., Warren, J., Wagner, E.P. (2002). Aligning general chemistry laboratory with a lecture at a large university. *School Science and Mathematics, 102,* 158-171.

Cohen, S. A. (1987). Instructional alignment: Searching for a magic bullet. *Educational Researcher, 16,* 16–19.

Cohen, S.A. & Stover, G. (1981). Effects of teaching sixth grade students to modify the variables in Math word problems. *Reading Research Quarterly, 16,* 175-200.

Elia, I.S.J., (1986). *An alignment experiment in vocabulary instruction: Varying instructional practice and test item formats to measure transfer with low SES fourth graders.* Unpublished Doctoral Dissertation, University of San Francisco.

English, F. W. (1992). Deciding what to teach and test: Developing, aligning, and audit ing the curriculum. In F. W. English (Series Ed.), *Successful school s: Guidebooks to effective educational leadership: Vol. 4.* Newbury Park, CA: Corwin Press.

Erickson, H.L. (2001). *Stirring the head, heart, and soul: Redefining curriculum and instruction.* (Second Edition). Thousand Oaks, CA: Corwin Press.

Fahey, P.A., (1986). *Learning transfer in main ideas instruction: Effects of instructional alignment on main idea test scores.* Unpublished Doctoral Dissertation, University of San Francisco

Freeman, D., Kuhs, T., Porter, A., Floden, R., Schmidt, W., & Schwille, J. (1983). Do textbooks and tests define a national curriculum in elementary school mathematics? *Elementary School Journal, 83,* 501–513.

Gentile, J.R., & Lalley, J.P., (2003). *Standards and mastery learning.* Thousand Oaks, CA: Corwin Press.

Goodman, K. S., Shannon, P., Freeman, Y. S., & Murphy, S. (1987). *Report card on basal readers.* Katonah, NY: Richard C. Owen.

Howson, G. (1995). *Mathematics textbooks: A comparative study of grade 8 texts.* Vancouver, Canada: Pacific Education Press.

Jacobs, H.H. (Ed.) (2004). *Getting results with curriculum mapping.* Alexandria, VA: Association of Curriculum and Supervision.

Kozar, M.L., (1984). *Effects of varying degrees of instructional alignment in posttreatment tests on mastery learning task s of fourth grade children.* Unpublished Doctoral Dissertation, University of San Francisco.

Levine, D.U, Block, J.H., Cox, B.E., Friedman, L.B., Huynh, H., Jones, B.F., Kennedy, M.M., Mamary, A., Menahem, M., Pringle, P.R., Robb, D.W., Rowe, L.A., Ryan, D.W., Smith, W.J., Spady, W.G., Tinzmann, M., Walberg, H.J., & Weisman, L. (1985). *Improving student achievement through mastery learning programs.* San Francisco: Jossey-Bass Publishers.

McGhee, J.J. & Griffith, L.K. (2001). Large-scale assessments combined with curriculum alignment: Agents of change. *Theory into Practice, 40*(2), 137-144.

Moss-Mitchell, F. (1998). *The effects of curriculum alignment on the mathematics achievement of third-grade students as measured by the Iowa Test of Basic Skills: Implication for educational administrators.* Unpublished doctoral dissertation, Clark University, Atlanta, GA.

National Center for Education Statistics (2007). *Mapping 2005 State Proficiency Standards Onto the NAEP Scales* (NCES 2007-482). U.S. Department of Education. Washington, DC: Author.

Porter, A. C., Kirst, M. W., Osthoff, E., Smithson, J. L., & Schneider, S. (1994) *Reform of high school mathematics and science and opportunity to learn.* Consortium for Policy Research in Education Policy Briefs. New Brunswick, NJ: Rutgers University, Consortium for Policy Research in Education.

Porter, A. C., & Smithson J. L. (2001). *Defining, developing, and using curriculum indicators* (CPRE Research Report Series RR-048). Philadelphia: Consortium for Policy Research in Education, University of Pennsylvania.

Posner, G.J. & Rudnitsky, A.N. (2006). *Course design: A guide to curriculum development for teachers.* Boston, MA: Pearson Education, Inc.

Price-Baugh, R. (1997). *Correlation of textbook alignment with student achievement scores.* Unpublished doctoral dissertation, Baylor University, Waco, TX.

Quellmalz, E., Kreikemeier, P., Haydel DeBarger, A., & Haertel, G. (March, 2006*). A Study of the Alignment of the NAEP, TIMSS, and New Standards Science Assessments with the Inquiry Abilities in the National Science Standards.* Center for Technology in Learning, SRI International. Paper presented at the American Educational Research Association, San Francisco, CA.

Schmidt, W. H., McKnight, C. C., Houang, R. T., Wang, H. C., Wiley, D. E., Cogan, L. S., & Wolfe, R. G. (2001). *Why school s matter: A cross-national comparison of curriculum and learning.* San Francisco: Jossey-Bass.

Squires, D.A., (2009). *Curriculum alignment: Research-based strategies for increasing student achievement.* Thousand Oaks, CA: Corwin Press.

Squires, D.A. (2012). Curriculum alignment research suggests that alignment can improve student achievement. *The Clearing House: A Journal of Educational Strategies, Issues and Ideas*, 85:4, 129-135.

Tallarico, I., (1984). Squires, D.A. (2012). Curriculum alignment research suggests that alignment can improve student achievement. *The Clearing House: A Journal of Educational Strategies, Issues and Ideas,* 85:4, 129-135.

Tomlinson, C.A., Kaplan, S.N., Renzulli, J.S., Purcell, J., Leppien, J., Burns, D. (2002). *The parallel curriculum: A design to develop high potential and challenge high-ability learners.* Thousand Oaks, CA.: Corwin Press.

Webb, N.L. (January, 1997). WISE Brief: Determining Alignment of Expectations and Assessments in Mathematics and Science Education [Electronic Version] *http://www.wcer.wisc.edu/archive/nise/Publications/Briefs/Vol_1_No_2/NISE_Brief_Vol _1_No_2.pdf].* Retrieved February 22, 2006.

Wiggins, G. & McTighe, J. (2005). *Understanding by Design.* (2nd Edition). Alexandria, VA: Association of Curriculum and Supervision.

Wise, L.L., Zhang, L., Winter, P., Taylor, L., & Becke, D.E. (2006). Vertical alignment of grade-level expectations for student achievement: Report of a pilot study. In Council of Chief State School Officers, *Aligning assessment to guide the learning of all students.* State Collaborative on Assessment and Student Standards: Washington, DC

Wishnick, K. T. (1989). *Relative effects on achievements scores of SES, gender, teacher effect and instructional alignment: A study of alignment's power in mastery learning.* Unpublished doctoral dissertation, University of San Francisco, CA.

In: Curriculum
Editor: David A. Squires

ISBN: 978-1-62948-673-4
© 2014 Nova Science Publishers, Inc.

Chapter 4

CURRICULUM STRUCTURE AND DISTRICT LEADERSHIP STABILITY

David A. Squires, Ph.D.
Southern Connecticut State University, New Haven, CT, US

INTRODUCTION

The purpose of this chapter is to show how a model curriculum structure provides a necessary attribute to a curriculum development process that produces improved achievement. Criteria are presented at the end of the Chapter for important structures to consider when designing a curriculum. "Don't teachers and administrators know this already?' My hunch is that there is not a specified structure that all curriculum use. This became obvious to me as a Board of Education member, when our first curriculum was presented, it was in a form that was useable if you wanted to check alignment to the standards, but not useable to help teachers in planning instruction. Further, most curriculum development models, such as Understanding by Design, Curriculum Mapping, The Concept-based Curriculum by Lynn Erickson contain little reference to the standards and the state and national assessments, and little attention is paid to aligning the standards to the curriculum. Carol Ann Tomlinson et al. (2002) in her Parallel Curriculum acknowledges the need to align the curriculum with standards, but emphasizes using the standards as a way to access the most important concepts in a subject area, rather than ensuring coverage of the standards (and the assessment) within the curriculum. For example, in the Parallel Curriculum there is no way to determine which standards have been covered by the curriculum. These curriculum designs are lacking some essential pieces of curriculum structure.

Why is structure needed? Structure is needed so that the curriculum will be powerful enough to improve student achievement. Although we aren't the first to propose these structures, we are the first to suggest that these structures, taken together, will produce results in improving student achievement. All school districts have the capability to use a curriculum structure so student achievement will improve.

Before introducing the components of the curriculum structure, we spend time understanding that one purpose of curriculum structure is to reduce the variation in teaching outcomes. We follow this with an explanation of the "common" definition of curriculum, followed by our definition of curriculum. Finally, we discuss the curriculum structure which includes Content, Time, Process, Alignment, Assessment and Management. We believe that districts who develop and implement curriculum using this structure, student achievement will improve. The districts described in this book provide the cases in point. We conclude the chapter by emphasizing district stability as a key ingredient of getting results when using curriculum to improve achievement.

CURRICULUM'S PURPOSE IS TO REDUCE VARIATION IN TEACHING OUTCOMES

Curriculum structure exists to reduce variation in teaching outcomes. For example, let's pretend that we just started a school, and the first year it only has one grade level. We have four teachers teaching that one grade level. We could let all the teachers teach whatever they felt was important for children to learn. As the teachers have different beliefs about what is important for students to learn at that grade level, we will probably get very different outcomes, because teachers made different decisions about what was most important to emphasize. And this would pose big problems for the next grade level, as students wouldn't have similar levels of prerequisite skills. Here are some strategies we could use, and districts also use, to reduce the variation.

1   Order books and/or adopt programs – Insure similar content and process. One way to reduce variation is to provide the teachers with the same text or program. We would assume that teachers would follow the text/program and thereby get similar results. However, most teachers know that the same material can be used in many different ways, and so providing the same text/program, without further specification, may not result in teachers getting similar results. This is one strategy to reduce variation in outcome across teachers at the same grade level or course that most districts use.

2   Develop Common Assessments – Work for Similar Outcomes. Wiggins & McTigh (2003) focused their curriculum development on adopting common assessments as one way to structure the curriculum. The rationale for adopting such a strategy is that if teachers know what the assessment will be, then they are more likely to teach so students will perform well on the assessment. Teachers won't have to guess what is on the assessment. By specifying what is on the assessment, this insures more consistent results, rather than each teacher developing their own assessment. This provides another strategy to reduce variation across teachers. Many districts are developing common assessments as this is one way to reduce variation in outcomes.

3   Mapping the Curriculum through Content and Time – Heidi Jacobs (2004) has proposed a curriculum mapping process that involves teachers spelling out the content that they cover over a specified time period (like a month). Teachers then come together and distill their maps to produce a map that all will use. In this way, the time teachers spend on a unit, and the content of that unit is spelled out in the curriculum map. Controlling time and content is another way to produce a curriculum that reduces the variation among teacher outcomes.

4   Consistency of Teaching - Roots and Wings (Slavin & Maddin, 2003) is a program that spells out exactly what a teacher does in the classroom during Reading/Language Arts. The program is made up of a series of scripts for teachers to use in their teaching. One key to the program's success is that variation among teachers is reduced, as everyone uses the same scripts for the same amount of time.

5   Aligning the curriculum – Squires (2009, 2012) has shown that aligning curriculum to state standards and assessments, results in improved achievement. Alignment insures that what is taught is aligned to (state) standards and assessments. If the teachers teach the curriculum, then variation is reduced because the curriculum is aligned to the (state) standards and assessments.

6   Management – Squires (2005, 2013) has also demonstrated that managing the progress of teachers through the curriculum helps to insure positive results. For the Balanced Curriculum, teachers indicate on-line when they have completed the curriculum units. Principals can see how the teachers in their school are progressing, and district can see all the teachers in the district; individual teachers can only view their own record. Managing the curriculum is one way to reduce the variation in teachers by ensuring that all teachers teach and complete the same curriculum.

All these curriculum models demonstrate different ways to reduce the variation in outcome for students. Some may violate district/school norms for what is permissible. For example, some districts/schools have found the program of Roots and Wings to be too highly structured. It removes creativity from the teaching process through the use of scripts (while insuring less variation among teaching staff).

The districts discussed in this book, as well as those who have used the Balanced Curriculum, have generally structured their curriculum so that dimensions of content, time, process, alignment to standards and assessments have been addressed. Districts in this book have uniquely developed a curriculum structure that combines many of these elements

Some researchers emphasized that textbooks or state or national standards are the curriculum as they provide guidance on what students know and are able to do. Others believe that it is the instructional material. The lesson plan s or the student assignments represent the curriculum to other researchers, as these elements specify what students know and should be able to do on a daily basis. These various definitions present different levels of specificity (e.g., a lesson plan versus state standards). The definitions also take into account different time perspectives (daily for lesson planning versus yearly or longer for state standards). Only by knowing how curriculum is defined and structured will we be able to ensure the continuous, positive achievement effects. Next we examine a "common" definition of curriculum.

THE "COMMON" DEFINITION OF CURRICULUM

We begin with the common definition of curriculum to show the way school districts typically define curriculum: Curriculum sets the goals for instruction; teachers independently decide how to achieve those goals. For many educators, curriculum is just a list of goals agreed upon by the educational organization. The educators decide how to meet the goals by making decisions about time –i.e., how much time to spend on achieving the goal – and the process of how to go about teaching to meet the goal. The common definition reinforces the "agreement" between the organization and educator about goals for instruction. In this case, teachers have the autonomy to interpret the goals for instruction in any way. Some call this academic freedom. Districts specify the goals and individual teachers decide how to meet the goals in their classes, with little or no accountability (i.e., checking to see if the goals were addressed or accomplished) from district or school level administration. Content is the focus of this curriculum model, as it specifies what content should be taught, but not how to tech it, or defining how much time is necessary to teach it. Many districts still operate in this manner today.

Enter the standards movement. Standards --what students should know and be able to do- - set the goals and content for instruction specified by the state or nation. The state replaced the district in setting the goals. Districts now have to find a way to meet those goals, as opposed to setting the goals themselves. Individual teachers still have the authority to decide how and when to enact the standards. Little checking on whether the goals are taught or met occurs. Again, many school districts continue these arrangements. As there are now national standards, they assume even more importance.

Standards increase pressure on districts because achievement is assessed by high stakes state or national tests with highly publicized results. These hold districts, superintendents, school s, principals, and teachers, responsible for progress, or the lack thereof, of students' performance on standards-based state assessments. Additionally, the "No Child Left Behind " legislation requires that all children be proficient on their state test by 2014. Many states and districts have a long way to go. States can now get waivers for their results.

Curriculum's "common agreement" that districts (or states, or the nation) propose the goals and that individual teachers decide how the goals will be realized needs to change in order to meet the current realities of the standards movement, accountability, and the "No Child Left Behind " legislation. The "Common Agreement" needs to change because teachers working individually have no way of aligning their instruction, or their individual curriculum, or determining how much time to spend on topics. There is also no testing to determine if students are meeting the goals, prior to state or national testing. If individual teachers would have to make decisions about time, alignment and assessment, the process would be too inefficient, cost prohibitive and time consuming for each individual teacher to enact.

Districts respond to this pressure created by the standards by enacting a combination of strategies that specify:

- When content is taught (Time)
- What content is taught (Content)
- How the content is taught (Process)

For example, pacing guides may outline *when* topics are taught and *what* topics are taught, thus leaving it to the individual teacher's choice as to *how* topics are taught within the time constraints (see Jacobs, 2004). The "how to teach" part of the curriculum structure is absent. Greater variability in teaching occurs if "how to teach" is not addressed. Test scores will reflect this variability.

To address this problem, some districts adopt prescriptive programs, like "Success for All - Roots and Wings for Elementary School Reading". These programs script what teachers say and do (Slavin, R.E. & Madden, N.A., 2003). Such programs address "how to teach" issues, by scripting individual lessons for all teachers. Unfortunately, they do not address how well the program's content may be aligned to state standards and assessments. The program's generally positive results suggest that controlling for teacher variability in implementing curriculum can result in positive achievement gains. To maximize these gains, alignment with state standards and assessments must occur in order to capitalize on alignment's ability to produce higher student achievement (Squires, 2009). So, not just one variable needs to be taken into account in designing a curriculum structure.

The "Roots and Wings" curriculum structure addresses what to teach, when to teach and how to teach, but many have found that following a script is too confining. Variation among teachers may be reduced, but the price is a lack of flexibility in the scripts. Curriculum structure can reduce the variability without having to require scripted lessons (see Squires, 2005a. 2005b. 2005c, 2012)

Alignment is another issue for curriculum structure. There is no way for individual teachers to align their instruction with the standards, except to naively hope that the professional teacher s have read the hundreds of standards statements for one subject area and integrated them when instructing their students. Such hope is futile as it is impossible for teachers to keep hundreds of standard statements in their heads while making thousands of decisions during instruction. If teachers individually decide what and how to teach, then there is little alignment between what is instructionally done in the classroom and the state standardized tests, variation among teachers increases, with poorer results happening on year end state or national tests. As a result this condition virtually guarantees that alignment of curriculum and standards across the professional teaching community of the school district will not and cannot occur. Consequently, standardized test results do not improve. A structured curriculum can help.

Implementing the "Common Definition" of curriculum will not work. It is not possible for the district to decide the goals for instruction, outside of state standards and assessment, and then hope that teachers will make correct instructional decisions that automatically take into account standards and test specifications. Therefore, a curriculum structure needs to specify:

- When the content is taught
- What content is taught
- How the content is taught
- The alignment to standards
- How the curriculum will be assessed and managed

Our definition of curriculum contains these elements.

OUR DEFINITION OF CURRICULUM

We call our definition of curriculum the "standards-based" definition and in contrast with the common definition, ours states:

"Curriculum is the district's written plan incorporating aspects of time use, content and process aligned to standards and assessments that establishes a focus for instruction, assessment, staff development and management so student achievement improves."

Let's examine each phrase in the definition to understand its implications.

Part 1: "Curriculum is the District's Written Plan..."

Curriculum, as part of the institutional structure, needs to be written. Having a written plan means that teachers can look at the written plan and make decisions about what they will teach. As there is only one plan for the district, having it written insures that it will be interpreted in nearly the same way across the district school s. This also assumes that district leadership has seen the need to bring together teachers from across the district to develop this plan through a consensus building process. This may be a big step, as schools may have been used to functioning independently of the district. Indeed, our upcoming stories of districts point out that many had to adopt a district curriculum, where none existed before. This represents a huge change in the culture of a district.

Part 2: "...Incorporating Aspects of Time Use, Content and Process..."

A curriculum needs to demonstrate how time will be used (Walberg, 1988). Many districts already have pacing guides, which specify how much time is used on particular topics or units (see, for example, Jacobs, 2004); therefore, a curriculum needs to specify the content to be covered during a particular time period. Time management for teaching core concepts, therefore, becomes an integral part of the process for covering important curricular content. No longer can individual teachers make individual decisions about when important content should be taught. Managing how time is used is an important function of curriculum structure.

Finally, the district stipulates the process by which important content is covered. For example, teaching the "main idea" concept by asking students to develop newspaper headlines is a powerful teaching technique that specifies the process by which the concept, "main idea" is taught. Linking content and process together in the standards-based curriculum is different from the common definition curriculum where only content goals are specified and the process is under the purview of the individual teacher. Under the common definition the "main idea" goal might be taught by using sample state test question of the "main idea" or any one of a hundred different instructional methods, increasing variability across the school and district. Experienced teachers can distinguish between powerful and weak ways to address content. Their expertise should be incorporated into the curriculum development process so the most powerful teaching strategies can be used by all on a systematic basis. If all of the curriculum's goals are addressed with powerful strategies that all students had access to, achievement would be likely to improve.

Part 3: "…Aligned to Standards And Assessments…"

Standards-based curricula require that time, content, and process be described and aligned to standards and assessments. The common definition does not even consider alignment to state standards. By demonstrating *in writing* how standards will be met, we fulfill a primary function of the education system – coverage of the standards.

The district is the definition's focus as it has the responsibility of determining how the standards are enacted, not the school s or individual teachers as occurs in the common definition. The focus emerges from a resource issue, as most schools and individual teachers do not have the time or resources to produce, maintain and improve a written plan for instruction, other than lesson plan s. (See chapter 3 for more details).

Part 4:… "That Establishes a Focus for Instruction, Assessment, Staff Development and Management"

A link has already been established between curriculum and instruction, but curriculum is also connected to assessment, staff development processes, and management functions. These issues have traditionally not been part of curriculum design.

If curriculum is a written plan for instruction, it must be linked to the instruction that takes place in the classroom. By now, it should be clear that this link includes the instructional process, how the content (standards) are actually delivered in the classroom, and specifying how time is used.

In addition, we must ask ourselves: How well did students know? How ably can they perform? These are assessment questions that are not separate from curriculum, but intimately related to it, as the *Understanding by Design* (Wiggins & McTigh, 2005) framework for curriculum development demonstrates.

Curriculum structures also require management. Through management processes, the district knows that the curriculum (written plan) is assessed and implemented. Unfortunately, many districts while having a curriculum don't have a systematic process in place for recording teacher's progress on teaching the curriculum. Nor do they have a way of collecting data (though this is changing) on collecting assessment results. Decisions, based on good data, can then be made on whether to improve, maintain, or modify the written plan. Many curriculum development plans do not have a consistent process whereby actors in the system record results of assessments.

Part 5: "…So Student Achievement Improves…"

Improved achievement is the outcome of a well developed, aligned and implemented curriculum. If student achievement is not improving, then districts need to reexamine their curriculum development plan. If the function of the district's curriculum is not to improve achievement, then developing a curriculum is not productive work. If the written plan (the curriculum) did not work the first time, then changes need to be made so it will work better the second time. Those changes to the written plan give the district the necessary data and tools to revise the curriculum.

For example, if achievement decreased in the "writing persuasive essays" section of the state assessment, is this a problem of:

- Time or lack of time spent on the content persuasive essays?
- The process of how persuasive essays were taught and learned?
- The alignment between instruction and standards and the way the instruction is assessed?
- The fact that assessment results from units do not align with the standardized assessments?
- The management of the curriculum? Was the concept taught by teachers in the district? Were there early warning s from district or unit assessments that there were problems? Did this data come to decision makers in a timely and useful fashion?
- The lack of staff development on teaching and grading of persuasive essays?

The different potential causes of decreased student achievement highlights the importance of a robust curriculum structure, as it allows questions like the ones above, to be answered using data produced by the curriculum. The curriculum structure must be designed to anticipate the problem solving if achievement doesn't improve.

The problem of curriculum design, therefore, must be integrated into the assessment, staff development, and management structures of a district if the district is to use curriculum as a tool for improving student achievement. All pieces of the definition of curriculum have to be in place for curriculum to effect student achievement.

Ralph Tyler said it best.

The primary educational function of organization is to relate the various learning experiences which together comprise the curriculum so as to produce the maximum cumulative effect in attaining the objectives of the school. The significant question to ask about any scheme of organization is: How adequately does it provide reinforcement of the several learning experiences so that they produce a maximum cumulative effect? (Tyler, 1977, p. 48.)

The definition of curriculum highlights the issues of content, time, process, standards, assessments and management. The next section describes each piece of curriculum structure.

CURRICULUM STRUCTURE

Curriculum structure deals with issues of content, time, process, standards, assessments and management. But not alone or individually, because individually they cannot provide the guidance that they can when taken together. Content means the issues or concepts studied. There might be a couple of units in Math dealing with the content of "Numeration". Time tells how much time is assigned to a particular content, for example a week to study density. Process defines the way the study of a content area is structured. For example, numeration might be taught using cooperative learning. Standards specify what students at particular grade levels need to know and be able to do, usually defined by state and/or national standards. Standards will generally include process and content considerations. In Science, for example, standards include both what is to be taught and how it should be taught. For example, the AASA science standards list the following standard as part of Scientific Inquiry,

Scientists differ greatly in what phenomena they study and how they go about their work. Although there is no fixed set of steps that all scientists follow, scientific investigations usually involve the collection of relevant evidence, the use of logical reasoning, and the application of imagination in devising hypotheses and explanations to make sense of the collected evidence.

So teaching this standard would involve the processes of "collection of relevant evidence, the use of logical reasoning, and the application of imagination in devising hypothesis."

Assessments function to help teachers know that students understand the concepts and processes. These structures need to be presented in two ways: so teachers can use the curriculum to guide instruction, and so school s will have the data they need to improve from the assessments. Lastly, is management; district leaders can check on teacher's progress in the curriculum and how much curriculum is associated with particular standards. This is particularly useful when analyzing test results which are aggregated by standard; having the curriculum organized by standard then allows school and district leaders to know how the curriculum that produced the results.

CONTENT

Content is defined as "what is taught in the curriculum." It is the most basic element of a curriculum structure, but not the only one. Content needs to be specific so that listing content will help the teachers in knowing what to teach. For example, specifying that "The middle ages" needs to be taught, might be a good beginning, but is too general to be of use. More detail is needed to focus instruction.

Help is available. Erickson (2001) believes that identifying the concepts that should be taught will help in specifying the curriculum. Wiggins and McTigh (2005) anchor their curriculum development process around assessments, then working backward from the assessments to instruction. Their process focuses on identifying enduring understandings and essential questions that is transferable and can be used in other situations. Tomlinson et al. 2002 divide the curriculum conceptualizing process into four areas: The core or basic curriculum, the curriculum connections, the curriculum of practice, and the curriculum of identity. Working across curriculum areas strengthens the process of identifying content appropriate for a specific curriculum. The Balanced Curriculum (Squires, 2005) relies on the personal expertise of the teachers creating the curriculum and the results of aligning the curriculum to state standards and assessments. All the curriculum models described in this book specify the content to be taught. Different models have different ways to describe the curriculum's content.

Time Most of the curriculum models in this book have a way to specify how much time to spend on teaching particular content. We believe this is a key issue: knowing that you have a week to spend on understanding the scientific method is different that if you had a month.

There are so many topics (content) that could be covered in a curriculum that it makes sense to identify those that are central to the curriculum, and then specify how much time is needed to teach those topics. This will be important in planning a year's worth of instruction. When I was a curriculum director in a small New Jersey school district, our students didn't do well in measurement in the third and fourth grade. The measurement unit was in the curriculum, but at the end. When I finally asked teachers if they covered that unit, all admitted that they had not, because they took all of the time with other units. In the future we paid more attention to completion dates for units, the students now received instruction on measurement, and the test results improved in that area.

As there are many demands on time, with interruptions for assemblies or fire drills, realistically specifying time is important. If content takes time to teach, then feeling an "academic press" to cover the content is just as important as having a written plan, consistent across school s, for making sure that all the specified content is covered. This may appear to be very basic, but many school districts don't have a way to manage what time they have for instruction in their schools.

Process

The process by which content is taught is just as important as specifying the time and content. This is where the districts in this book made sure that not only the content, but the process, be specified. For example, you might have the content of "teaching for the main idea". It might be contained in a unit that covers a month worth of instruction. But there are many ways to teach the main idea. Not specifying how the main idea is taught leaves a new teacher with no models on how to teach. The new teacher might decide, given the district emphasis on test scores that she will teach the main idea by taking models of how the main idea is tested by the state, and giving students practice using those models when teaching in her classroom. An experienced teacher may link a newspaper study with identifying the main idea. He would eliminate headlines from articles, and then ask the students to read the articles and develop a headline. He organized his instruction using cooperative groups. If the new teacher had this model of specifying the headline of a news article, she may have adopted this strategy too. As time is an issue, which activity would you rather your students participated in? The stories in this book, will illustrate ways that districts were able to specify how to teach, as well as what to teach and the amount of time for teaching particular content. Expertise is available in all district with the best, the brightest, and the most caring able to identify strong ways that particular content may be taught.

By specifying how content should be taught, there will be an advantage when analyzing yearly test results. If results for a particular topic was not up to expectations, then experienced teachers can review how the topic was taught, how much time was needed, and suggest changes that might improve the curriculum next time. Those changes might be increasing the amount of time spent on a topic, revising how the topic was taught, by specifying a different way to teach the topic, or combining it with another similar topic. These options are all available if one knows how the topic is taught. If one doesn't know how the topic is taught, then there is little to do in revising the curriculum based on yearly scores. (Of course, this type of analysis is also available if there are common formative assessments).

Alignment

Alignment is a theme that goes throughout the stories of the districts in this book. All used alignment processes in developing their curriculum. As mentioned previously, it is surprising to me that major curriculum development systems (Erickson, 2001; Jacobs, 2004; Wiggins & McTigh, 2005) do not reflect the importance of alignment in their curriculum structures. Most have no way of recording how much of the curriculum is aligned to the standards and state assessments or reporting which of the standards are over or under emphasized. Yet the districts reported in this book who improved their student achievement all used alignment processes as an important structure in their curriculum development processes.

Deciding on a way to align is difficult. We use the Balanced Curriculum here as it provides the clearest model of how to structure alignment. The first difficulty is identifying what the district will align the standards and assessments to. For example, on could align standards and assessments to unit descriptions. Let's assume that there were approximately 15 units a year. Standards statements have anywhere from 100 – 300 standard statements. So 15 units divided by 300 (the top number of standards) and you would need to align 20 unique standards to each unit in order to get all the standards covered. What would be the impact on a teacher of having 20 unique standards per unit let's say, as part of a unit introduction. I believe, that if a district chose this way, teachers would ignore the unit introduction, and possibly miss some of the standards in their instruction.

Another possibility might be to align lesson plan s with the 100-300 standard statements. Let's assume that there are 150 "real" teaching days in a year that aren't interrupted and are not before a holiday. That would mean that each lesson plan would need to be aligned to 1 or 2 unique objectives. That appears to be doable. However, that would mean that all would have to follow the same lesson plans. From my experience as a teacher, the lesson plan is to small an amount of time, and it would be too difficult to require that all teachers of a grade or course, teach from the same lesson plan.

The structure used in the balanced curriculum is to define significant tasks, or assured activities that everyone will teach, using their own lesson plan s so they can fit the lesson plan to their specific classes. If each of the 15 units had 4 significant tasks, then there would be about 60 significant tasks per year. If the alignment was to 180 standard statements then three unique alignments would be needed for each significant task. In the Balanced Curriculum, there are usually 5 alignments for each significant task, allowing for some standards that go across significant tasks to receive double or triple billing. The difficulty with this is that teachers who develop the curriculum, as well as all the staff in the district, needs to deeply understand what makes a good significant task, as it falls between a lesson plan and a unit.

When significant tasks are aligned, a teacher centered report can be printed which shows the standards each significant task is aligned to. So a teacher can examine the alignments to the significant task and know that they will need to cover those five standards when teaching the significant task. (Without alignment, teachers would need to keep the hundreds of standards in their heads, an impossible feat.)

The web site where the Balanced Curriculum is housed also produces a report that for the course shows what standards have been aligned and which standards have not been aligned. The teachers working on the curriculum can use this report to determine standards that have been under or not emphasized and standards that have been overemphasized. Basically the report lists all the standards and then the number and title of the significant tasks to which they have been aligned. This report can also be used when analyzing test results. Teachers would examine the test results aggregated by standard. Those with excellent results may be fine or could be de-emphasized. Results that indicate a weakness, then teachers could decide whether:

- there was enough time spent on the significant task,
- the significant task was difficult enough,
- the assessment was too easy,
- the significant task gave an adequate way to teach to content,
- it needed to be replaced with a more difficult significant task,
- there should be more significant tasks addressing the similar standards

In this way, based on a yearly review, the curriculum can be revised and updated on a yearly basis based on the newest results from the state testing program. This would be an excellent activity for a district data team to work on.

Alignment needs to be reported in two different ways, as illustrated above. First, there needs to be alignment to the taught curriculum (in this case the sequence of specific tasks). Second, the alignments need to be organized by standards. In this way we will know how many significant tasks (or assured activities) are aligned to each standard. When test results come back, it will be important to examine those reports to identify areas that need to be improved. Having an aligned curriculum is important for continued district improvement of test scores, as demonstrated by the forth coming district stories.

Assessment

A system of assessment will reinforce the curriculum. If a district specifies what is to be taught, the amount of time for teaching the content, the process by which the content is addressed, and how the instruction is aligned to state standards, then having a system of assessment allows a district to know whether students are actually learning what has been defined in the curriculum. In this way assessment coupled with these other areas promotes an integrated view of curriculum structure.

The length of time the assessments address matter. An assessment is designed to cover a specific length of time. With state tests, the length of time is usually one year. The development of the assessments is generally quite rigorous, as the test needs to fairly represent the standards that are covered throughout the year. And these tests are generally tried out on a sub-population of the state to insure fairness to various important groups throughout the state. They have high reliability and validity. We can judge the test to be a fair way to assess students' knowledge because of the technical dimensions of the test. Having a test that covers a year's worth of material is problematic for teachers and districts because it is difficult to know exactly what will be tested; there are quite a few options. This also increases the importance of aligning to the test specifications that the state may make available, as well as aligning to the standards. Specific content of the state test must remain secret so that validity and reliability can be maintained (see Squires, 2005a for a discussion).

Since everyone must take the yearly state test, many districts have district-developed tests that are given during the year, let's use the example of those given on a quarterly basis. Where the tests are aligned to the format and content of the state test, the results can be predictive (Squires, D.A. and Feinn, R., (January, 2008)). In this case the authors found that the four scores of the quarterly assessments, taken as a whole, did the best in predicting outcomes on the state test. Again, one of the reasons the tests are used in this large urban district, is that it helps to reinforce what is on the state's test and gives teachers a way to benchmark how well their class may be doing.

Some districts have reduced the time between tests to a month. The small scope of the test allows districts to collect data about student performance during an even smaller time period, thus partially assuring that topics covered during the month will yield results that will show how well students are doing on important topics covered during that month.

Districts may give tests in addition to teacher made tests that are given after a unit of instruction or on quizzes in the classroom. Again, districts will need to do a cost /benefit analysis. If teachers give a test after each unit, and there are 15 units a year, then 15 days per year are spent on testing by the teacher. If district testing is once per month for 8 months, then testing covers a total of 23 days per year. The state or national test may take an additional 5 days out of instruction for a total of 28 days. If there are 180 days of instruction, testing then approximately 1/6 of the instructional time is spent in testing students or 1 day every 6 instructional days. The state test in these circumstances may receive more importance in terms of time, than the data received is worth (but this needs to be determined by the district). If districts constructed their own unit tests, instead of individual teachers, then only 20 days (15 on unit tests, 5 days on the state test) would be spent during the year on testing. This amount of time is only for one subject area. The district will need to arrive at a figure that includes all subject areas so a decision can be made on the "proper" amount of testing the district requires.

Using the results of the tests provide one criteria for assisting in making decisions about test results. Many districts have adopted the use of data teams as a way to use the data from testing to improve results. School data teams meet and identify patterns in the test results, and then link those patterns to changes in instruction that will take place in the future. District data teams can make district-wide recommendations about the testing results, that might yield staff development plans for the future. What you will notice in the district stories is that data teams and formative testing are used as a way to improve performance; coupled with specifying content, time, and process, using results from assessments form one of the benchmarks of these improving systems described in the later chapters of this book.

Management

Curriculum needs to be managed in order to be effective. Administrators need to have some way to check on individual teacher's progress through the curriculum. Principals could do this through monitoring lesson plan s. In Balanced Curriculum there is an on-line management tool that teachers use to indicate unit completion. Principals can see the results for their school; district officials can see results for the whole district. With one report, administrators can know at a glance who has completed the curriculum in a timely fashion. For curriculum to have an impact, it must be managed through recording at a minimum, which has completed various units of the curriculum. Unfortunately, many districts that have a curriculum have no provisions for managing the curriculum.

SUMMARY

This chapter has provided the rationale for six structures that need to be in place for a curriculum to have an effect on student achievement.

Str-1 Does the curriculum specify the Content (subject matter) of the curriculum?
Str-2 Are Time parameters used so teachers k now how much time should be devoted to particular content?
Str-3 Does the curriculum specify the Instructional Process used to teach the curriculum content?
Str-4 Is Alignment included in the curriculum design? Is there at standard way to align within the curriculum? (See the Alignment section.)
Str-5 Does the curriculum specify the parameters for Assessment? (see the Assessment section)
Str-6 Does the written curriculum design specify how the curriculum will be Managed? (Who is responsible for seeing the curriculum is being completed?)

Figure 4.1. Structure of Curriculum.

Current curriculum development processes deal with some of these structures, but few deal with all of them in an integrated whole. If curriculum is going to affect student achievement, we propose that a system of curriculum development needs to address all six.

LEADERSHIP STABILITY

As important as having an appropriate curriculum structure is the importance of having stability of leadership at the district level. The districts cited in this book have all had stability at the superintendent level during the development of curriculum as a means for district improvement. When reading the district stories, you will invariably be impressed by the scope of hurdles these individual districts faced when making the curriculum the center of the district's improvement efforts. This is an important consideration, especially for members of school boards, as research shows that the average tenure for a superintendent is less than five years, while almost a quarter serve less than three years (Lashway, 2002). To put into place a curriculum structure that will improve student achievement will take a superintendent an extended period of time.

Our next chapter addresses implementation. A strong implementation plan of action is necessary to ensure that all members of a district actually implement the curriculum. A downfall of some districts is that there is not enough emphasis on implementation of the curriculum once it is developed.

Stab-1 Does the district have stability at the upper levels of administration so that a 3 to 5 year curriculum development process can be conceptualized and completed?

Figure 4.2. Stability.

The next chapter summarizes the research about implementation and comments on building district infrastructure for curriculum development.

REFERENCES

AAAS, *http://www.project2061.org/publications/bsl/online/index.php?chapter=1#B3*, retrieved on March 23, 2011.

Briggs, T.H. (1926). *Curriculum problems.* New York: Macmillan.

Erickson, H.L. (2001). *Stirring the head, heart, and soul: Redefining curriculum and instruction.* (Second Edition). Thousand Oaks, CA: Corwin Press.

Jacobs, H.H. (2004) *Getting results with Curriculum Mapping.* Alexandria, VA: Association of Supervision and Curriculum Development.

Lashway, Larry. (2002). The Superintendent in an Age of Accountability. *ERIC Digest 161, Clearning House on Educational Policy and Management, College of Education, University of Oregon, http://eric.uoregon.edu/publications/digests/digest161.html*

Slavin, R.E. & Madden, N.A. (2003). Success for all / Roots & wings: Summary of Research on Achievement Outcomes. (Report no. 41 (revised)) Baltimore, MD: Center for Research on the Education of Students Placed at Risk. Available on the web at: *http://www.successforall.net/_images /pdfs/SummaryofResearch-2003.pdf.*

Squires, D.A. (2005a). *Aligning and balancing the standards-based curriculum.* Thousand Oaks, CA: Corwin Press.

Squires, D.A. (November, 2005b). *The relationship between aligned curriculum and student achievement.* Charleston, WV: Edvantia, Inc.

Squires, D.A. (June, 2005c). *Curriculum Alignment: Literature Review.* Appalachian Educational Lab., Inc., Charleston, WV.

Squires, D.A. (2009). *Curriculum alignment: Research-based strategies for increasing student achievement.* Thousand Oaks, CA: Corwin Press.

Squires, D.A. (2013). *The balanced curriculum model: Description and results.* SAGE Open, January-March 2013; vol. 3, 1: 2158244013478012, first published on February 27, 2013.

Squires, D.A. (2012). Curriculum alignment research suggests that alignment can improve student achievement. *The Clearing House: A Journal of Educational Strategies, Issues and Ideas*, 85:4, 129-135.

Squires, D.A. & Feinn, R. (January, 2008). *Correlation of Bridgeport's, CT. quarterly assessments in Mathematics with the Connecticut Mastery Test for Third Grade Mathematics.* Eastern Connecticut State University: CSU Research Conference.

Tomlinson, C.A., Kaplan, S.N., Renzulli, J.S., Purcell, J., Leppien, J., Burns, D. (2002) *The parallel curriculum: A design to develop high potential and challenge high-ability learners.* Thousand Oaks, CA: Corwin Press.

Tyler, R.W. (1949). *Basic principles of curriculum and instruction.* Chicago: The University of Chicago Press.

Tyler, R.W. (1977). The organization of learning experiences. In A.A. Bellack & H.M. Kliebard (Eds.), *Curriculum and evaluation* (pp. 45-55). Berkeley, CA: McCutchan Publishing.

Walberg, H.J. (1988). *Spending More While Learning Less*. Fordham Report, Volume 2, Number 6.

Wiggins, G. & McTighe, J. (2005). *Understanding by Design.* (2nd Edition). Alexandria, VA: Association of Curriculum and Supervision.

In: Curriculum
Editor: David A. Squires

ISBN: 978-1-62948-673-4
© 2014 Nova Science Publishers, Inc.

Chapter 5

IMPLEMENTATION AND INFRASTRUCTURE

Meagan Martins, Ph.D.
Administrator in the Danbury Public Schools, Danbury, CT, US

INTRODUCTION TO FACTORS AFFECTING TEACHER, PRINCIPAL AND CENTRAL OFFICE EFFECTIVENESS

In the current era of educational accountability, school districts are under unprecedented pressure to demonstrate improved student achievement results. The No Child Left Behind Act requires State Education Agencies to select from a menu of federally-approved sanctions to impose upon districts when they fail to meet Adequate Yearly Progress targets for four consecutive years (U.S. Congress, 2001). One such available sanction is that districts must implement a new curriculum. This certainly stands to reason as *what* students are taught directly impacts how well they learn. However, as many seasoned teachers and administrators will tell you, what is in the curriculum binder is not always found happening in the classroom. This chapter will explore the context of improvement planning in school districts, frequent challenges encountered when districts attempt to implement improvement strategies and a research-based framework school and districts leaders can consider when preparing to embark on improvement efforts.

Implementing a new curriculum for a school district is a major improvement strategy. A new curriculum may require teachers to learn new content, instructional delivery models, and assessment and management systems; an undertaking of these proportions requires resources and support if it is to be done so effectively. Before embarking upon the long journey of curricular development and implementation, district and school leaders must assess the current state of affairs, with respect to both existing curriculum and faculty attitude towards implementing something new. This chapter will present a framework for considering common improvement strategy implementation challenges so leaders can proactively plan for potential issues. It will also present a framework that can be utilized when developing, implementing, and monitoring district improvement strategies, such as instituting a new curriculum.

Improvement planning is about fundamentally and simultaneously changing three things: the values and beliefs of people, the conditions in which the work is done, and the ways in which people learn about the work (Elmore, 2008). The exercise of improvement planning is good practice for any organization that seeks to improve (Fidler, 2003; Senge, 1990), but simply developing a plan will not effect change. Implementation gaps loom large in many school s and so even the best-laid plans may not be implemented and therefore cannot positively impact student achievement (Fullan, 2005).

Since many school districts are required to engage in the strategic exercise of developing improvement plans and are still not demonstrating improvement, it is critical to understand the barriers and challenges experienced when implementing plans. While the actual size and complexity of the plan can in and of itself be a barrier to implementation (Fullan & Stiegelbauer, 1991; Schmoker, 2004), Martins (2010) has identified five broad categories of challenges commonly encountered by teachers and leaders when implementing improvement strategies:

1 Loose-coupling of system levels and lack of impact that district improvement strategies have on instruction;
2 Change process as experienced by the organization and individuals within the organization;
3 Lack of resources, politics, and policies to support improvement;
4 Lack of capacity in leadership and faculty; and
5 Lack of monitoring and communication systems.

LOOSE-COUPLING OF SYSTEM LEVELS AND LACK OF IMPACT ON INSTRUCTION

Elmore (2008) has suggested that an essential element in tackling the issues of instructional improvement is the need to preserve the connection between district-wide improvement strategies and the daily practice of teachers. This presents the challenge of how to infuse classrooms with better instruction, ensure that teachers have the requisite skills and resources needed to implement the change, and monitor that the adults in the system are in fact changing their behavior in a way that does not cause great variation of implementation across the smallest and most critical units of the system—classrooms. District improvement necessarily means instructional improvement (Connell & Klem, 2000).

School districts are complex systems with several levels within the organization. The central office, individual school s, grade level clusters or content area clusters, and individual classrooms are the primary units found within the school district. As a result of the multi-layered system that exists in school districts, it becomes increasingly more complicated to effect change at the critical unit, the classroom, because the central office most often devises improvement strategies and is often far removed from individual classrooms (Elmore, 2008). In large part because of the system's structure, improvement plans do not often impact instruction (Fullan, 1993), which is "the central work of school" (Tyack & Cuban, 1995, p. 84).

The disconnect between the levels of the system which prevents all levels from working in harmony towards a common goal is referred to as loose-coupling (Meyer & Rowan, 1978;

Rowan, 1990; Weick, 1976). Elmore (2008) stated that the danger of loose-coupling lies within the lack of impact on teachers' instruction:

> Derived from institutional sociology, this view [loose-coupling] posits that the'technical core' of education – detailed decisions about what should be taught at any given time, how they [students] should be grouped within classrooms for purposes of instruction, what they should be required to do to demonstrate their knowledge, and, perhaps most importantly, how their learning should be evaluated – resides in individual classrooms, not in the organizations that surround them. (p. 46)

As a result of this phenomenon, the challenge for educators engaged in improvement planning efforts becomes one of tightening the links within the system so that improvement plan strategies directly impacts classroom learning and teaching.

Stigler and Heibert (1999) have argued that school and district improvement in the United States has not been impacted by research because education is largely a cultural process in America. Teachers are often impervious to so-called systematic efforts to improve instruction and, because of the isolation that is inherent in the profession, often continue with their old ways. Daily practice will only evolve to mirror best practice as outlined by research if schools are restructured so that teachers are expected to be lifelong learners and are given the requisite time during the school day that is needed for collaborative lesson study, peer observation, and team planning. Too frequently, improvement plans ignore harsh realities, such as the lack of available time for teacher collaboration during the day. This enormous oversight provides would-be implementers with a convenient reason not to attempt to engage in new practices because they simply do not have the time (Hess, 2004).

CHANGE PROCESS

School improvement requires systemic change, which in turn requires a change in the activities of the organization (Adelman & Taylor, 2007). In a school system, this usually translates into a need for the adults in the system to change their behavior to implement a new practice. Change takes time and major commitment (Hall & Hord, 1987). Consequently, the change process can be an enormous barrier to improvement processes and must be attended to in both the planning and implementation phases. This section will explore the change process as it is experienced by organizations and individuals, as well as the need to change culture in order to sustain new practices in the school system.

Change is an unavoidable process in the quest for continuous organizational improvement. This is particularly true of school systems as the children who require teaching change each year in terms of their demographics, needs, and talents. Change is particularly difficult in school systems as all educators are the product of a school system, and so it is often difficult to imagine another way of doing business other than the way that it was experienced (Cuban, 1984). However, the proliferation of educational research in the last few decades requires a re-examination of how schools operate, and this often means that organizations must change to be responsive to what research identifies as best practice.

Organizational change is extremely complex because it does not only deal with changing the practices of the organization as a whole, but it also requires attending to the change process as it is experienced by the individuals who comprise the organization. Change is frequently experienced as a grieving process whereby individuals must let go of old practices (Marris, 1974). Individuals move through the grieving process in their own time, which makes the leadership task of supporting individuals as they navigate the process difficult because it is not linear and occurs at a different rate of time for each person who is experiencing it.

RESOURCES, POLITICS, AND POLICIES

Every aspect of education in the United States is political in nature. From the standards-based reform movement to the adoption of local curricula by elected boards of education, the decisions made regarding what knowledge is important to ensure students learn are governed by a political process (Spring, 2001). The process for obtaining and distributing resources is also mired in the political process (Stone, 2002). Successful school districts enact comprehensive, coherent policies to support sustaining reform over long periods of time (Dailey, Fleischman, Gil, Holtzman, O'Day & Vosmer, 2005). Policies for adopting curricula and distributing resources are negotiated on a political platform, and improvement planning strategies must take into account who is distributing what to whom since a change in the adult actions of the organization usually requires a change in resource allocation (Waters & Marzano, 2006).

A common mistake made in improvement planning exercises is the development of strategies for which there are simply not enough resources to support (Schmoker, 2004). Resources for implementation, including professional development and teacher release time, and resources for strategy monitoring must be allocated. Often, the impossibility of implementing a strategy lies in the lack of resources, which causes great frustration, negativity, and cynicism within the teaching force. In a study of high-quality instruction in high-poverty classrooms, Knapp and Shields (1995) found that the pattern of district involvement in instructional improvement was commonly chaotic and incoherent, which resulted in few supporting resources being provided to teachers. In the successful school districts analyzed in a meta-analytic study, Waters and Marzano (2006) found that superintendents ensured alignment between district goals and resource allocation. They suggested that "Effective superintendents ensure that the necessary resources, including time, money, personnel, and materials are allocated to accomplish the district's goals" (p. 4).

CAPACITY OF LEADERSHIP AND FACULTY

Improvement in a school district necessarily requires that individuals in the organization have the capacity to change their beliefs (DuFour, DuFour, & Eaker, 2005; Hess, 2004). This is the case for both leaders and teachers alike. Leaders must develop their capacity to be instructional leaders, and all levels of the organization must build capacity to change adult behaviors. In order to change student outcomes, there must be a shift in belief of what defines success for a school district. Successful school districts are those that are goal oriented with a laser-like focus on student achievement, and goals are framed in terms of student achievement

(Fidler, 2003; Reeves, 2004; Waters & Marzano, 2006). This shift requires a change in adult beliefs and skills, and it has deep implications for leadership behaviors, including ensuring a common belief in a vision of improved student achievement as a result of adult actions, establishing a community of learners, and building infrastructures of distributed leadership to facilitate transformational leadership.

COMMUNICATION AND MONITORING PROCESSES

Communicating expectations, strategies for change, available resources to facilitate the change, and regular reports on progress are key to ensuring that all members in the school district have a clear understanding of the improvement efforts. Without ensuring clarity of purpose, leaders are by default allowing individuals to continue working in isolation (Hess, 2004). Waters and Marzano (2006) emphasized the role of the district superintendents and stated that "Effective superintendents continually monitor district progress toward achievement and instructional goals to ensure that these goals remain the driving force behind a district's actions" (p. 4). Effective leaders also communicate progress and make time to celebrate short-term wins to sustain members of the organization for the duration of improvement efforts and effective change process (Fidler, 2003). Monitoring the implementation of strategies and their impact on student achievement is equally critical to successful improvement plans (Reeves, 2006).

Senge (1990) identified feedback loops as one of the critical components found in all learning organizations. Feedback loops are formal structures of communication that allow for information to flow horizontally and vertically throughout the organization. These structures offer all stakeholders with the opportunity to provide input into the development of improvement plans, as well as to provide feedback on the successes and challenges of implementing plans once they are established on the individual, group, and total levels of the organization.

THE RESEARCH

Martins (2010) conducted research in order to identify and analyze the challenges experienced by educators in 12 Connecticut Partner School Districts as they implement improvement plans. This research also investigated how these challenges are being addressed so that policy and practice can be informed for future districts that will be required to engage in the district improvement planning process.

Since no instrument existed to investigate these challenges, an exploratory mixed methods design was employed to develop a survey instrument that became the basis for identifying and analyzing challenges experienced by educators. Two phases of instrument development were performed. In phase one, focus groups were held to gather data to inform the survey development. Once the instrument had been developed and piloted, it was administered to educators in the 12 Connecticut Partner School Districts in phase two.

The survey responses indicated that both leaders and teachers identified four distinct categories of action that they have used to address improvement strategy implementation challenges:

1   Ensuring a targeted and common focus that informs school practice;
2   Involving teachers in improvement strategy development and monitoring;
3   Allocating appropriate resources (specifically funding for teacher release time, professional development for teachers and principals, and support staff to assist in and monitor classrooms); and
4   Providing individualized and team support for teachers and principals on the process of district improvement planning as well as the strategies that are expected to be implemented.

These categories can serve as a framework for developing, implementing, and monitoring improvement efforts, such as curriculum changes.

Ensuring a targeted and common focus informs school practice. Survey participants indicated that keeping a sharp focus on a limited number of actions was effective in ensuring DIP strategy implementation. This is supported by the literature (Fullan & Quinn, 2004; Reeves, 2006; Waters & Marzano, 2006). Communicating the focus and ensuring that clear expectations were understood and acted on by all were cited several times. Examples of these included ensuring that the curriculum reflected district goals and is followed consistently by all teachers, requiring teachers to develop common formative and summative assessments so strategy implementation and effectiveness in terms of student outcomes could be monitored, expecting lesson plans to connect to district goals, and using classroom walkthroughs as a monitoring and support mechanism.

Respondents also indicated the critical nature of ensuring that school improvement actions were aligned with district expectations. As improvement efforts evolve, strategies change which requires frequent alignment checks between district goals and school realities. The changing nature of the work served as a source of frustration for some teacher respondents. While many researchers highlight the importance of making midcourse corrections if strategies are not yielding the desired results (Fidler, 2003; Fullan, 2001; Reeves, 2004, 2006), this is often perceived as "changing the rules in the middle of the game" by teachers. District and school leaders must be clear not only about the change in strategy, but they must also communicate the reason that the strategy has changed. Districts must create structures to link the central office and schools. Such structures can be used to inform district leaders on how efforts are progressing at school, and to inform schools about reasons for changes asked by the central office.

Several respondents highlighted the critical role that principals play in translating district expectations into school practice and in providing support to teachers so they can implement expected changes. School leadership has been identified as one of the determining factors in the success or failure of improvement efforts (Marzano, Waters & McNulty, 2005), and so it is extremely important that school principals receive ongoing professional development and support in the strategies expected to be implemented and in the process of leading change.

Involving Teachers

The importance of involving teachers appeared as both a challenge that teacher respondents elaborated on, and as an action being taken by those respondents who felt that they were addressing implementation challenges. Leaders also identified involving teachers as a critical step, but they saw this as an area of success. This was a different point of view than that held by most teacher respondents which evidences very different perceptions. A few respondents highlighted the importance of involving the teacher and administrator unions in the development, implementation, and monitoring of the plans. Many teachers indicated that they felt as though the central office and those who determine improvement strategies were out of touch with current classroom reality and that the inclusion of more teachers in the process would have been beneficial. While many leaders cited that teacher involvement in strategy development was a success, teacher responses indicated that they seemed unaware that teachers had been involved in the process. Teachers merely participating in the writing of an improvement plan is not enough to qualify as distributing leadership (Spillane, 2006); a critical component of teacher participation is returning to the stakeholder group that they represent so that regular reports of the efforts can be made. This research suggests that a more complete definition of teacher involvement whereby "after meeting" responsibilities are more clearly delineated is needed.

Allocation of Resources

Teachers and leaders alike both cited the lack of resources to be an immense challenge in implementing improvement strategies. Specifically, the lack of time for additional work to be done and the lack of funding to hire more teachers and support staff to improve instruction are the biggest resource issues that were cited. Many respondents indicated that the lack of resources was an insurmountable challenge and that without additional time and funding for more personnel it would be impossible to make the changes outlined in strategies. Interestingly, only two respondents cited the lack of materials as an impediment. Fullan (2005) underscored the importance of leaders structuring an environment in school s whereby scarce resources are marshaled to support classroom performance. Respondents clearly indicated that, overwhelmingly, the greatest need is for additional human resources.

Providing Individualized and Team Support for Teachers and Principals

The most frequently cited action taken to successfully implement improvement strategies was to provide appropriate professional development on the strategies expected to be implemented. Proportionately, leaders identified this as an action taken more frequently than teachers. Both groups underscored the importance of professional development. Some teacher respondents indicated that there was not enough sustained professional development and that they were expected to implement new practices after a single in-service session. Several leaders cited the importance of providing professional development that supported both the growth of individuals and teams of teachers. Central office respondents highlighted the need to differentiate professional development for school s, both for teachers and for principals.

Superintendents and assistant superintendents identified building the capacity of principals through professional development to be critical.

To summarize the content of this chapter, questions are posed that school folks in the process of designing or refining a curriculum should attempt to answer.

I-1 Has the district established a common focus on curriculum?
I-2 Have teachers b een involved in the designing and refining the curriculum design or development strategy?
I-3 Have appropriate resources been allocated to the curriculum plan? (specifically funding for teacher release time, professional development for teachers a nd principals, and support staff to assist in and monitor classrooms)
I-4 Has an individualized and team support for teachers a nd principals on the process of curriculum improvement planning as well as the strategies that are expected to be implemented?
I-5 Is the plan for implementation written down, with processes for evaluating the implementation done on a regular basis?

Figure 5.1. Implementation and Infrastructure.

The next chapter examines one way to insure that implementation plans have the necessary power to drive implementation down to the teacher level.

REFERENCES

Adelman, H. S., & Taylor, L. (2007). Systemic change for school improvement. *Journal of Educational & Psychological Consultation, 17*(1), 55-77.

Bertani, A., Fullan, M., & Quinn, J. (2004). New lessons for change at the district level has 10 crucial components. *Educational Leadership, 61*(7), 42-46.

Connell, J. P., & Klem, A. M. (2000). You *can* get there from here: Using a theory of change to plan urban education reform. *Journal of Educational and Psychological Consultation, 11*(1), 93-120.

Cuban, L. (1984). *How teachers taught: Consistency and change in American Classrooms from 1890-1980*. New York: Longman.

Dailey, D., Fleischman, S., Gil, L., Holtzman, D., O'Day, J., & Vosmer, C. (2005). Toward more effective school districts: A review of the literature. Washington, DC: American Institutes for Research.

DuFour, R., DuFour, R., & Eaker, R. (2005). *On common ground*. Bloomington, IN: National Education Service.

Elmore, R. F. (2008). *School reform from the inside out: Policy, practice, and performance*. Cambridge, MA: Harvard University Press.

Fidler, B. (2003). *Strategic management for school development: Leading your school's improvement strategy*. London: Paul Chapman.

Fullan, M. (1993). *Change forces: Probing the depths of educational reform*. Bristol, PA: The Falmer Press.

Fullan, M. (2001). *Leading in a culture of change*. San Francisco: Jossey-Bass.

Fullan, M. (2005). *Leadership and sustainability: Systems thinking in action*. Thousand Oaks, CA: Corwin Press.

Fullan, M., & Stiegelbauer, S. (1991). *The new meaning of educational change.* New York: Teachers College Press.

Hall, G. E., & Hord, S. M. (1987). *Change in school s: Facilitating the process.* New York: State University of New York Press.

Hess, F. M. (2004). *Common sense school reform.* New York: Palgrave MacMillan.

Knapp, M. S., & Shields, P. M. (1995). The school and district environment for meaning-oriented instruction. In M. Knap (Ed.), *Teaching for meaning in high poverty classrooms.* New York: Teachers College Press.

Marris, P. (1985). *Loss and change.* London: Routledge & Kegan Paul.

Marzano, R. J., Waters, T., & McNulty, B. A. (2005). *School leadership that works: From research to results.* Alexandria, VA: Association for Supervision and Curriculum Development.

Meyer, J., & Rowan, B. (1978). The structure of educational organizations. In M. Meyer (Ed.), *Environments and organizations* (pp.78-109). San Francisco: Jossey-Bass.

Morgan, G. (2006). *Images of organization.* Newbury Park, CA: Sage Publications.

Owens, R. G. (2004). *Organizational behavior in education: Adaptive leadership and school reform.* Boston: Pearson.

Reeves, D. B. (2002). *The daily disciplines of leadership.* San Francisco: Jossey-Bass.

Reeves, D. B. (2004). *Accountability for learning: How teachers and school leaders can take charge.* Alexandria, VA: Association for Supervision and Curriculum Development.

Reeves, D. B. (2006). *The learning leader: How to focus improvement for better results.* Alexandria, VA: Association for Supervision and Curriculum Development.

Rowan, B. (1990). Commitment and control: Alternative strategies for the organizational design of school s. *Review of Educational Research, 16,* 353-389.

Schlechty, P. C. (2002). *Working on the work: An action plan for teachers, principals, and superintendents.* San Francisco: Jossey-Bass.

Schein, E. (1985). Organizational culture and leadership. San Francisco: Jossey-Bass.

Schmoker, M. (2004). Tipping point: From feckless reform to substantive instructional improvement. *Phi Delta Kappan, 290*(2), 424-432.

Schmoker, M. (2006). *Results now: How we can achieve unprecedented improvements in teaching and learning.* Alexandria, VA: Association for Supervision and Curriculum Development.

Senge, P. M. (1990). *The fifth discipline: The art & practice of the learning organization.* New York: Doubleday.

Sergiovanni, T. J. (1996). *Leadership for the schoolhouse: How is it different? Why is it important?* San Francisco: Jossey-Bass.

Spillane, J. P. (2006). *Distributed leadership.* San Francisco: Jossey-Bass.

Spong, D. (2007). Leading organizational improvement: Finding structure within culture. *Plant Engineering, 61*(7), 27-28.

Spring, J. (2001). *American education.* New York: McGraw-Hill.

Stigler, J. W., & Heibert, J. (1999). *The teaching gap: Best ideas from the world's teachers for improving education in the classroom.* New York: The Free Press.

Stone, D. (2002). *Policy paradox: The art of political decision making.* New York: W. W. Norton.

Tyack, D., & Cuban, L. (1995). *Tinkering toward utopia: A century of public school reform.* Cambridge, MA: Harvard University Press.

U.S. Congress. (2001). *No Child Left Behind Act of 2001*. Public Law 107-110. 107th Congress. Washington, DC: Government Printing Office.

Vaill, P. B. (1989). *Managing as a performing art: New ideas for a world of chaotic change.* San Francisco: Jossey-Bass.

Waters, J. T., & Marzano, R. J. (2006). *School district leadership that works: The effect of superintendent leadership on student achievement.* Denver, CO: Mid-continent Research for Education and Learning.

Weick, K. E. (1976). Educational organizations as loosely-coupled systems. *Administrative Science Quarterly, 21*, 1-19.

Wiklund, H., & Wiklund, P. S. (2002). Widening the six sigma concept: An approach to improve organizational learning. *Total Quality Management, 13*(2), 233-239.

Wirt, F. M. & Kirst, M. W. (2005). *The political dynamics of American education.* Richmond, CA: McCutchan.

In: Curriculum
Editor: David A. Squires

ISBN: 978-1-62948-673-4
© 2014 Nova Science Publishers, Inc.

Chapter 6

IMPLEMENTATION: A MODEL FOR MAKING IMPLEMENTATION PLANS

David A. Squires, Ph.D.
Southern Connecticut State University, New Haven, CT, US

INTRODUCTION

This chapter proposes a generic planning model that can assist principals, teachers and central office personnel in generating plans that are "doable" and that can insure consistency and fidelity in implementation. This process was originally developed to help in the implementation of the Balanced Curriculum. The planning process is guided by the answers to four questions:

- Who is affected by the reform, process, or program?
- What should these people know and be able to do?
- Who will manage the professional development?
- Who will know that the professional development is completed and having an effect and how will that be recorded?

Each bullet will be discussed, then, an example will be given at the end showing the answers to the questions. The term "planners" is used to indicate the people who put together the plan.

WHO IS AFFECTED BY THE REFORM, PROCESS, OR PROGRAM?

Here planners list all the people affected, generally listed by roles they play in the organization. For example, with the Balanced Curriculum, most roles in a district would be affected: students, teachers (such as regular classroom teacher s, special area teachers like art, bilingual teachers, and special education teachers), aides, mentors or coaches, assistant principals, principals, curriculum director, special education director, assistant superintendents, superintendents, board members, and parents /guardians. This may also included non-educational staff such as secretaries, cafeteria workers, and janitors. Being detailed and precise in identifying roles is important so that all the roles are listed who will be affected, for all affected will need some form of staff development. For a big project, such as implementing a new curriculum, most of the roles in the district will have a role to play, at the very least; will need to know something about the curriculum's implementation. As roles intersect, such as with a teacher and an aide who works in the teacher's classroom, making sure that both parties understand what their roles should be is important.

WHAT SHOULD THESE PEOPLE KNOW AND BE ABLE TO DO?

Much of the difficulty in implementation is not having a thorough understanding of all the roles that are involved and what we want each role to know and be able to do. Yes, we want teachers to implement the curriculum, but what does implementation mean? Below is a record of what a teacher needs to know and be able to do in implementing the Balanced Curriculum:

Role: Math Teacher to implement the Math Curriculum (already developed)
Know and Do

A   Familiar with web site's structure and practiced accessing web site.
   – Use user name and access code to log onto web site.
   – Choose a course
   – Choose a significant task
   – Examine attachments
   – Comments
      – Unit Comments
      – Significant Task Comments
   – Reports
      – Request a report
      – Print a requested report
      – Waiting for a requested report
B   Practice using significant tasks to generate lesson plan s.
   – Turning in lesson plan s for inclusion on web site
   – Access attachments for other helpful information
   – Role of grade level team.
   – What the principal will be looking for
   – Grade level teams collaborate on making lesson plan s for first unit.
   – Notes to Math Specialist about suggestions for other attachments
   – Lesson plan submission for inclusion in attachments on web site
C   Entering completions/comments
   – How to do this on the web site
   – How this information will be used

- Who has access to this information
D Relay expectations to classroom aide
- (assume aide has received an overview of Balanced Curriculum)
E Discussion at Grade Level Meetings
- Role of Grade Level Meetings in Implementing BC
- Role of Math Specialist in implementing BC
- Principal's Role in visiting grade level meetings
- Review lesson plan s
- Send to Math Specialist
- Set aside grade level meeting time to enter completions.
- Set aside grade level meeting time for generating and entering
- Report to Superintendent/Assistant Superintendent
- Enter comments on units and significant tasks
F Show parents how to access site with parent access during back to school night
- Script that shows what to do and say
G Request Math Specialist assistance for grade level or individual assistance.

Figure 6.1. What a Math teacher needs to know and do for implementation of the curriculum.

By being this specific, in knowing what each role should know and be able to do when implementing the balanced curriculum, ensures that significant details haven't been overlooked and that the written plan will be put in place for all to follow. The role of the teacher also interacts with other roles, such as the Mathematics Specialist or the principal, so what is listed for one role also impacts the roles of others. Doing this depth of planning is important because the district needs to develop a systemic plan that relates and is consistent with all the roles listed. As the plan is developed and additional areas that a role player needs to know and be able to do are added, planners will need to ensure that cross checking for consistency of role is featured. When we have implemented this planning process we find that planners go back and forth between our understanding of various roles and what we want the role players to know and be able to do.

WHO WILL MANAGE THE PROFESSIONAL DEVELOPMENT?

In the last step we spelled out what each role player should know and be able to do. Usually this involves new learning for folks that have the role. Professional development needs to be organized, sequenced and provided to ensure that all the people that occupy the role will know and be able to do what is specified for that role. Planners will find that they can meet multiple needs of different roles by providing professional development to multiple roles. For example, many roles in the district needed similar introductions to the Balanced Curriculum process, such as aides, parents, teachers, and administrators. Planners decided to design an "Overview Module" which would be appropriate for a large numbers of roles, in getting a general idea of what the design of the Balanced Curriculum is, and why it is important for the district.

The planners decided to develop a power point presentation for the "Overview Module" so that the message would be consistent across presentations. As there was a Math Specialist as well as a principal in each school, the planners decided to train the Math Specialist and the Principal in giving this presentation. Then they would be responsible for giving the presentation to others, such as teachers, aides, special education teachers, bilingual teachers, and parents of each school.

The planners also thought it was important for teachers who will implement the program to know more detail about the program, so again the Math Specialists and the Principals were selected to be the "trainers" of the teachers in how to implement the Balanced Curriculum.

Different districts and school s will have different configurations of personnel, so plans will vary according to school and district. Generally, we use the following "rules " to help to insure good implementation.

1   Always train at least two role players to deliver the training. Then a backup is available if needed, or the two can divide the training.
2   Think through issues of collaboration. While training only one role player might appear more efficient, it is sometimes more helpful to have a partner with whom to collaborate. In addition, this might also strengthen implementation if more than one person has a stake in training.

We have found that usually people are more than happy to collaborate around training needs.

WHO WILL KNOW THAT THE PROFESSIONAL DEVELOPMENT IS COMPLETED AND HAVING AN EFFECT AND HOW WILL THAT BE RECORDED?

Most implementation is weak because it is not well managed. People assume that if it is written in the plan that it will happen, which is not always the case. Folks also assume that if it happens, it will have the desired effect, again, not always the case.

To confront these problems, we suggest that districts have a "Point Person" in charge of the project's implementation to whom all the data about the implementation can flow. For large projects, such as curriculum implementation, a person needs to use data from the implementation process to sense, confirm and solve implementation problems. Depending on the district, for curriculum implementation, an assistant superintendent, might be assigned the point person's role. The main idea for the point person is to use as much of the district's infrastructure as possible to gather and report the information. (Different districts will have different configurations around infrastructure, so no two plans will be the same.) Thus, it will be important to be able to conduct an infrastructure analysis. This could be a first step in devising an implementation plan.

Rather than telling about an implementation plan, we would like to illustrate how one assistant superintendent, Jeff, accompanied by his district Math Supervisor, Neil, thought through the infrastructure that already existed in the district.

Sometimes infrastructure can be difficult to think about, because it is like air that surrounds the district all the time; it is present but not often thought about because it is "just a fact of life".

Jeff: Neil, I'd like you to take notes so we won't let anything slip through the cracks. Let's begin thinking about infrastructure at the school level. Lesson plans are already required on a weekly basis and are checked by the principal. That would give us one way to see if the teachers were implementing the curriculum, assuming if they wrote about using the significant tasks in their lesson plan s that would be one indication that the curriculum is implemented.

Neil: Yes and the teachers have a daily grade-level meeting where they meet to discuss what they are doing. Notes from those meetings, which are commonly shared with principals, might be another indicator that the curriculum is being implemented. You'll remember that we were able to incorporate grade level meetings into our implementation plan.

Jeff: Principals also have a weekly individual meeting with me where we go over concerns that affect principals and school s. We could collect the notes from that meeting as one more way to assess implementation of the curriculum.

Neil: There are also the math supervisors in each of the elementary school s, and department chairs in the middle and high school s. The middle and high school s have department meetings on a once per month basis. The math supervisors could be available on a weekly basis to meet with grade level groups. Since there are usually 7 grades in the elementary schools, if the building-based math supervisors did one meeting a week with the seven grades, they could meet with 3 to 4 grade level meetings each day and they could get done in two days, which would allow them to be available the rest of the time for individual issues of particular teachers. (Although we may not want to require that much time meeting together once we are a couple of months into the process.) The department chairs, because of released time they have each day, could meet with their math teachers around curriculum implementation.

Jeff: Let's not forget that all school s have monthly faculty meetings, where curriculum work could also be accomplished.

Neil: If we are done with the school, could we do some thinking about the District Level infrastructure that's available.

Jeff: One important thing is that the principals submit monthly reports to my office and the Superintendent's office. We could set up a structure for the principals to report what happens at the school level around curriculum implementation during the month.

Neil: There is also, at the beginning and ending of the school year, days in the district calendar when just teachers and other school personnel are present. That might be a time to begin the curriculum professional development on a district basis followed up by activity at each school.

Jeff: Don't forget there are two staff development days during the year we could also use.

Neil: Of course, the superintendent might also play a role, not just making a speech that she supports this work. As a matter of fact, the Superintendent does conduct school level walk-throughs where they examine what is happening in the class. Maybe for the first half of the year she could concentrate on walking though classrooms to see about the implementation of the Math curriculum. And for the few classroom observations that she does, they could be in Math classrooms.

Jeff: That also reminds me that the Superintendent receives a monthly report from me. I should probably think of an appropriate format for that information.

Also, the math supervisors and department chairs also meet twice a year to discuss Math related concerns. It seems to me that if we get the agendas for those meetings, with the approval of the "head" Math Supervisor, these reports could also focus on the Math curriculum implementation.

Neil: And don't forget about the math supervisor's monthly report to you, the Assistant Superintendent. This would be another way to communicate about successes and problems that is already built into the system.

Neil and Jeff, in completing an inventory of existing infrastructure, concentrated on time that was already built into the school and district schedules, and the reporting functions of who reported what to whom. It also concentrated on the "meetings" of groups that had already been built into the schedules of the schools or district. We are sure that you can see how the existing infrastructure could easily support Mathematics curriculum implementation as long as a plan that took advantage of that infrastructure was in place. Districts may have more of less infrastructure, but cataloging time, meetings, and reporting functions that could be used to support Mathematics implementation. If a district already has a solid infrastructure, there will be little need for additional infrastructure to provide for good curriculum implementation. On the other hand, if the district did not have Math supervisors in each elementary school and no department chairs with released time in the secondary schools, other infrastructure, like faculty meetings, may have to be more heavily used and depended upon. Or if notes were not usually taken during meetings, then the infrastructure may need to be changed so notes could be a communication tools to pass information along up the line.

Neil and Jeff then used this infrastructure analysis to devise a yearly plan for implementing the math curriculum. They used their work in Figure 5.1 now transferred to Figure 5.2 as a basis so that the infrastructure analysis supported all elements of the what the teacher should know and be able to do (Step 1). To complete the full plan, they would need to fill out a similar sheet for each role.

Role: Math Teacher to implement the Math Curriculum (already developed)

Know and Do?   How will it be managed
And   Recorded?

A   Familiar with web site's structure and practice accessing web site. Principal and
    Math Super.
    —   Use user name and access code to log onto   lead meeting before School
        web site
    —   Choose a course   begins in Sept
    —   Choose a significant task
    —   Examine attachments   Meeting notes passed onto
                                                           Principal Assistant
                                                           Superintendent.
    —   Comments
        – Unit Comments

- Sig Task Comments
- Reports
    - Request a report
    - Print a requested report
    - Waiting for a requested report

B   Practice using significant tasks to generate lesson plan s   Principal/Math Super.
- Turning in lesson plan s for inclusion on web site   conducts
- Access attachments with other helpful information   Meeting notes passed
- Role of grade level team   to assistant superint.
- What the principal will be looking for
- Grade level teams collaborate on making lesson plan s for first unit.
- Notes to Math Specialist about suggestions for other attachments
- Lesson plan submission for inclusion in attachments on web site

C   Entering completions   Same as B above
- How to do this on the web site
- How this information will be used
- Who has access to this information
- Goal:

D   Relay expectations to classroom aide   Teacher
    - (assume aide has received an overview   reports completion to
        of Balanced Curriculum)

                                                            Principal in report.
E   Discussion at Grade Level Meetings   Math Spec. or Principal
                                                            Notes sent to principal
                                                            who
- Role of Grade Level Meetings in Implementing BC   uses them to send a
                                                            school
- Role of Math Specialist in implementing BC   summary to ass't super.
- Principal's Role in visiting grade level meetings
- Review lesson plan s
    - Send to Math Specialist
- Set aside grade level meeting time to enter completions.
- Set aside grade level meeting time for generating and entering
- report to Superintendent/Assistant Superintendent
    - Enter comments on units and significant tasks

F   Show parents how to access site with parent access during   Teachers follow script
- back to school night   reported in teacher's
- Script that shows what to do and say.   Monthly Report to
                                                            Principal

G   Request Math Specialist assistance for grade level or individual assistance. Reported
    by Math Specialist

Figure 5.2. How will what is Known and Done be Managed and Recorded?

The point person's role is to make sure district leadership, including building principals, understands the plan's components and requirements. They will need to know that the point person will be using the data from their reports to monitor whether the plan is being implemented. Such a plan takes time to complete. For someone who is familiar with the format, the plans for the district as a whole can be developed in one day's work by the point person. Obviously, more time would be needed in existing district and school meetings to fully communicate what the plans will be for curriculum implementation.

The next chapter looks at a case study of assessment strategies used by two Pennsylvania school districts, Philadelphia and Cumberland, PA. There has been much research done around assessment; we chose to concentrate on the research around how these two districts used assessment results because many of the assessment issues are covered in these two case studies. Also the study reflects a theme of the book of using district practices to reinforce findings.

In: Curriculum
Editor: David A. Squires

ISBN: 978-1-62948-673-4
© 2014 Nova Science Publishers, Inc.

Chapter 7

ASSESSMENT RESEARCH

David A. Squires, Ph.D.
Southern Connecticut State University, New Haven, CT, US

INTRODUCTION

In this chapter we review a case study of two school districts, Philadelphia, Pa and Cumberland, Pa., one urban and one suburban who had been using the same math program (Everyday Mathematics) and had developed ways to use interim assessments, in addition to the curriculum for Everyday Mathematics, which were widely used and accepted by the staff. We review the strategies used by these districts because they provide strong examples of how assessments can be used in strengthening curriculum.

We conclude the chapter with a list of things to consider if embarking on or refining an assessment system in a district. The study, by Margaret E. Goertz, Leslie Nabors Oláh, Matthew Riggin, entitled "From Testing to Teaching: The Use of Interim Assessments in Classroom Instruction" was published by CPRE (Consortium of Policy Research in Education) from the University of Pennsylvania in 2009 and is available on line. We include the study as it is the most comprehensive and thorough study of school district interim assessment we know about.

We concentrate here on the structure of the interim assessment systems the two districts set up, although the study goes into great detail about what teachers learned from participating in an interim assessment system with extensive attention paid to teacher capacity to utilize assessment data within those systems.

SCHOOLS CHOSEN

Nine school s in each district were chosen for in-depth study using three criteria:

- All school s made Annual Yearly Progress for the year before the study (2004-05).

- Schools were chosen to represent school s around the district's average achievement on the Pennsylvania state exam.
- Schools were chosen to reflect the racial and economic diversity within the districts.

DATA COLLECTION

Data was collected from six sources: classroom observations, teacher interviews, school and district leader interviews, observation of district and school meetings, artifacts, a survey for teachers' Content Knowledge for Teaching Math.

QUESTIONS ADDRESSED

The major questions addressed in the study are:

1 What policy supports at the school and district levels enhance the use of interim assessments to change instruction? How does instructional support, the nature of professional development, the sophistication of local data systems, and the school- and teacher-level incentives for improved instruction affect teachers' use of interim assessment data?
2 How do elementary school teachers, individually and collectively, learn from interim assessment results in mathematics and apply that knowledge to instructional decisions about content, pedagogy, and working with individual students?
3 In what ways are interim assessments situated within the wider context of teachers' formative assessment practices and tools?
4 What is the relationship among teacher capacity, analysis of assessment information, and teaching practice?

We were interested in the first question, particularly since the system of interim assessments was so well developed in both districts. For each district we describe the cycle of assessment, teachers' and administrative use of the assessment data.

CYCLE OF ASSESSMENT – PHILADELPHIA

The math curriculum was divided into eight week chunks. The first six – seven weeks were spent teaching the curriculum which was aligned with the Everyday Mathematics Program. Teachers then used the assessment results for re-teaching or enrichment activities during the last week or two of the eight week cycle. Teachers also had a pacing guide which specified weekly goals and processes for teachers to use. Assessments were given sometime during week seven, graded by an assessment contractor, and contained 20 multiple choice questions. After grading, the results are posted on SchoolNet by Princeton Review, a service which translated the results to an on-line report. Most useful for teachers is the item analysis report. Parents also have on-line access to a version of these reports.

Class-Wide Summary
How the class performed as a whole on each test item

23 students in this section
20 students took this test

	Total	1 View	2 View	3 View	4 View	5 View	6 View	7 View	8 View	9 View	10 View	11 View	12 View	13 View	14 View	15 View	16 View	17 View	18 View	19 View	20 View	Total	
Standard ID	--	2.2.5.A.1	2.2.5.A.1	2.2.5.C.1	2.2.5.A.1	2.2.5.C.1	2.11.5.A.1	2.1.5.D.1	2.11.5.A.1	2.2.5.E.1	2.4.5.A.1	2.2.5.B.1	2.1.5.B.1	2.1.5.B.1	2.1.5.B.1	2.4.5.A.1	2.6.5.A.2	2.1.3.2.1	2.4.5.A.1	2.2.5.B.1	2.2.5.C.1	--	Standard ID
Correct Response	--	A	D	A	C	C	C	B	D	A	A	A	B	D	B	D	B	C	B	C	C	--	Correct Response
Point Value	20	1	1	1	1	1	1	1	1	1	1	1	1	1	1	1	1	1	1	1	1	20	Point Value
Summary Score (Points)	327/400	16/20	16/20	12/20	16/20	12/20	20/20	19/20	12/20	16/20	20/20	20/20	18/20	18/20	12/20	13/20	20/20	18/20	18/20	17/20	14/20	327/400	Summary Score (Points)
Summary Score (Percent)	82%	80%	80%	60%	80%	60%	100%	95%	60%	80%	100%	100%	90%	90%	60%	65%	100%	90%	90%	85%	70%	82%	Summary Score (Percent)

Student-by-Student Data
The list below reveals how each student answered each test item. You can select one or more students to add to a Student Group.

Go

	Total	1 View	2 View	3 View	4 View	5 View	6 View	7 View	8 View	9 View	10 View	11 View	12 View	13 View	14 View	15 View	16 View	17 View	18 View	19 View	20 View	Total	
Alex Z.	95%	✓	✓	✓	✓	✓	✓	✓	✓	✓	✓	✓	✓	B	✓	✓	✓	✓	✓	✓	✓	95%	Alex Z.
Amanda Y.	50%	D	B	✓	D	B	✓	✓	C	B	✓	✓	D	✓	A	B	✓	✓	✓	✓	B	50%	Amanda Y.
Ali X.	70%	✓	✓	C	✓	B	✓	✓	C	✓	✓	✓	✓	✓	✓	✓	✓	✓	C	A	B	70%	Ali X.
Cheyenne W.	90%	✓	✓	C	✓	✓	✓	✓	✓	✓	✓	✓	✓	✓	✓	✓	✓	A	✓	✓	✓	90%	Cheyenne W.
Deiondre V.	95%	✓	B	✓	✓	✓	✓	✓	✓	✓	✓	✓	✓	✓	✓	✓	✓	✓	✓	✓	✓	95%	Deiondre V.
Dakota U.	65%	✓	✓	D	✓	B	✓	C	C	✓	✓	✓	✓	✓	D	B	✓	✓	✓	A	✓	65%	Dakota U.
Dwayne T.	75%	C	✓	✓	B	✓	✓	✓	✓	B	✓	✓	✓	✓	C	B	✓	✓	✓	✓	✓	75%	Dwayne T.
Jacy S.	70%	✓	✓	D	✓	B	✓	✓	C	✓	✓	✓	✓	✓	A	B	✓	✓	✓	✓	B	70%	Jacy S.
Jariah R.	85%	✓	✓	C	✓	B	✓	✓	A	✓	✓	✓	✓	✓	✓	✓	✓	✓	✓	✓	✓	85%	Jariah R.
Kendis Q.	95%	✓	✓	✓	✓	✓	✓	✓	✓	✓	✓	✓	✓	✓	✓	✓	✓	✓	C	✓	✓	95%	Kendis Q.
Lakin P.	90%	✓	✓	✓	✓	✓	✓	✓	✓	✓	✓	✓	✓	✓	A	C	✓	✓	✓	✓	✓	90%	Lakin P.
Lenelle O.	50%	C	B	D	D	B	✓	✓	C	B	✓	✓	D	✓	A	✓	✓	✓	✓	✓	B	50%	Lenelle O.
Mekdia N.	95%	✓	✓	✓	✓	✓	✓	✓	✓	✓	✓	✓	✓	✓	✓	B	✓	✓	✓	✓	✓	95%	Mekdia N.
Mancel M.	90%	✓	✓	✓	✓	✓	✓	✓	✓	✓	✓	✓	✓	✓	✓	✓	✓	A	✓	A	✓	90%	Mancel M.
Nara L.	100%	✓	✓	✓	✓	✓	✓	✓	✓	✓	✓	✓	✓	✓	✓	✓	✓	✓	✓	✓	✓	100%	Nara L.
Shandi K.	80%	✓	✓	D	✓	B	✓	✓	A	✓	✓	✓	✓	✓	✓	✓	✓	✓	✓	✓	B	80%	Shandi K.
Sidone J.	65%	B	C	✓	B	✓	✓	✓	✓	B	✓	✓	✓	B	A	B	✓	✓	✓	✓	✓	65%	Sidone J.
Talisa I.	100%	✓	✓	✓	✓	✓	✓	✓	✓	✓	✓	✓	✓	✓	✓	✓	✓	✓	✓	✓	✓	100%	Talisa I.
Tate H.	100%	✓	✓	✓	✓	✓	✓	✓	✓	✓	✓	✓	✓	✓	✓	✓	✓	✓	✓	✓	✓	100%	Tate H.
Yancy F.	75%	✓	✓	C	✓	B	✓	✓	A	✓	✓	✓	✓	✓	A	✓	✓	✓	✓	✓	B	75%	Yancy F.

Figure 7.1. Format of Philadelphia's Interim Assessment Scores.

The teachers then used these reports to decide what their emphasis would be for individuals or student groups for re-teaching and/or enriching mathematics concepts. The assessment only covered those areas that were covered in the curriculum during this time period.

Guiding this decision making process is the Benchmark Data Analysis Protocol (PDAP), required by most principals for all teachers to use based on the item analysis provided by SchoolNet to make decision about the organization of instruction for the next week, the week when re-teaching and enrichment takes place. "This district-created protocol is designed to help teachers identify weak points in their students' performance, and articulate strategies for regrouping, re-teaching, and reassessment.

Additionally, it asks teachers to reflect on how they can better differentiate their instruction to meet the needs of all students (Goertz, et al., 2009, p. 132)." Also available on the web site were ideas for re-teaching the concept. Teachers use the PDAP to make decisions about using the results of the formative assessment during the six days in the cycle allowed for re-teaching and enrichment.

CYCLE OF ASSESSMENT – CUMBERLAND

Cumberland also has an eight week instruction/assessment cycle shown below.

The practice end of unit test is the test teachers use to base their re-teaching and enrichment decisions during the next three day time span.

The report used by the teachers is not as sophisticated as in Philadelphia, and they must grade the assessments and put the results in a spread sheet (See figure 7.4 below).

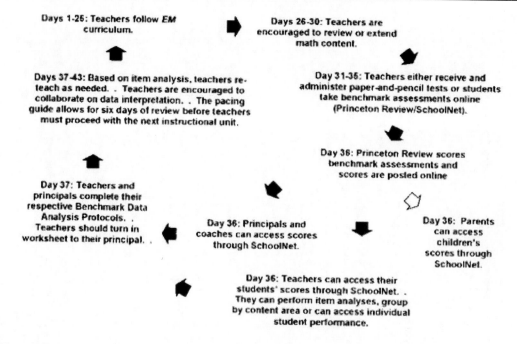

Figure 7.2. Instructional Cycle for Philadelphia here.

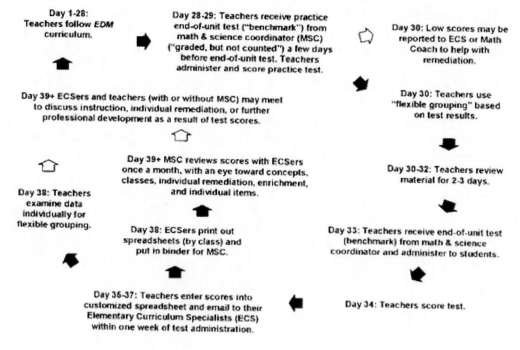

Figure 7.3. Cumberland's Instructional Cycle.

Administrators pass out a district developed pacing guide to teachers for the Math program, identifying the number of lessons in each EM unit and the number of days to cover the lesson content, as well as the expected completion date for each unit. This pacing guide includes time devoted to re-teaching and enrichment after the formative test.

Practice test problem numbers	19,20,21,22	3,4,5,6,7,8	9,10	11, 12, 14	1,2,13	15,16,17,18
Learning Goal	Equivalent mixed numbers	Adding & subtracting fractions and mixed number	Percent-decimal-fraction correspondence	Comparing or ordering fractions	Finding common denominators	Multiplying fractions
Proficiency level	S	D/S	S	D/S	S	D
Number of items	4	6	2	6	2	4
Name	Number wrong on Practice test					
1. Michael Ambruster		1		1		
2. David Bridgewater	1	2	1	4	2	1
3. Brittany Cooper				3	1	
4. Skye Davidson		1				
5. Hodgkin Eames	1		1	1		
6. Paige Fairly	1	5	2	4	2	1
7. Tony Garafalo				1		
8. Sorrell Hill	3	2		2	1	
9. Madelaine Isaak	4				1	
10. Alexander Jacob				1		
11. Kiki King			1	2	1	
12. Anton Lang	2	4	2	3	2	1
13. KC Monroe						
14. Clay Nailor			1			
15. Daniel Ooster	1	1	1	2	1	1
16. Adam Powell						1
17. Elif Ross						
18. Jenna Smith	1		1	2	1	1
19. Randal Tatum		1			1	
20. Ari Urbinski			1	3	1	
21. Jonah Valdez	4			2		
22. Ambrosia Wallace		1	1			
23. Ynes Yaragosa				1	1	

Figure 7.4. Cumberland's spreadsheet for reporting results to teachers.

"The formal and routinized assessments for elementary mathematics include practice (formative), end-of-unit (formative/summative), end-of-book (summative) and benchmark (predictive) tests. Every three to four weeks, the district's Mathematics and Science Coordinator (MSC) sends out to the elementary school s "practice tests" that align with the pacing guide for the mathematics program and that are modeled closely on the district's end-of-unit mathematics tests " (Goertz, et al. 2009, p. 90).

At the end of the unit two tests are given: one practice test (considered by this study to be the interim assessment) and one chapter test.

The practice test is given before the chapter test. Both tests contain five multiple-choice items, a number of constructed response items and one open ended item aligned to the Pennsylvania Assessment Anchors as part of the districts "integrated PSSA prep." The practice tests contains anywhere from 11 to 20+ items.

Students are automatically highlighted in yellow if they are below expectation, assisting teachers in re-grouping for instruction. The spread sheet is then emailed by the teacher to the Math/Science district coordinator. Teachers also can report the information to building administrators or others who might help the teacher.

PHILADELPHIA: ROLE OF
ADMINISTRATORS AND
SUPPORT PERSONNEL

All the teachers involved in this study used interim formative assessments, which suggests strong administrative support and follow through. The district also structured a way that principals would know that interim assessments were being analyzed and used in re-teaching called the BDAP (Benchmark Data Analysis Protocol). The teachers used the BDAP as a way to sift through the data. For principals, it provided the "proof" that interim assessment data was being properly used by teachers to make decisions about re-teaching or enrichment, as the teachers when they completed the BDAP, handed it in to the principal. Principals also did their own review of the data to determine where teachers might place emphasis in their re-teaching. Principals also held regular meetings with grade levels to discuss the implications of the interim assessment data. Principals also had regular staff development in SchoolStat meetings where they shared information across school s, about the assessment process. Principals also received training in the SchoolNet program that was used to report results to teachers. In the SchoolStat meetings, they also learned how to access data, interpret the results of grade level groups of teachers, with practice in identifying patterns in the data that they could use in their teacher supervision. Principals were also encouraged to plan the school day so that grade-level teachers would have the same planning time so that results could be discussed. School results were also highlighted during principal meetings held by the district. Other support personnel, specifically SBTLs or School Based Teacher Leaders were also available to assist teachers to use the system. However, many SBTL's had classroom or other responsibilities which restricted the amount of time they could devote to helping others. Generally, teachers were on their own to conduct re-teaching and enrichment in their classrooms, although the SBTL's would often help teachers in using the data to plan re-teaching or enrichment instruction. Not mentioned in the study was the decision to structure EM (Everyday Math, the district's math program) so that there was time built into the schedule for the assessment (a couple of days) and re-teaching (at least one week). This took the scheduling of these assessment activities out of the teachers hands, so all participated.

CUMBERLAND: ROLE OF ADMINISTRATORS
AND SUPPORT PERSONNEL

Administrators have no role in the administration or examining the results of the "practice" interim assessments. Unlike Philadelphia, students would not bring these assessments home.

Results of the practice tests however, are reported to the Math/Science Coordinator (MSC) of the district using the spread sheet in figure 7.4. The Elementary Curriculum Specialist (ECS) is also entitled to see the results. Teachers can call on the ECS or the MSC to assist or to help design interventions. The district expects the teachers to use the assessments as regular pieces of the Math program, so there is no need to intervene. End of unit tests, given after the "practice" interim assessments, receive most attention from the administrators, as they are considered "predictive" of students scores on state tests. Principals reviewed data on student performance (the chapter tests, not the "practice" tests, with their curriculum team in order to identify students in need of additional assistance.

"Teachers in the Cumberland school s had considerable instructional support available to them. The school-based curriculum specialists provided remediation and enrichment to students, usually in a pull-out or push-in setting. The ECS directed a fulltime instructional aide who worked with students in the classroom. The district mathematics coach also provided remedial services in three of the district's schools. Some teachers scheduled their practice tests for a time when the ECS, mathematics aide and/or mathematics coach would be available to assist with flexible grouping. The ECSs and mathematics coach also used the results of the district's end-of-book assessments to "pre-teach" groups of students at the beginning of the following school year (Goertz et al., (2009), p. 100).

PHILADELPHIA / CUMBERLAND - DEVELOPING AND REVISING THE ASSESSMENTS

During the study, the benchmark assessments were co-created by the district's curriculum and assessment administrators and Princeton Review in the weeks prior to their administration. This continued throughout the study. The assessments were designed to be aligned to Pennsylvania's Assessment Anchors, to the district curriculum (EM) and to the state standards, although the district had no formal documentation that this was the case.

In Cumberland, the practice tests are teacher designed and occasionally revised, under the leadership of district curriculum staff through the MSC (Math/Science District Curriculum Specialist). There was no mention of attempts to align the assessments to state standards or assessments.

PHILADELPHIA – TRAINING FOR USING AND MONITORING THE ASSESSMENTS

Teachers, Principals and other school staff, and district administrators all had to be trained for using and monitoring assessments. We address each in order.

Teachers received training in the Math program (EM) before beginning their teaching of the Math curriculum. All teachers in the district received in-service on EM before beginning teaching. Those who came on later received at least a day of EM in-service before beginning their teaching. Teachers also received training in School Net through principals and technology staff, the program that produced the reports for the interim assessment.

The training focused on accessing the data, not using the data to regroup for instruction. Teachers reported that they relied on grade level discussions to provide in-service in this area.

Principals also received training in the Math program along with teachers. SchoolStat meetings focused the principal on the use of data from the interim assessments in the SchoolNet program.

Principals were expected to review the most recent assessment in SchoolNet and bring the documentation to SchoolStat meetings where the data was discussed, strategies developed, and results compared. Principal's meetings also took a look at summary data across the school s. It was not clear how SBCA's received training.

Neither was it clear how district administrators received their training or what the content of that training might be. Because the implementation at the school s was at such a high level, I would assume that training was delivered to district staff.

CUMBERLAND – TRAINING FOR USING AND MONITORING THE ASSESSMENTS

The district mathematics coach and individual school's ESC's provided training on using the data from interim assessments, the district developed spreadsheet for reporting results, and the process for regrouping for instruction before the Unit test. Training areas were not detailed very specifically in the monograph.

PHILADELPHIA AND CUMBERLAND SUMMARY

Six clear themes emerge from the reports of interim assessment use in Cumberland and Philadelphia.

First, both districts aligned their interim assessment with state content standards and the district curriculum, thereby ensuring that the assessment data teachers used was actually covered in their teaching.

Second, both districts created and communicated expectations for assessment data use at all levels of the systems. School leaders in both districts expected teachers to use assessment results to reflect on their instructions and share common problems and instructional solutions for remediation in the time following the assessments.

Third, both districts designed "user friendly" data systems to analyze the data, based on the use of computers for the entire test and associated state learning standards.

Fourth, "both districts provided *professional support* in curriculum, the use of the IMSs, analysis of assessment data, and, to differing extent, instructional approaches. Both districts designated school -based mathematics coaches for instructional and content support—a full-time specialist in the suburban district, but only limited release time for a grade-level teacher in the urban schools (Goertz, et al. (2009), p. 103."

Fifth, dedicated time was provided by the districts for teachers to discuss results, ensuing instructional techniques to address the results and to participate in professional development. Sixth, school leadership and a culture of data use became utilized in supporting teachers' data use. (Goertz et al., (2009) p. 102-104.)

PLANNING FOR USING FORMATIVE ASSESSMENTS (THE PHILADELPHIA MODEL)

In chapter 6 we described a planning model to use to insure fidelity of implementation. We would like to model this process for implementing an assessment system similar to the one described in this chapter for Philadelphia. In this case we assume that district leadership has designed a system that is congruent with Philadelphia's, so the design phase of the work is already completed, and the design is ready for implementation. We use the four questions to organize our implementation taken from the last chapter:

- Who is affected by the reform, process, or program?
- What should these people know and be able to do?
- Who will manage the professional development?
- Who will know that the professional development is completed and having an effect and how will that be recorded?

Who Is Affected by the Reform, Process, or Program?

Here we concerned with the major actors: teachers and principals; and the minor actors of students, parents, and district office staff (the staff developers and school support personnel).

What Should These People Know and Be Able to Do?

Teachers:

Provide a rationale for why a formative assessment process is a valuable addition, to the teach/test instructional model, with accompanying weaknesses.

Use individual and class assessment data to determine instructional needs of the class.

Group the class into smaller groups based on needs.

Schedule groups during a 4-6 day reteaching/enrichment period.

Review the plan for introducing a 4-6 day re-teaching/enrichment period on the yearly schedule for the subject area.

Based on the needs, make recommendations of how you would teach these topics next year.

Use SchoolNet's reports to decide on the needs of the class during the re-teaching period.

As a grade level group, preview how students will take the interim assessments on line. Develop a plan for introducing this in the classroom. Anticipate problems that may occur.

As a grade level group, participate with others, (grade level colleagues, the principal and the school's instructional specialist) in a grade-level meeting to discuss how each would structure instruction during the 4-6 day period for re-teaching, based on the needs of the class. Debrief this meeting for implications for future meetings of this type.

As a grade level group, provide an introduction plan for your classes in introducing this process to the children.

As a grade level group, provide an introduction plan in introducing this process to the parents, during a parent meeting. Plan for reviewing the introduction during parent/teacher conferences for those that don't attend the meeting.

Principals

Provide a rationale for why a formative assessment process is a valuable addition, to the teach/test instructional model, with accompanying weaknesses.

Use individual, class assessment data and cross class data to determine instructional needs of the grade level. Report your analysis to other principals.

Suggestions that teachers will understand about grouping the class into smaller groups based on needs.

Make suggestions that teachers will understand about schedule groups during a 4-6 day re-teaching/enrichment period.

Understand the use and role of SchoolNet (the software program that produces results in many different report formats) for the formative assessments to understand what the general needs of the grade level are.

Schedule the introduction of students to formative assessments, including taking the assessments on line.

Work with grade level groups of classroom teacher s to develop a plan for introducing formative assessments to children and parents.

Practice developing reports for principal meetings that shows how you have completed an assessment of a grade-level groups and come up with findings and recommendations for sharing at a principal's meeting.

Practice collaborating with other principals on improving interim assessment in your school.

While these are a list of very specific considerations to be gleaned from this study, we would also like to propose some general criteria for assessment when designing or refining curriculum development plans.

This chapter dealt with assessment by examining two assessment frameworks for math in two different districts in Pennsylvania that used the same Math program. The chapter concluded by demonstrating how a "plan for assessment implementation" might be developed for a district, reviewing the contents of Chapter 6 on Planning for Implementation.

A-1 Are uniform assessments employed across the curriculum? (Uniform assessments means that everyone who teaches a course gives the same assessments.)

A-2 Is additional time built into the yearly schedule for teachers to use the results of the assessments to re-teach or enrich the curriculum? (Is time provided for reteaching and/or enrichment after, for example, each unit?)

A-3 Is there a way to monitor and evaluate whether the extra time is producing anticipated results?

A-4 Do teachers teaching the same course collaborate on using the test results to improve instruction?

Figure 7. 5. Assessment Criteria.

This completes the second section of the book which gives research backing up the four areas of the ASIA model: Alignment, Structure of the Curriculum and Stability, Implementation and Infrastructure, and Assessment. The next section of the book contains chapters telling the stories of curriculum development and implementation by school districts.

REFERENCES

Goertz, M. E., Oláh, L. N., Riggan, M. (2009). *From testing to teaching: The use of interim assessments in classroom instruction.* Philadelphia, Pa.: Coalition of Policy Research in Education (CPRE).

INTRODUCTION TO PART THREE: CHAPTERS 8, 9, 10, 11 AND 12

The third part of the book describes six other districts that have used curriculum as a framework for improving student achievement. Chapter Eight in this section describes three urban districts that won the Booker Prize: Aldine, TX, Garden Grove Unified School District, CA, Norfolk Public Schools, VA; and focused on curriculum as a way to improve student achievement. Then four separate chapters are offered, by Superintendents and Assistant Superintendents of districts in Connecticut serving three different levels of Socio-Economic status: high, medium and low. The four chapters tell the stories of how the district leadership organized their successful achievement gains on state tests, through emphasizing curriculum which incorporated the ASIA framework.

In: Curriculum
Editor: David A. Squires

ISBN: 978-1-62948-673-4
© 2014 Nova Science Publishers, Inc.

Chapter 8

CURRICULUM DEVELOPMENT IN 3 URBAN DISTRICTS THAT HAVE RAISED ACHIEVEMENT

Heather Zavadsky, Ph.D.
Director of EdPractice Connect, Austin, TX, US

THE ROLE OF CURRICULUM IN EDUCATION REFORM

Ever since the U.S. education system came under fire in 1983 in the infamous report, A Nation at Risk, the quest to improve student achievement has held a front seat as both a policy and economic concern. Decades of education reform rolled out after that report, some lasting and most fleeting. Despite the common assertion that nothing has changed for decades in education, some people believe that while we do not have the ultimate solution, we have learned a lot along the way.

In my book, *Bringing School Reform to Scale: Five Award-Winning Urban Districts*[1], I highlight five urban districts that moved from poor to laudable student performance by strategically applying systemic reform across their entire district. The districts were selected based on their national recognition for making great gains in student achievement and winning the prestigious Broad Prize for Urban Education.[*] Their success is largely attributed to their focused approach that clearly defined desired outcomes and goals, and then mapped backwards from the end of the system to the beginning, and then putting in appropriate supports and monitoring to ensure they were leaving nothing to chance. This chapter will highlight three of the five districts for their systemic work in curriculum reform.

Books and articles on reform often highlight the important pieces that need to be in place, like a powerful human capital strategy to ensure teacher and leader quality, the need to use data to inform instruction, and the need to connect all pieces of the system, from Pre-K to 12th grade. The one area that does not gain enough attention in education reform is the importance of attending to curriculum. Even the best selected and supported teachers cannot achieve ultimate success unless they have a well defined and aligned curriculum. Having data

---

[*] The Broad Prize…

to inform early intervention is not efficient if the curriculum does not adequately prepare all students for the next grade. (See the next to the last chapter of the book for more examples.)

One important commonality shared by Aldine (TX), Boston (MA), Garden Grove (CA), Long Beach (CA), and Norfolk (VA), the districts featured in *Reform to Scale,* is their understanding that affecting student achievement to scale requires aligning the parts of the system around core elements directly linking to teaching and learning. Since the term *Curriculum* has expanded over time to describe all of the teaching, learning, and assessment materials available for a given course of study, one can begin to understand why these districts began their improvement strategies by focusing on practices that would most impact instruction; curriculum. The ASIA Framework is unique in that it covers all elements that are affected by curriculum and should be considered to make meaningful impact on the instructional core. The descriptions below detail how all the elements in the ASIA Framework are applied by urban districts to achieve system-wide improvements in teaching and learning by viewing the curriculum as integral to reform work.

CURRICULUM REFORM WITHIN THE ASIA FRAMEWORK

Even though each of the selected districts had a set of state standards to follow, they all underwent an intense curriculum development process to better define their state standards for the district, *align* the standards across all grade levels, apply more rigor to what they felt were minimal state standards, move particular subjects down to lower grades (such as algebra), or increase focus in some areas (as Norfolk did with literacy). Regarding alignment to the state standards, most districts felt the need to enhance their state-adopted standards to ensure students were on the path to college and workforce readiness. Note that while the ASIA framework refers to curriculum alignment with state standards and across grades, references in this chapter will additionally define alignment as the aligned instructional sequence from Kindergarten (or pre-school) to 12th grade.

For *Structure (management and process),* curriculum development was facilitated through central office curriculum directors and instructional experts, who convened teams of school instructional leaders and teachers from all grade levels to engage in a collaborative curriculum overhaul. Following a structured approach, the teams used data and teacher input to identify instructional gaps and problems to create a more seamless and aligned PK–12 instructional sequence in each subject. The process was often approached by backward mapping from the system's end-point—what a graduate from the system should know and be able to do—to lower grades.

The curriculum in each district was broken down into smaller, more manageable units (*time*)—often called benchmarks —that were articulated across each district's annual instructional calendars in the form of curriculum or pacing guides. The benchmark units typically lasted six weeks and had accompanying benchmark units or quarterly assessments to make sure students mastered the content for each unit (*assessment*). Additional tools provided to teachers included model lessons and uniform instructional activities such as warm-ups or homework assignments to ensure instructional continuity regardless of student mobility.

Although there were some exceptions, most teachers interviewed saw the curriculum guides and tools as sources of support rather than as constraints on their professional judgment. This was particularly true for new teachers, who found the clarity of the standards and their pacing to be extremely helpful. Other teachers asserted that the curriculum guides put the issue of pacing, or *what* to teach, on central office but left the decision of *how* to teach to teachers. The districts seemed dedicated to helping teachers adjust to the new curriculum and new expectations: in the instances when teachers thought that the pacing guides put unreasonable expectations or inappropriate constraints on classroom instruction, those teachers were provided flexibility and support by central office staff, who helped them adjust the pace to fit their needs.

Each district also had an annual curriculum revision process that included teachers, central office curriculum specialists, and district leaders. The inclusive process added a crucial element of vertical and horizontal alignment of district standards, sparking ongoing dialogue between district, school, and classroom staff about what students needed to know in every grade and subject. The districts believed that their curricula gained better clarity and refinement each year. While developing and maintaining a detailed and aligned curriculum might be considered a basic and straightforward process, many systems fail to create a seamless PK–12 curriculum containing no skips or unnecessary repetitions in content. Teacher comments from all five districts indicated that the districts had been successful in developing such seamless curricula; teachers believed that students were coming to their classrooms better prepared for their appropriate grade or subject. Additionally, teachers appreciated being involved in the curriculum-development process as an acknowledgement of their professional knowledge and as an opportunity for them to take on leadership roles.

Regarding *Implementation*, faithful implementation of the curriculum was crucial in all five districts and was handled through multiple communications, monitoring, and support processes. The districts communicated curriculum content to school leaders and teachers through numerous trainings, curriculum guides, and vertical and horizontal team meetings, and by allowing teachers to observe in each other's classrooms. Additionally, in most cases, the curricula and accompanying tools were easily accessed online.

To ensure the curriculum was being fully taught and identify supports for teachers, the districts regularly used benchmark or quarterly *Assessments* and walkthroughs by instructional specialists or school leaders. When issues arose, teachers had many sources of support, such as instructional coaches, principals, or other teachers. Curriculum interventions were frequently described by teachers as a welcome provision of support rather than an opportunity for administrators to criticize.

In addition to pacing guides and formative assessments, instructional coaches or specialists, principals, and other teachers supplied immediate classroom -based support for curriculum implementation. Boston's Collaborative Coaching and Learning model is an example of a successful structured coaching model in which teachers work with each other.

OTHER CURRICULUM SUPPORTS

Curriculum directors provided another strong source of support from each district's central office. Multiple site visits and interviews at the districts pointed to very strong, extremely knowledgeable curriculum directors who facilitated the curriculum-development process. In addition to their knowledge base, part of the strength of the curriculum directors lay in their ability to create and manage participative curriculum processes that mined district expertise and subsequently generated stakeholder support.

The district and school goals were also an important driver of the districts' curriculum development process. Often goals began with a simple mission or vision, like "Ensure academic achievement for all students" or "Build a world-class education system." From there, the necessary components of the vision/mission were defined and became the goals. The most important and common elements of the districts' goal planning processes were that goals be clear, measurable, and few in number. Additionally, the goal-planning processes had to balance alignment between district and school goals with affording some level of customization to meet the unique needs of schools. Districts accomplished this balance by providing a basic framework or focus areas for goals—such as the two specific goals in Garden Grove related to academic and ELL achievement—and then having schools work in committees to review data and add sub-goals that provided appropriate benchmarks on the way to those goal.

EXAMPLES OF SUCCESSFUL DISTRICT-LEVEL CURRICULUM REFORM

This chapter features three of the five Broad Prize winning districts in Reform the Scale. They were selected for their comprehensive, focused approach to refining, implementing, and monitoring their curriculum as a crucial piece of their overall comprehensive reform strategies. Rather than break the case studies out by discrete ASIA Criteria, each district's curriculum approach has been detailed holistically to see the Framework in application. References to Appendix A – Summary of the ASIA Criteria -- are provided throughout the cases to illustrate which criteria are being illustrated.

Aldine Independent School District, Texas

Aldine Independent School District (ISD) has gained attention in Texas for its history in strong performance with high poverty high minority students. The district is located near Houston, TX in an unincorporated area in Harris County, near Bush Intercontinental Airport. It is the seventy-third-largest school district in the nation and is the tenth-largest school district in Texas. Aldine's population has remained relatively similar, although it has seen some recent growth. In the 2008-09 school year, the districts served 61,299 students, with a demographic breakdown of 29.6% African American, 65.3% Hispanic, 3.3% White, 1.8% Asian, 85% economically disadvantaged, and 13.8 Limited English Proficient.

Aldine is a district that embraced the accountability movement early and showed success with a challenging population before the implementation of the No Child Left Behind (NCLB) Act. Aldine was nominated twice as a Broad Prize finalist between 2002 and 2006, and 2008. Highlights of the performance contributing to the district's 2009 Prize win include:

- Higher performance than other similar districts in Texas in reading and math at all school levels (elementary, middle, and high school).

- Higher average proficiency rates than their state counterparts in reading and math at all levels.
- Math achievement gaps between income groups at all school levels were among the smallest in the state.

District vs. State Math Proficiency 2007

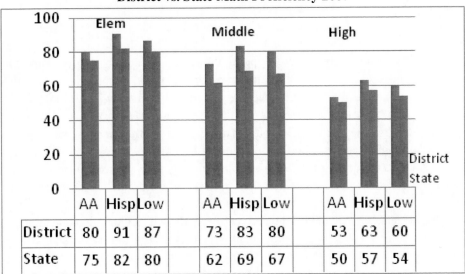

	AA	Hisp	Low		AA	Hisp	Low		AA	Hisp	Low
District	80	91	87		73	83	80		53	63	60
State	75	82	80		62	69	67		50	57	54

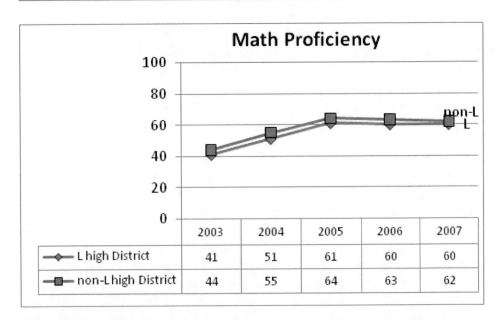

	2003	2004	2005	2006	2007
L high District	41	51	61	60	60
non-L high District	44	55	64	63	62

Aldine's "reform story" began around 1997 (Stab-1-Stability), when the district agreed that they needed to redefine what was to be taught to better prepare their students, and then align instruction seamlessly across all grade levels. The district developed its curriculum by starting with the state standards, which district and school staff felt lacked the clarity needed for teachers to know exactly what to teach and when to teach it (AL-1-Included, Str-4-Alignment, (AL-2-Standard Way). To tap into their "in-house" expertise, the district solicited feedback from teachers at all grade levels to determine how to pace the scope and sequence into six-week instructional units (I-2-Teacher Involvement, Str-2-Time Parameters). Teacher input was also important in this process to create buy-in and ensure the end result was something that teachers felt was appropriate and useful for planning and implementing instruction. Additionally, district leaders and teachers wanted to improve curriculum and instruction alignment (AL-1-Included, Str-4-Alignment), to ensure that no essential skills would be missed or unnecessarily duplicated.

In addition to clearly defining what was to be taught and learned, a second important step was to mandate that everybody teach the entire curriculum, because, as district leaders stressed, "We knew some people were skipping things or staying too long on some topics." They monitored adherence to the curriculum by using data (Str-6-Managed). During the first few years of curriculum refinement, it became apparent which teachers did not follow the curriculum, as they received poor results on their benchmark assessments (A-1 –Uniform assessment, A-Str-5-Assessment, A-3-Monitor and Evaluate). Another principal mentioned a situation with a science teacher who focused most of her time on her favorite topic: genetics. Most of the students in her class missed numerous quarterly exam items that were not covered during that quarter, providing "a real wake-up call," as one principal described, for that teacher.

Looking at data was an important part of the entire curriculum revision process and helped uncover some early gaps in instructional sequencing. For example, teachers found that rounding numbers was taught too late in the sequence, so the team added an instructional strand to address that gap (I-6 Revise). Additionally, the curriculum developers found that the state standards were not rigorous enough to prepare students adequately for graduation and college readiness, so they aimed to extend the standards beyond the minimum state requirements for each grade level (AL-6-Other Categories). Changes made through the review process created a more seamless "spiraled," or continuous, scope and sequence focused on higher academic levels. When we visited Aldine school s in 2004 and 2005, we saw evidence of their focused professional development (I-4-Group Support) on moving instruction from concrete to more applicative higher cognitive level s through the application of Bloom's Taxonomy (Al-6-Other Categories).[1] During one team meeting, we observed elementary teachers identifying the cognitive level of their lesson questions based on Bloom's model. Teachers explained that they identified each cognitive level for all their lessons to ensure that their instruction moved beyond basic knowledge and comprehension to higher-level skills, such as application and evaluation (I-4-Group Support).

Instructional alignment across classrooms and school s is extremely important in districts that serve highly mobile student populations. For a student to learn one reading approach only to change schools a few months later and find reading instruction to be completely different is highly disruptive to the learning process. Aldine ensures alignment through curriculum guides that divide a year's instruction into six-week units that are implemented uniformly across the district (Str-1-Content, Str-2-Time Parameters). To reinforce alignment, teachers are provided collaborative planning time to co-develop daily warm-ups, lesson plan s, practice and review exercises, and homework assignments (I-4-Group Support). As explained by one teacher, "The curriculum alignment throughout the district works well for our highly mobile population. With our alignment, whatever kids do on one side of the district feeds over to all of the vertical teams." This proved to be true. During two separate visits to Aldine, site visit team members reported seeing similar math warm-ups in different school s and locations. They also saw posted academic objectives of each lesson and a "word wall" in every elementary classroom.

In addition to coordinating instruction across classrooms, the school leadership takes the lead on monitoring implementation of the curriculum and providing supports where they are needed. Implementation is monitored by principals, assistant principals, and core subject "skills specialists," who work together to monitor instruction frequently as well as participate in regular teacher team meetings (I-4-Group Support, Str-6-Managed). Concerns are addressed from a service-oriented perspective, with questions like, "What do you think about that lesson?" or "What might you do differently next time?"

> Our classroom visits and focus groups with teachers yielded many positive comments about the curriculum, its components, and the development process. Teachers appreciated having a role in curriculum development (I-2-Teacher Involvement) and felt that the alignment between grades had a positive impact on their students. One teacher commented
> I think the biggest strength is that our district provides an aligned curriculum for all of our teachers. It addresses the curriculum for every six weeks. It puts the bulk of defining teaching and learning at the district level so that new teachers are not stressed with what they should be teaching. The curriculum addresses each objective and the prior knowledge that should be there. When I started teaching, there was just a guideline, but now there is no question about what you should be teaching.

There is much controversy around the idea of "managed curriculum;" that it stifles instructional creativity and takes away from professionalism in teaching. However, the teachers we interviewed did not appear to feel stifled by having instruction outlined in specific six-week increments. They asserted they could easily strike a balance between covering the designated objectives in each six weeks and having freedom to decide exactly how to teach. New teachers in particular thought that having clear guidelines for instruction and pacing was helpful (Str-1 Content & Str-2-Time Parameters). One new teacher said, "Our curriculum is strength, as I know where I am going day to day. It has helped me prepare for future planning."

While it is difficult to determine causation between a reform effort and achievement, many Aldine teachers and leaders believe their curriculum work was a huge factor in their success. When asked how their intense curricular focus affected student achievement (I-1-Curriculum Focus), district interviewees stated that the link between benchmarks, pacing guides, and common assessments moved the district from Academically Acceptable to Recognized status in a year's time.[1] (A-1–Uniform Assessment, Str-5-Assessment) Interviewees asserted that this performance jump was not owing to a tighter focus on test scores, but rather to a focus on exactly what teachers should teach and when. One district leader said, "We can't close the door and just teach dinosaurs in a vacuum just because we always did that unit. If you teach the curriculum, the test takes care of itself."

The point about the tight focus being a function of alignment and instructional coordination for students rather than test prep is important. Throughout the three or four research studies I have conducted in Aldine, district and school personnel over the years have always said, "We don't care about the test. We care about good instruction. If you teach well, the test will take care of itself."

Garden Grove Unified School District

Garden Grove Unified School District is one of the growing number of "urban suburban" districts in the United States, serving 50,030 students in parts of seven municipalities in the Los Angeles area. The district's student population is urban, with 61 percent low-income students, 53 percent Hispanic, 31 percent first-generation Asian American, 15 percent white, and 1 percent are African American.[2] The district is heavily populated by families who immigrated recently to the United States. English is the second language for approximately 75 percent of the district's students, who speak sixty-eight different languages.

After being named a finalist for the first three years of the Broad Prize, Garden Grove won the award in 2004. Highlights contributing to its 2004 win showed that Garden Grove had:

- Met its Adequate Yearly Progress (AYP) targets in 2004 for 100 percent of its schools
- Consistently performed higher than demographically similar districts between 2001 and 2004
- Narrowed the external gap (the gap between the district's disadvantaged group and the state's advantaged group) for all groups in reading and for low-income and Hispanic students in math

To better serve their diverse student population and increase academic performance, district leaders decided they needed more focus and alignment in their overall educational practices. As part of this process, the superintendent worked with central office and school leaders to better define goals for academic performance overall and for ELL students. To meet these goals, the district divided the state standards into specific "focus standards" supported by curriculum and pacing guides, which they continually revise using student data and current research on best practices (AL-1-Included, Str-4-Alignment & I-6 Curriculum Revision). The focus standards further specified what students should be able to do in each grade, executed by backward mapping from the 12th grade to Kindergarten. The guiding principles behind the development of the focus standards, according to central office interviewees, were that "what is being tested is not all of what kids need to know" and that teachers' input on the standards was critical.

The curriculum articulation process in Garden Grove was developed through collaborative groups of teachers and district administrators (I-2-Teacher Involvement) who worked with experienced consultants to construct the curriculum guides, quarterly benchmark assessments (A-1–Uniform assessment, Str-5-Assessment), and pacing guides for all grade levels (Str-2-Time Parameters).[3] Having test-writing experts help develop the benchmarks was very important, according to now retired superintendent, Dr. Schwalm, for ensuring proper correlation with the standards (A-1 –Uniform assessment, Str-5-Assessment). She felt their expertise added more usability and validity to the end product and was a worthwhile investment. In addition to the benchmark tests, many Garden Grove school s have developed common units and assessment pieces to customize instruction based on the unique learning needs of their students.

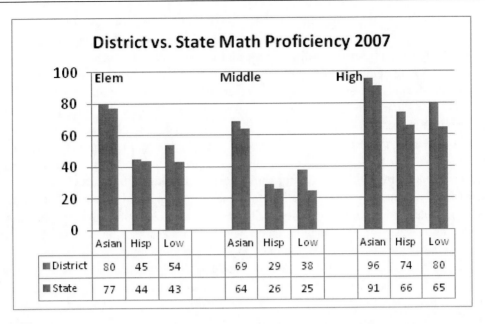

District vs. State Math Proficiency 2007

	Elem			Middle			High		
	Asian	Hisp	Low	Asian	Hisp	Low	Asian	Hisp	Low
District	80	45	54	69	29	38	96	74	80
State	77	44	43	64	26	25	91	66	65

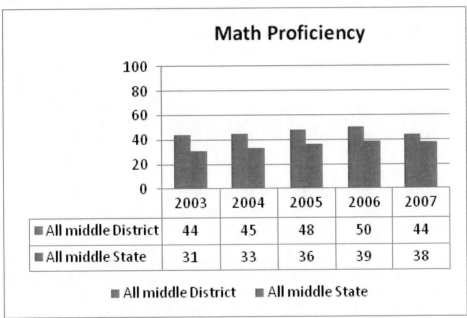

Math Proficiency

	2003	2004	2005	2006	2007
All middle District	44	45	48	50	44
All middle State	31	33	36	39	38

■ All middle District   ■ All middle State

Clearly articulated and aligned curriculum standards are important; however, their effectiveness is limited without appropriate implementation (I-3—Resources, I-4-Group Support). To support full implementation of district standards, Garden Grove provides intensive training for teachers and principals in the use of curriculum guides and research-based instructional strategies. Training is offered throughout the year and often includes opportunities such as classroom observations by teacher teams to see curriculum implementation firsthand. Additionally, principals and department chairs monitor curriculum implementation through classroom walkthroughs (Str-6-Managed) and assessment data culled from their data monitoring system (A-1–Uniform assessment, Str-5-Assessment).

Although focus, structure, and monitoring are important for providing immediate interventions as problems arise, putting some of these practices in place can be difficult. In 2003, not all teachers embraced the increased focus on standards and adherence to the instructional pacing guides. While some teachers felt they saw improvement with the level of preparedness students had for the next grade, others still believed that many students were not improving, particularly in high school. Additionally, the increase in structure put some teachers out of their comfort zone; something the superintendent and her team anticipated and addressed. Describing the teachers' feelings as "standing near the edge of a cliff (their comfort zone)," districts leaders voiced their confidence in the teachers, and provided numerous supports to help them step forward "closer to the edge" to the extent possible (I-2 Teacher Involvement, I-3—Resources). With the additional encouragement and support, the teachers gradually bought into the utility of the standards and curriculum guides. Their buy-in cemented as they saw improvements, which began with a marked increase in math skills, which they attributed to improved alignment in the math curriculum (AL-1-Included, Str-4-Alignment). When we returned for a separate study in 2005, teachers seemed to find more consistency across subjects and grades in the schools. A team of teachers interviewed mentioned that the pacing guides (Str-2-Time Parameters) helped create a common vocabulary, which seemed to help them work more effectively together to create instructional consistency (Str-2-Time Parameters). Illustrating more confidence in the preparedness of students, one teacher noted, "If a student moves anywhere in the district and is in Algebra I, I'm confident that child will know 'XYZ' because the teachers all follow the pacing guide."

The process Garden Grove used to create teams to work on the curriculum and supporting documents was a collaborative and structured process (I-2-Teacher Involvement, I-4-Group Support). Each project is called a "Consult," and is coordinated between the Garden Grove Educator's Association and district leadership, who solicit teacher and leader volunteers to work on a particular issue (I-4-Group Support). The team typically sets an outcome goal for the Consult, and then build a rubric or strategic plan to structure the process. Site visit interviews with teachers found a sense of satisfaction with their involvement with the development of the focus standards (Al-6-Other) and curriculum guides. Because teachers work in teams to develop and revise those standards, they believed the revision created a more seamless and aligned district curriculum. As one teacher described it:

> Being able to get into vertical teams and talk to your grade levels helps to actually create an effective plan. In that way, you are able to remind [other teachers] about current skills to be addressed and then go on to the next skill and spiral instead of spending more time teaching what they already know. We are trying to meet the background knowledge of our kids.

This process has been very effective for helping teachers view the curriculum in larger pieces across numerous grade levels. Another teacher who has been involved in the curriculum revision process said:

> We look at the results of California STAR test and also look specifically at the weak areas (Al-4-Assement Specs). At a grade level, we look at those results and decide what we need to emphasize for the year. We also look at the standards that have changed over time so that it is not just a set of standards. We see what it looks like from kindergarten to sixth grade, so we take a strand, like "word analysis" and talk about how that strand looks at different

levels so that every student is receiving the standards, but it may be at a different level, depending on where their ability is.

Once the district established greater clarity on what was to be taught and learned, they were better able to communicate that information to parents (I-4-Group Support). To help parents understand how well their children are mastering the standards, the district developed a standards-based report card for kindergarten through sixth grade. Instead of using simple letter grades, the report cards detail the specific skills that students have or have not mastered (Str-6-Managed). This helps parents and students know exactly what has been learned and where there may be cause for concern. In 2004, Garden Grove was piloting an electronic version of these report cards translated into the major languages spoken in the district in preparation for a district wide implementation.

Norfolk Public Schools

Norfolk Public Schools (NPS) is located in the Norfolk, a major port city in southwest Virginia that hosts the region's international airport and one of the busiest international ports on the east coast of the United States. It is also home to the world's largest naval base and NATO's North America n Headquarters.[4] The area includes five centers of higher education, and the military employs 25 percent of the local workforce. The student population tends to be highly mobile from the flux of military families, and diverse. Of their slightly more than 35,000 students, 56 percent are low-income, 64 percent African American, 4 percent Hispanic, and 24 percent are white.

NPS was a Prize finalist in 2003 and 2004 and won the Prize in 2005. NPS has done well with a challenging student population. The district's results demonstrate higher levels of achievement than demographically similar districts in Virginia. Highlights contributing to their nominations for and win of the Broad Prize in 2005 include:

- Met Adequate Yearly Progress (AYP) targets in 2004 for 76 percent of school s.
- Increased the number of elementary students who reached proficiency in reading by 14 percent between 2001 and 2005, and increased the number of middle school students who reached reading proficiency by 12 percent.
- Increased the number of elementary students who reached proficiency in math by 14 percent from 2001 to 2005, and increased the number of middle school students who reached proficiency in math by 23 percent.
- Reduced achievement gaps in elementary reading for Hispanic students (by 11 percent) and in middle school math for African American students (by 10 percent).
- Narrowed the achievement gaps in elementary reading between African American and White students.

Since winning, the district has gained numerous distinctions. In 2006, it was recognized by the National School Boards Association as having the top school board in the country, and since 2007, several Norfolk schools have won honors such as the U.S. Department of

Education Blue Ribbon award, and the bronze medal in *U.S. News & World Report*'s annual ranking of high school s.

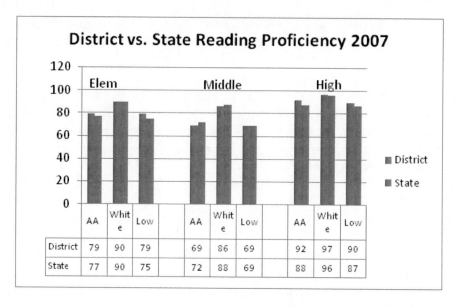

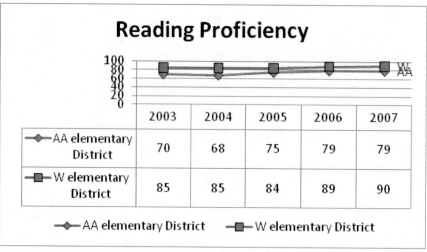

This successes and honors were not always present in NPS. Back in 1998, when John Simpson became superintendent in Norfolk (Stab-1-Stability), he was alarmed by the district's poor student performance. His first step was to recentralize many functions that had been decentralized and left to the school s, with his first act to be recentralizing curriculum and instruction (I-1-Curriculum Focus). Believing that district-wide alignment was crucial for their highly mobile student population, district leadership began the process by reducing twenty-four different reading programs down to one used by the successful schools. The selected reading program and other subsequent programs were selected based on their ability to address high levels of thinking (AL-6-Other Categories). Once well-defined, the curriculum and instruction was coordinated across grade levels, and then district leaders worked to create a structured system that would ensure alignment, faithful implementation, and tools and supports for schools and teachers (Al-1-Included, Str-4 –Alignment, I-4-Group Support, I-3—Resources).

Similar to Aldine and Garden Grove, NPS used their state standards as the foundation for their curriculum (AL-3-State Standards), but considered them to be the "floor, not the ceiling" for the district's instructional program. To ensure that everyone clearly understood the state standards, the district broke them down into specific skills in literacy, math, and other core-content areas (Str-1-Content). This process was completed through collaboration between teachers, central office, parents, and higher education partners (I-2-Teacher Involvement). When the process was complete, teachers were given specific learning objectives (Str-1-Content), curriculum maps, quarterly pacing calendars (Str-2-Time Parameters), monitoring rubrics, and multitask performance assessments (Str-5–Assessment, A-1-Uniform Assessment) to support the curriculum.

The supporting curriculum documents were always viewed as a work in progress, and revised or improved upon as needed (I-6 Curriculum Revision). During the site team's second Broad Prize visit to NPS in 2005, we found that the already-comprehensive curriculum maps had been improved by including: "essential questions" that help clarify the purpose of each lesson; an additional one-page view of the objectives aligned to the quarterly tests (A-1 – Uniform assessment, Str-5-Assessment); and support resources and extra materials for teachers (I-3—Resources). Additionally, pacing guides had been burned to CDs that provided hyperlinks to specific activities and common technical vocabulary to align content across the district.

NPS's curriculum is developed and revised by teams of teachers who use notes of suggested changes that all teachers write in their curriculum guides throughout the year (I-6 Curriculum Revision). During the revision process, vertical teams of teachers work together to analyze and discuss a particular issue, such as introducing algebra at lower grade levels (I-2-Teacher Involvement), to ensure that instruction is aligned appropriately from higher to lower grades (AL-1-Included, Str-4-Alignment). To expand that example—vertical teams of teachers met to discuss the instructional gaps students tended to display in algebra (I-4-Group Support). The teachers wanted to focus on laying the basic skills as a foundation, and then scaffolding upon it, rather than just teaching superficial skills, such as prime and composite numbers, repeatedly. The end result was a well-articulated strand from pre-K to grade 7 that prepared students on an in-depth level for algebra.

To assist with pacing and alignment, instructional objectives are grouped into six-week increments, giving teachers flexibility to decide how to cover a given topic, with remediation and acceleration built into daily lessons as needed (Str-1-Content, Str-2-Time Parameters). Quarterly benchmark assessments are given at the end of each six-week period to monitor progress on the objectives (Str-5–Assessment, A-1-Uniform Assessment, A-2-Time in Schedule). The district-wide quarterly assessments (A-1-Uniform Assessment, Str-5-Assessment) (and in some school s monthly assessments) are administered, and extensive walkthrough observations are provided to struggling schools to ensure that the curriculum is being consistently implemented (Str-6-Managed). The district's quarterly assessments are also used to determine regrouping of students according to their learning needs (A-2-Time in Schedule, A-3-Monitor and Evaluate).

District core-content teachers, department chairs, and grade-level leaders are responsible for helping teachers learn about and fully align the curriculum (I-4-Group Support). Additionally, the district provided central office support for classroom instruction by requiring all central office instructional support specialists to spend 70 percent of their time in classrooms helping teachers appropriately implement the curriculum. This central office school connection provided an efficient avenue for quick intervention, and added more alignment and opportunity to adjust the curriculum as needed. Interviews at all levels within the district illustrate the importance the system places am making these supports into a collaborative problem-solving process (I-4-Group Support) rather than a "gotcha." As in the other examples, most conversations in Norfolk sound like, "We looked at the data and thought, wow, that's interesting. We ask the teacher, what do you think happened? Is it the test question or something with instruction? How can we help you with this?"(I-4-Group Support) These conversations and monitoring occur throughout the district on an ongoing basis during the entire school year (Str-6-Managed).

The new focus on centralizing curriculum and instruction was a difficult change for some leaders and teachers in the district. In an early interview in 2003, Dr. Simpson mentioned that a certain number of NPS teachers ultimately left the district, leaving a "critical mass " of personnel that embraced the district's new curriculum and standards. However, in focus groups conducted in 2005, principals and teachers primarily spoke favorably about the curriculum, stating that it was clear, and that the pacing guides were particularly useful (Str-2-Time Parameters). Principals and teachers felt that the district communicated the curriculum throughout the system and gave appropriate support for implementation (I-4-Group Support).

DISCUSSION AND LESSONS LEARNED

The three districts highlighted in this chapter all moved from a point of what they describe as "unacceptable" student performance to winning the prestigious Broad Prize for Urban Education. They provide examples of districts that made impressive in-roads in raising achievement within a challenging urban context, while narrowing income and ethnic achievement gaps. While their approach is systemic and addressed all aspects that support instruction, each one illustrates the importance of curriculum; clearly defining and monitoring what is to be taught and learned.

When looking across these three districts (as well as the other two in Bringing School Reform to Scale), there are strong similarities in their approach to revising, aligning, communicating, and structuring their curriculum. The common themes found within all three examples provide potential lessons for other districts focused on improving their instructional program for students. Elements of the ASIA Framework are embedded within these lessons that form recommended curriculum practices outlined below:

- [Alignment] Create a clear and specific curriculum that communicates exactly what students should know and be able to do. The curriculum should align with state standards, and consider extending beyond them. A recommended process is to seamlessly map backward from the end-product of the system—a graduate prepared for college or skilled careers—down to preschool. There should be no unnecessary repeats or gaps between the instructional objectives.

- [Structure & Implementation] Communicate the curriculum across the entire system and support fidelity of implementation through curriculum documents like pacing guides, training, support, and monitoring.
- [Structure & Implementation] Create an open culture that welcomes feedback on the curriculum contents, instruction, and that focuses on providing supports when needed rather than blame.
- [Structure] Creates structures that allow collaboration and discussion around curriculum and instruction, in the form of common planning time, team observations of instruction, or a clear curriculum revision process for example.
- [Assessment] Create benchmark or quarterly assessments to monitor student performance and curriculum implementation as frequently as possible. Provide results to teachers and principals as soon as possible.

CONCLUSION

Education will continue to be a prime concern in our nation, and education reform will remain a constant. Incremental improvements found in national results show areas where we have made in-roads in raising student achievement. Close examination of those positive results show districts and school s that approach their reform efforts strategically and systemically by aligning the parts of the system around expectations for student learning. The end result is that all practices and activities--be them parent communications, school board meetings, budgeting, or planning professional development for instance- directly support the instructional core of the system. Aligning those parts must involve a constant laser-like focus on curriculum, and a comprehensive approach to developing, refining, communicating, and supporting the curriculum. One way to ensure all the pieces are in place for full curriculum support it to follow a structure like the ASIA framework.

The next two chapters highlight the work done in Norwalk Public Schools, CT. The first chapter explains how the superintendent fashioned district improvement by using curriculum as the center piece. The second chapter gives a more in-depth look at curriculum development in Mathematics.

End Notes

[1] Zavadsky, H (2009). Bringing School Reform to Scale: Five Award-winning Urban Districts. Harvard Education Press, Cambridge, MA. http://www.hepg.org/hep/book/110/BringingSchoolReformToScale
[2] National Center for Education Statistics, "Common Core of Data: Public Education Agency Universe" (Washington, DC: U.S. Department of Education, 2004).
[3] The district stopped using the same curriculum guides around 2005 because it found that teachers were torn between following the guides and trying to follow guidelines in their textbooks. To eliminate the confusion, the district focused more on instructional strategies; the guides are available for reference for pacing.
[4] Norfolk Public Schools, "NPS Fast Facts," http://www.nps.k12.va.us/index.php?option=com_content&view=article&id=673/.

In: Curriculum
Editor: David A. Squires

ISBN: 978-1-62948-673-4
© 2014 Nova Science Publishers, Inc.

Chapter 9

BUILDING INFRASTRUCTURE FOR IMPROVED ACHIEVEMENT IN NORWALK, CT

Salvatore J. Corda, Ph.D[1] and John Keogh[2]

[1]Previous Superintendent in Norwalk School District, Norwalk, CT, US
[2]Previous Math Supervisor in Norwalk School District, Norwalk, CT, US

ABSTRACT

This chapter outlines the plan we followed to organize the district for high achievement in Norwalk, CT. The next chapter describes how, in one content area in Norwalk, mathematics, the process of curriculum revision unfolded over time. The District did demonstrate steady progress in improving student achievement on State tests in Reading, Mathematics, and Writing for all subgroups identified in the No Child Left Behind legislation. The chapter shows that improved achievement comes about by having a clearly developed plan (I-5 Written Plan) that will help the infrastructure of the district be driven effectively toward improving student achievement. (I-3-Resources) (References to Appendix A – Summary of the ASIA Criteria for Refining or Designing Curriculum Process and Product are given after important criteria are mentioned. The I-3-Resources at the end of the sentence indicates that criteria I-3-Resources from Appendix A is referenced here).

THE DISTRICT PERSPECTIVE

Figure 9.1 provides a graphic representation of our work.

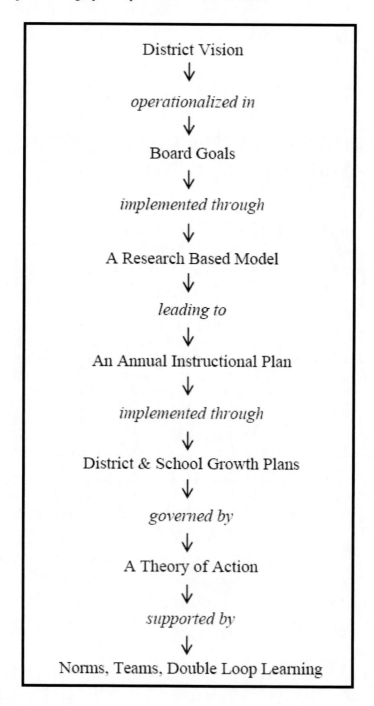

Figure 9.1 District Perspective.

Headings for the chapter follow these steps, with additional steps added to tell the story.

BACKGROUND OF THE DISTRICT

Norwalk, Connecticut is a community that combines both urban and suburban elements. Multi-racial and multi-cultural, the city is the sixth largest in the state and has a population of about 83,000. The economic diversity in the city covers a wide spectrum represented by multi-million dollar homes to public housing. The median family income is about $76,000 compared with $96,000 for Fairfield County (where Norwalk is located) and $52,000 nationally. The white population is about 59%; African Americans comprise about 13% and the Hispanic population, representing the fastest growing subgroup, accounts for about 23% of the city's population.[1]

The Norwalk Public Schools are part of District Reference Group H. District Reference Group (DRG) is a classification system in which Connecticut districts are rated according to their socioeconomic status. DRGs are based on seven variables: income, education, occupation, family structure, poverty, home language and district enrollment. They include nine groups, from group A (very affluent suburban districts) to group I (high-need, low socioeconomic urban districts).[2]

According to the District's Strategic School Profile for 2007/2008, the Norwalk public schools served 10,591 students as of October 1, 2007 in twelve elementary school s, four middle school s, two comprehensive high school s and a small secondary alternative high school. Figures 9.2 and 9.3 describe the poverty level, percentage of students for whom English is not their first language, and the racial and ethnic breakdown of the District compared with DRG H districts and State averages.

	Norwalk %	DRG H %	State %
Students Eligible for Free/Reduced-Price Meals	29.7	41.8	28.7
K-12 Students Who Are Not Fluent in English	12.6	12.0	5.4

Figure 9.2 Demographic Descriptors for the Norwalk Public Schools, DRG H and the State of Connecticut.

Race/Ethnicity	Norwalk %	DRG H %	State % (2006 data)
American Indian	0.2	0.4	0.4
Asian American	4.6	5.6	3.7
Black	23.6	20.6	13.9
Hispanic	30.8	32.3	16
White	40.9	41.2	66

Figure 9.3. Race/Ethnicity Descriptors for the Norwalk Public Schools, DRG H and the State of Connecticut.

---

[1] Source: U.S. Census Bureau, 2006-2008 American Community Survey, retrieved from http://factfinder. census.gov/home/saff/main.html?_lang=en March 23, 2010

[2] Charter school s, Connecticut Technical High Schools and Regional Educational Service Centers are not given DRGs. For additional information, see http://www.csde.state.ct.us/public/cedar/databulletins/db_drg_ 06_2006.pdf.

Dr. Salvatore Corda came to the district in April 2001 (Stab-1 Stability) as the new superintendent after it had been through three years of tumult resulting from a contentious relationship between the Board and the previous superintendent, serious budget reductions that stripped the central office of its instructional support infrastructure, little curriculum development, and even less focused teacher professional development. The clear sentiment from the Board, staff, and community was the need to get the system back on track with a focus on education. The school s were noted for many positive elements and many students did well, but there was a strong feeling that the district was capable of doing better, especially when it came to closing the achievement gap. This issue, usually perceived in terms of the difference in performance levels between white and minority students, had to be addressed. More importantly, however, and not as clearly articulated, was closing the gap for all groups of students' current performance in relation to State goal levels and having more students perform at higher levels.

The vision for the District needed to articulate our desired state. The goals (See Figure 9.4.) of the District had to make clear that the expectation for high achievement was for all groups and the goals would describe how we were going to do that.

VISION AND GOAL DEVELOPMENT

The work of school system improvement began in the 2001/2002 school year with a new superintendent, Dr. Corda, in place and the District's Board of Education committed to improving student performance. The Board expected a focused, systemic plan to improve student achievement recognizing that it would require a multi-year effort. The Board indicated its willingness to work together, despite political differences, and exemplified its intent by meeting with the Superintendent to develop goals (Figure 9.4) that would drive the work of the district and set the stage for the work to begin. After several meetings, the Board adopted five goals in June, 2001 (I-1-Curriculum Focus):

GOALS OF THE NORWALK PUBLIC SCHOOLS

Goal One - Instruction

We will build the Norwalk Public Schools into an exemplary district characterized by a cohesive and coordinated academic system with a set of clearly defined performance based outcomes for all students. Our work as a learning community will:

- emphasize mastery of knowledge, strategies and skills;
- develop in our students the habits of thinking, cooperation, and self-discipline;
- focus on results;
- ensure excellence and equity of opportunity
- value diversity;
- instill respectfulness and responsibility.

Goal Two – Community Participation

We will actively seek the input and involvement of staff, parents, students, and the community when making the educational decisions necessary to ensure every student's success.

Goal Three - Communication

We shall effectively communicate to the public our plans, progress, and successes for the implementation of our goals.

Goal Four - Finance

We will develop annual operating and capital financial plans to implement the objectives necessary to achieve our goals and meet our contractual obligations in a manner that is fiscally responsible to our community.

Goal Five – Long Range Planning

We will develop, communicate, and implement long range educational and facilities plans based on student needs, program needs, equity and excellence, and fiscal responsibility.

Figure 9.4. Goals of the Norwalk Public Schools.

The Board did not wish to pursue the crafting of a vision statement. To them the purpose of our work was clear—high achievement for all students and do what is necessary for the District to get there. In 2002, however, they did adopt a mission statement.

> The mission of the Norwalk Public Schools is to create a supportive learning community rooted in the belief that all children can learn.
> Our educators will challenge all students to demonstrate high levels of achievement on a wide variety of clearly defined standards.
> Our students will graduate with the skills, knowledge, attitudes and experiences necessary to ensure their highest potential for success and life-long learning. (I-1-Curriculum Focus)

The administration, on the other hand, did grapple with developing a District vision. During the annual administrators' three-day workshop in June, 2002, after reading Fullan's Change Forces (1993), the administrative team discussed the crafting of a District vision. We were concerned about crafting a District vision that did not include the participation of the larger community, teachers, other district staff, and the community. Administrative staff made comments like, "Building a vision takes time." Our vision has to be developed to bring about change." "Creating and implementing our vision is a collective process. We have to bring resistors to nurture the vision and empower those who don't buy in—They have to become a part of it." District and School leadership acted mindful of Fullan's comment that collective vision can come later as long as the key leadership is clear about the desired state. The administrators felt the Board and Superintendent were clear in the District goals about what our District needed to be. The administrative team left their workshop with an agreement to wait to craft a District vision, but we were clear about and committed to the following:

- Every student had to learn.
- We had to do what was best for kids.
- You can't have a learning society without students who learn; you can't have students who learn without teachers who learn, and you can't have teachers who learn without administrators who learn. (I-5 Plan Written)

SELECTING THE LEVERAGE POINT – CURRICULUM

Recognizing that the improvement work of the District could most effectively be approached from a focus on professional tasks, the Superintendent recommended and the Board approved a decision to begin an ambitious process of curriculum revision. (I-1-Curriculum Focus) Elmore (2002) has identified a variety of leverage points as the means to improve the focus on the instructional core, i.e., the interaction between teacher and student in the presence of content. These include resources; knowledge, skills, and expertise; accountability; assessment; curriculum; capacity building and professional development, and structure. These elements are interconnected and while one may begin the work of system improvement by focusing on any one of them, what becomes quickly apparent is that the system must pay attention to all of the elements because of their interconnectedness.

A focus on curriculum, what will be taught, and the accompanying discussions about how it will be taught, to whom, what resources would be needed, and with what effect provided the greatest opportunity for several reasons. (I-1-Curriculum Focus) First, the staff recognized that the curriculum needed to be revised in every content area. Second, curriculum revision would provide the opportunity for making clear the need for restoring the instructional support infrastructure. Third, the process would enable the expertise of the District staff to be utilized and reinforce the need for developing a culture of mutual support and professional growth (I-4-Group Support). Fourth, the need for new textbooks [3] and materials, professional development, and support staff essential for the implementation of revised curricula would document the need for resources when the annual budget was prepared (I-3-Resources). Fifth, with new curricula in place and the resources provided for its implementation, a sense of urgency would be created for the development of a meaningful and growth (I-1-Curriculum Focus) enhancing teacher evaluation and supervision plan which was followed by a similar plan for administrators. (More information on the actual process of curriculum revision in Chapter 10). Politically, the focus on curricul revision avoided any implication that the District's stagnant performance was the result of teacher or administrative performance.

The extremely talented Dr. Karen Lang was hired as the Assistant Superintendent for Instruction to lead an ambitious five-year plan for curriculum revision of every content area (I-5 Plan Written). At the beginning of the 2001/2002 school year, Corda presented a multi-year plan to reorganize central office instructional support staff by eliminating the position of supervisors who had responsibility for multiple disciplines and replacing them over a three year period with Instructional Specialists in the content areas of Language Arts, Mathematics, Social Studies and Education for Gifted Students, Science, English Language Learning, and Early Childhood Education. By 2004/2005, the Instructional Specialists were in place. The plan also included, over time, adding a Director of Secondary Education (Fall, 2001/2) and a Director of Elementary Education (2003/4) who had the primary responsibility of supervising and working with principals in the implementation of curricula and the development, supervision, and evaluation of instructional staff. (I-3-Resources)

This configuration was selected since it provided an instructional support infrastructure staffed by experts in content areas, and professional development and accountability by the principals through the supervision and evaluation of the Directors. Of critical importance was

---

[3] In fact, the District developed an innovative, systemic, multi-year financial plan for the expenditure of more than a million dollars to replace textbooks and received the support of the city for those funds.

the need to be politically sensitive to avoiding what some might perceive as a bloated central office administrative group. Specific titles were chosen with care to avoid this perception.

BUILDING CAPACITY FOR INSTRUCTIONAL SUPPORT

During this initial set-up period, financial constraints enabled rethinking about how to enhance administrative support for the important instructional work of teachers. Each elementary school had a half-time assistant principal, irrespective of its size. Given the expectation for regular and focused interaction between administrators and teachers around matters related to instruction and the introduction of a more intensive teacher supervision and evaluation plan that necessitated longer and deeper discussions about instructional practice, it would be necessary to ensure that each elementary school had a full time assistant principal. In 2003/04, the Superintendent, with the support of elementary principals and central office staff, proposed eliminating Reading Recovery teachers in the twelve elementary schools and replacing them with six additional elementary assistant principals, each of whom would have strength in literacy. The Board agreed to do so. The Board demonstrated significant courage in coming to this decision. Unfortunately, the public perception of administrators, many times, does not acknowledge the value of administrators as instructional leaders. Teachers are perceived as providing service to students while administrators are thought of more as managers, and not as intimately involved in instruction. To its credit, the Board recognized that instructional leadership and support were needed and, while Reading Recovery was a successful program, the capacity for impacting a larger number of students would be increased by full time elementary assistant principals. (I-3-Resources) As a result, each elementary school had an assistant principal with expertise in literacy, and every school in the District had the necessary administrative staff to implement a rigorous teacher supervision and evaluation process based on the work of Charlotte Danielson (1996, 2000).

FRAMING THE WORK OF THE DISTRICT

In order for the work of systemic improvement to proceed, the staff and community needed to understand that the work was being guided by a clear vision, supported by stable goals approved by the Board of Education, and a research based model of implementation (See Figure 9.5.) for system improvement. This model would be the framework of the annual instructional plan and would guide the work of the District over time. Heavily influenced by Corda's work with the Connecticut Superintendents' Network, which was guided by Richard Elmore and Lee Teitel of Harvard and Andrew Lachman, Executive Director of the Connecticut Center for School Change, the model made clear that the work of the District was to focus on the work of the classroom. Building administrators were expected to provide strong instructional leadership and the work of central office was to provide both leadership and support. The Annual Instructional Plan model was developed from an earlier version Corda had constructed with his colleague, Dr. Sally Kuralt, and used in his previous District. The document was designed to fit on a single page so that the focus of the district was explicit and efficiently stated for all to understand. (I-5 Written Plan)

A Research-based Planning Model
Guiding Implementation of the Annual Norwalk Instructional Plan

Focus on the Instructional Core

i.e., the interaction between teacher and student in the presence of content.

Instruction

- Uses a variety of strategies that recognize the differences in student learning styles
- Instructional tasks are academically rigorous and require students to focus on instructional problems in all content areas
- Intervention is provided when assessment determines need for further instruction, rather than remediation at a later point in time
- Instruction is assessed based on its impact on student learning
- Requires that teachers routinely meet with each other around matters of instructional practice

Curriculum

- Focused to identify those standards in each content area that:
  - endure, i.e., recur in the skills and knowledge that students must display
  - provide leverage, i.e., are associated with success in other standards, and,
  - are essential for the next level of instruction

Assessment

- Periodic, short term, and meaningful to provide feedback to students and to guide teachers in making instructional decisions
- Consistent across grades and levels across the district

Professional Development

- Develops the capacity of teachers to collectively work on problems of instructional practice
- Develops individual knowledge and skills

Results-Driven

- Effective means of assessing student progress in attaining valued outcomes based on benchmarks and other measures
  - Student Portfolio
  - Student Performance
  - Traditional/standardized measures
- GAP analysis of actual and desired results
- Reporting of performance data by racial and ethnic groups
- Needed and existing capacity and resources
- Data-driven dialogue to guide district and site-based planning for student growth
- Public reporting of student progress

Learner Centered

- Shared body of knowledge of how students construct knowledge and strategies for effective teacher decision-making
- The emphasis of teaching and learning in the classroom is on:
  - The student as worker
  - The teacher as coach and modeler
  - Honoring student voice/choice
- Focuses on students' instructional tasks
- Instructional "Match"
  - Task analysis
  - Essential understandings and strategies
  - Backward design
- Spiral curriculum
- High expectations for all students
- Individual and collective accountability for students' affective and academic needs

Systems Thinking

- Common understanding of Essential 21st Century Outcomes and standards linked change
- Community of Learners Culture which develops norms that provide:
  - Thoughtful, continuous, and respectful dialogue with a focus on instructional work
  - Adults providing learning models for students
  - Administrators learning with teachers and students
  - Board and Community understanding and support of the instructional program
- Common Language of Instruction
- Focuses evaluation/supervision on examination of the teaching/learning process, not inspecting teachers
- Centralized (District) and De-centralized (School) Strategies which include those that are identical, similar, and different across all schools
- Using points of high leverage as vehicles for planned change
- Continuous assessment of system progress

Figure 9.5.

Focus on the Instructional Core

Corda had been involved with the Superintendents' Network, which was developed and supported by the Connecticut Center for School Change. Influenced strongly by the continuing and rich dialogue among the superintendents about the importance of focusing on the instructional core (City, et al., 2009) and the continued observation of the work of teachers in the classroom, Corda sought to instill in Norwalk this same commitment to creating communities of practice and to foster continuing conversations about instructional practice. (I-1-Currriculum Focus) The emphasis on the instructional core was based on instruction grounded in an articulated curriculum aligned to the District standards. The District had spent considerable time familiarizing itself with the work of Reeves (2002) and Ainsworth (2003). As the District conversation progressed about how the work would go forward, the importance of formative assessments (Popham, 2006, Stiggins, 2006) became clear, and work began on developing common formative assessments in a number of content areas and grades. (A-1 Uniform Assessments, Str-5-Assessment)

Results Driven

The importance of assessing student performance was underscored by the adoption of the No Child Left Behind legislation. The District, long committed to closing the achievement gap both between minority and white students, and, more importantly between all students and performance at goal on State tests, felt increased pressure because of the labeling of school s and the District as 'In Need of Improvement' because the federal benchmarks were not met.

Mindful, however, that State tests were not the only means by which student performance ought to be judged, the District also examined student work both in student portfolios and in other performance assessments. It was a review of all of this data that enabled school s to examine grade and school performance as a prerequisite to the development of school growth plans.

By using multiple data sources, the conversation at the school and district level was the driving force in making decisions about what to do. It is fair to say that this conversation was more of an internal dialogue since the general public, and, increasingly as the membership on the Board of Education changed, there was little understanding of the importance of any performance measures other than the CAPT and CMT (Connecticut State Tests) scores (Al-4-Assessment Specs). Any State Education department decision was driven only by these measures because of the overbearing pressure of the No Child Left Behind legislation.

Learner Centered

Constructivist thinking recognizes that for students to make meaning of the world around them, they must engage in addressing instructional problems of pronounced rigor and that the role of the teacher is one of problem framer and developer, coach, modeler, and resource. The work of the classroom, therefore, is a personification of the instructional core. The student, through the facilitation of, and interaction with, the teacher, is establishing and making meaning about content. This model demands that the thinking and perspectives of students (student voice) are as critical as the thinking and perspective of the teacher in framing the connection to the content. The duality of the student/teacher relationship is only valid in the presence of the instructional content (Str-1-Content). The teacher's responsibility includes collaboration with others in defining rigorous instructional tasks, expectations for understanding and content knowledge, assessment of student performance, and addressing the needs of individual students as they emerge. In academically and culturally heterogeneous classrooms, the work of the teacher is particularly challenging. Given the standards articulated by the State which will be measured by the State tests, teachers must know, and have a common understanding of, the critical understandings required for students, what it is that students are expected to do, and how performance can most effectively be assessed. The requirement for an aligned curriculum becomes self-evident. It is this work that demands collaboration among teachers as one of the norms of professional practice. (I-2-Teacher Involvement)

Systems Thinking

The literature is replete with illustrations of individual school s that have developed as learning institutions where students perform at high levels. Finding school systems that meet this criterion is a different story. If the Norwalk Public School District was to become a high performing district where all of its students, irrespective of background, were to be adequately prepared for the demands of the twenty-first century, it would be important to create a system which had the following characteristics:

- A common understanding of essential outcomes and standards (A-3-State Standards)
- A Community of Learners culture with established norms that expected:
  o Thoughtful, continuous, and respectful dialogue with a focus on instructional work
  o Adults providing learning models for students
  o Administrators learning with teachers and students
  o Board and Community understanding and support of the instructional program
- A common language of instruction
- An evaluation/supervision process that focused on examination of the teaching/learning process, not the inspection of teachers. This element is a bit of a slippery slope, however, since the role of the adsministrator is both supervisor, i.e., one who focuses on improving teacher practice, and evaluator, i.e., one who is responsible for the continuation of a teacher's employment.
- Centralized (District) and De-centralized (School) strategies which included those that *must* be identical, *might* be similar, and *could* be different across all school s
- Recognized points of high leverage as vehicles for planned change
- A continuous assessment of system progress and process (A-1- Uniform Assessment, Str-5-Assessment)

Clearly, this represented the desired state and would be achieved only after years of hard work and continuous reassessment about how the work was being done. The human dynamics of individual personalities and agendas, on many levels—Board, Union, Administration, and Community, in some cases accelerated the achieving of that state and, in other cases, created strong impediments. (I-4-Group Support) Where these stakeholder groups are aligned in focusing on high achievement for all students and function within their roles[4], progress is made. When they are not, progress ceases.

THE DISTRICT'S ANNUAL INSTRUCTIONAL PLAN

Each year the Superintendent submitted for Board approval an Instructional Plan that outlined the focus of the District's instructional work in Curriculum Development and Instruction. The plan also highlighted the professional development focus for all district staff recognizing that further professional development would be identified on a school by school basis and by the instructional specialists for particular groups of teachers based on the curriculum review, development, or implementation that was occurring. Finally, because these were areas that needed to be continually developed, the plan regularly highlighted the continuing priorities:

- Strong instructional leadership
- Developing learning communities through articulated norms of practice
- Continuous assessment of system capacity
- Accountability through assessment of stated objectives in the school growth plans
- Effective supervision to improve performance
- Academic intervention to ensure student success
- Enhanced academic opportunities for all students
- Strong parental and community involvement
- Strong connections with pre-school and after school programs
- Strong linkages with community agencies and organizations.

The plan would change from year to year depending on where the District was in implementing the instructional plan of the previous year. The purpose of the plan, among other things, was to provide a measure of public accountability for the work that was being done and to make explicit to the staff the work of the current school year (I-5-Written Plan). The most difficult challenge was to sustain support for the plan since the change in student achievement was sporadic for the first few years. However, in the early years of the work, to the Board's credit, there was a commitment to stay the course.

With the implementation of No Child Left Behind in 2002 and the District performance in the ensuing years, the situation became exacerbated because progress was not being made at the rate that the law required. The misguided emphasis of No Child Left Behind on making judgments about the effectiveness of school s and the district based on Adequate Yearly

---

[4] See Elmore, Richard. (2000) *Building a New Structure for School Leadership*. pp. 21-22 for a description of the functions of stakeholder groups.

Progress on State tests, and the sanctions it imposed, created a political climate that eroded support for the plans supported by an earlier enlightened Board of Education which recognized that systemic improvement was a long term process marked by peaks and valleys.

Figure 9.6 provides a sample Instructional Plan.

Norwalk Public Schools – Instructional Plan 2004 - 2005

Board of Education Instructional Goal

- Standards based expectations
- NPS graduation requirements
- High expectations for all students
- Access for all students to challenging content
- Close the achievement gap by focusing on the performance of all students who have not met expected standards
- Value diversity, respectfulness and responsibility

Indicators of Achievement

- State Tests
- Graduation Rates
- Assessments based on student work

Curriculum Development

Implementation of Five-Year Plan

Evaluation ⟶ Development ⟶ Phase-in

2004/05

- ➢ Phased-in Implementation of 6 - 12 Math
- ➢ Implementation of HS enhancement curriculum in Language Arts, Mathematics, and Science
- ➢ Implementation of 6 - 12 Social Studies
- ➢ Implementation of K - 8 Science
- ➢ Development of curricula in:
  - 9 - 12 Science,
  - 6 - 12 Technology Education,
  - 6 - 12 Family & Consumer Science,
  - 3 – 8 Academically Talented
  - 6 - 8 Computer Science
- ➢ Evaluation of World Language Program

Best Practices/Staff Development Priorities

- Higher level thinking and problem solving in classroom tasks
- Interdisciplinary planning
- Emphasis on active learning and student work
- Appreciating diversity
- Integrating technology into the curriculum
- Using student performance data to plan instruction

Focus: 2004/2005

- Continued refinement of Teacher Evaluation Plan
- Implementation of Administrator Evaluation Plan
- Development and implementation of School Growth Plans
- Enhance the learning organization through instructionally focused norms of practice
- Development of Curriculum Benchmarks and Assessments

Multi-Year Priorities

- Strong instructional leadership
- Developing learning communities
- Appropriate and current textbooks, resources, and materials
- Accountability through assessment of stated objectives
- Strong supervision
- Academic intervention to ensure student success
- Enhanced academic opportunities for all students
- Strong parental and community involvement
- Strong connections with pre- and after school

Figure 9.6. Instructional Plan of the Norwalk Public Schools for 2004/2005.

The implementation of the Instructional Plan is accomplished through a District and individual School Growth Plans (I-5 Written Plan). The District's Instructional Plan outlined the work of the District as it related to curriculum development and revision, professional development activities to encourage best practices, and other system enhancement activities. The School Growth Plan indicates the work of the school specifically related to the improvement of student achievement in the school. These plans outline in detail what the district and school intends to focus on in order for high achievement to occur for all students. Before a plan can be developed, however, there needs to be thoughtful reflection on the theory of action that will guide the work. (I-5-Plan Written)

A THEORY OF ACTION[5]

A theory of action is essentially a series of "If, then…" statements that describe how a particular objective may be achieved. The theory represents what we felt we needed to do if we were going to create a system that functioned effectively for all students. A critical assumption in a theory of action include the recognition that the evidence of what occurs as a result of the actions may disprove the theory and that using a theory of action requires a willingness to revise proposed actions as one learns about the consequences of the actions.

A theory of action to improve student achievement for all students relates to equally important actions by *both* central administration and building staff. One cannot succeed without the other. Over time, theories of action should become more specific and more focused as new information becomes available and as people become more sophisticated in their use. Corda began with the following:

For the Administrative Staff

If Norwalk Public School leaders consistently engage in using a continuous improvement model for district work by (1) focusing on the instructional core, i.e., the work of teachers with students in the presence of instructional content, and (2) reflecting on the learning emanating from that practice, *then* the Norwalk Public School system will become a learning organization.

If we say that this is our theory, then there are things we must do. This means that our administrators must:

- Demonstrate and nurture strong instructional leadership
- Develop learning communities through articulated norms of practice
- Continually assess our system's capacity to develop and sustain staff professional growth

---

[5] Argyris and Schön (1974, 1978) first articulated the concept of a Theory of Action. Richard Elmore, Gregory R. Anrig Professor of Educational Leadership at the Harvard Graduate School of Education, in his work with the Superintendents' Network, supported by the Connecticut Center for School Change, stressed the importance of articulating a theory of action as an essential ingredient in creating and nurturing systemic reform. To understand Elmore's thinking about the need for a Theory of Action see City, Elizabeth A., *et al.* 39 – 57.

- Hold ourselves accountable for high student performance through assessment of stated objectives in the school growth plans
- Nurture and develop effective supervision to improve performance
- Provide academic intervention to ensure student success
- Provide enhanced academic opportunities for all students
- Encourage and support strong parental and community involvement

For the Instructional Staff

If the Norwalk Public Schools sustains and increases its efficiency as a learning organization by (1) developing the reflective and analytical skills of administrators and teachers about teacher and student work, (2) providing the organizational support and structure for teachers and administrators to engage in this work, (3) always treating each other in a professional and courteous manner, and (4) devoting the resources necessary for improving in this work, *then* student achievement will improve.

If we say that this is our theory, then there are things we must do. This means that our instructional staff must:

- collaborate with each other in thinking about classroom practice, assessing student work, planning instruction, and observing each other's practice;
- align the work of the classroom around particular variables that research has demonstrated influence student achievement;
- ensure that students are engaged in instructional tasks of high academic rigor;
- ensure that students collaborate with each other and with their teachers in their work;
- continually assess the progress of students and use this information to inform instruction.

The articulation of a theory of action lays the groundwork for the development of growth plans for both school s and the district (I-4-Group Support).

SCHOOL GROWTH PLANS

We defined School Growth Plans as the agreed upon measurable objectives to improve student achievement accomplished by being goal oriented and data driven, attained through a continuous process of instruction, assessment, and reflection. These plans make operational a theory of action for student achievement. Research has demonstrated that the school is the center for change. Marzano (2003) states, "The school (as opposed to the district) is the proper focus for reform. Indeed, this is a consistent conclusion in the research literature." (p. 10.)

The purpose of the plan is:

- To guide and organize school building efforts to advance achievement for all students;

- To demonstrate the link between the work of the school s and the instructional goal of the district;
- To foster the development of the learning community through a strategic effort on improving student achievement by focusing on the instructional core.

In the 2003/2004 school year, each school began developing its school growth plan. Each year the format was refined and its format annually reviewed for its effectiveness. The review of the indicators at the end of each school year, as well as other objectives that might emerge, provides the basis for the focus for the following year (I-4-Group Support).

CENTRAL OFFICE GROWTH PLANS

Two components are part of the definition of Central Office Growth Plans:

1. The agreed upon objectives of central office instructional staff to support the instructional program in curriculum development, implementation, and professional development.
2. The agreed upon objectives of the Pupil Personnel Services department to support special needs students through inclusion, co-teaching, and the integration of our special needs population into the mainstream life of the school s.

The school is the center for change because the mechanism for high achievement is through a focus on the instructional core, i.e., the interaction between teacher and student in the presence of content. However, the school district, as a system, has a critical role in supporting that work. One of the essential purposes of central office instructional support staff is to serve as a resource, catalyst, and leader to the instructional staff. Just as it is essential for building staff to articulate their plans for improving student achievement, instructional support staff need to delineate how they will support the work of building staff, as well as meeting their responsibilities for curriculum development and program improvement.

Similarly, Pupil Personnel staff has the responsibility for identifying, planning, and supporting the needs of special education students. This involves fostering inclusion and co-teaching as the model for the delivery of this service. A thoughtful and goal oriented plan for meeting these needs is necessary if all of our students are going to be served. This plan must be coordinated with the work of the school s to meet the special needs of a particular part of our student body.

Finally, for English Language Learners, efforts to provide bi-lingual and ESL services must coordinate with the work of the buildings in meeting the needs of these students (I-4-Group Support).

The purpose of the plan is:

- To demonstrate the link between the work of central office instructional staff, building instructional staff, and the instructional goals of the district;
- To provide a clear articulation of the plans to address the needs of Special Education students and English Language Learners.

DISTRICT GROWTH PLAN

The definition of the district growth plan includes the agreed upon objectives designed to improve student performance across the District articulated through efforts in curriculum development, implementation, and professional development to incorporate best practices, i.e., those instructional strategies and efforts that have been documented to improve student achievement.

A District Growth Plan is necessary. While the essential work of improving student performance is best accomplished by the work that takes place in school s, the responsibility of the Superintendent of Schools, assisted by the work of central office and building administration and influenced by professional staff and parents, is to provide direction for the District's instructional work and to prepare a District plan for the approval of the Board of Education. In a system that is committed to high achievement for all students, there is room for diversity in the approach that is taken, but there are also some essential components that must be consistent across the District. For example, the focus on academic rigor in all lessons must be consistent across the school system but the practices that teachers may use in that effort may differ. These systemic efforts must be articulated in a District plan to guide and influence the school growth plans and to provide a benchmark against which school growth plans may be assessed.

In the 2006/2007 school year although student achievement had improved, the District had still not made sufficient progress under the requirements of the No Child Left Behind legislation. As the State Education Department began to provide assistance to the District, what became clear was that there was a need for a District Improvement/Growth Plan in order to provide a stronger sense of coherence and alignment across the District (I-4-Group Support, I-5-Written Plan).

The District Plan's purpose is:

- To guide and organize the efforts of the District that focus on improving student achievement with an emphasis on data driven instructional objectives;
- To provide a framework for improvement to be used by school s in the developing of the school growth plans;
- To serve as a vehicle for the identification and planning for the use of best practice in instruction.[6]

NORMS

The work of system improvement cannot be done well in the absence of norms, those agreed upon rules of behavior and action that guide the work of the district/school /department team. Each school will develop a set of norms that articulates how the entire staff will interact with each other and with students. Norms help to reinforce a climate of mutual respect and support. We need to state clearly how we will interact with each other and hold each other accountable for our behavior. Additionally, we need to assess routinely if the

---

[6] A model that may be useful is attached as Appendix A.

norms are being followed. It is only through a continuous monitoring that we can reinforce the agreed upon norms and take steps to address when the norms are not being followed.

Norms are important because:

- Norms curtail unproductive behaviors.
- Norms give us permission to be bolder than we otherwise might be.
- Norms acknowledge that people learn in different ways.
- Agreed upon norms allow others to enter the conversation at any time.
- Norms allow us to navigate through "tricky" conversations.
- Norms are guides; they are not rules.
- Norms require flexibility; yet provide guidance.
- Norms need to be periodically and routinely assessed for their effectiveness.
- Norms can be changed-- by the people who live by them.

TEAMS (PROFESSIONAL LEARNING COMMUNITIES)

Katzenbach and Smith (1993) define a team as a small number of people with complementary skills who are committed to a common purpose, set performance goals, and an approach to work for which they hold themselves accountable.

In contrast, a working group is a small number of individuals who focus on specific tasks that are designed to produce specific outcomes usually led by a particular individual. This is an absolutely appropriate pattern for meeting individual goals. But we also need to function as a team.

Figure 9.7 describes the differences, as delineated by Katzenbach and Smith (1993), between working groups and teams.

Working Group	Team
Strong, clearly focused leader	Shared leadership role
Individual accountability	Individual & mutual accountability
The group's purpose is to help each individual perform better	The team's purpose is to magnify the impact of individuals by what the team itself delivers
Individual work products are the outcome	Collective work products are the outcome
Runs "efficient" meetings	Encourages open-ended discussions and active problem solving meetings
Measures its effectiveness indirectly by its influence on others, but also on its own results	Measures performance directly by assessing collective work products and the impact on overall system performance

Figure 9.7. A Comparison between Working Groups and Teams.

A professional learning community is an educational manifestation of the team concept. As Ann Delehant of the National Staff Development Council draws the connection, "A Professional Learning Community is a *team* with an intentional focus on learning." Morrisey (2000) says, "A school that operates as a "Professional Learning Community" engages the entire group of professionals in coming together for learning within a supportive, self-created community."

The following are some guiding principles about professional learning communities:

1. The discussion is *always and only* about what is, and needs to be, done in terms of instructional practice to ensure student achievement.
2. The emphasis is on creating and sustaining a culture of collaboration.
3. The continuous question is, "Are all students learning and how do we know?"

Functioning as a PLC has advantages:

- Teacher and administrator learning is more complex, deeper, and more fruitful in a professional setting where participants can interact, test their ideas, challenge their inferences and interpretations, and process new information with each other.
- When new ideas are processed in interaction with others, multiple sources of knowledge and expertise expand and test the new concepts as part of the learning experience.
- The professional learning community provides a setting that is richer and more stimulating.
- Kids learn more!

Professional Learning Communities follow norms in order to ensure a focused and professionally respectful discussion. They rely on teachers assuming a variety of leadership roles in selecting topics, leading discussions, and collaborating about instructional practice. Many times, professional learning communities use protocols as the means for facilitating discussions and the work of the group in a way that includes the active participation of all of the members.

Effective teams, including professional learning communities, formally assess their effectiveness both in using the norms and in accomplishing the purposes of the group. They use this data to improve their own practice. It's how the team gets better in the way in which it works (I-4-Group Support).

Here are some ways we went about developing PLC's.

✓ Identify shared norms and values
✓ Make sure collaboration (working as a team) is embedded into daily work. The work must be:
  - Purposeful
  - Structured
  - Facilitated
  - Accountable for results
  - Research-based

- and must have a
  - o Focus that is instructional
  - o Collaborative adoption process for agreed upon best practice
  - o Commitment to continuous improvement

DOUBLE LOOP LEARNING - REFLECTIVE DIALOGUE ON THE PROGRESS OF THE PROCESS

If you don't ask yourself, "How are we doing?" you'll never really know. Formal and informal self- and collective feedback is an important tool to get better at the process of school improvement.

Teams form over time and their level of effectiveness is different at different times. Assessing one's functioning as a team is assessing its place along a continuum, rather than thinking of a team as functioning in a "good" or "bad" way. Tuckman (1965) describes the stages of team building as Forming, Storming, Norming and Performing. Teams can move from one category to another depending on the work of the team. In other words, as new phases of the work are begun, teams may return to an earlier stage and evolve back into a more effective way of performing as it gains expertise in the new level of work. Team assessment is a conscious act designed to help the team get better at what it does.

At the same time, it is important to continually examine the theory of action to determine its continued utility. To understand the importance of paying attention to the effectiveness of the process and its impact on the growth of the organization, we again turn to Argyris and Schön (1974) and to Smith (2001). They distinguish between single and double loop learning, characterizing double loop learning as a hallmark of learning organizations.

As Elmore (2009) describes it,

> Single loop learning describes the situation in which we act on the world, receive feedback on the consequences of our actions, and adapt our behavior to the feedback.
> Double loop learning is the process of single loop learning, with the additional stage of reflection on the process by which we read and adapt the consequences of our action, and try to improve how we learn from our action

Quite simply, with the understanding that we are willing to change, if we don't ask ourselves if what we are doing and how we are doing it, is getting us what we say we want, we won't get better at doing it. To do this well, a system needs to gather data from multiple sources, multiple times, and make the inferences and decisions necessary to change practice.

CONCLUSION

The work of school systems and schools must be well organized, thoughtful, understood by all who have a vested interest in its success, and subject to continuous revision based on results. Some things have to be "non-negotiables".

These include:

1. A written vision statement that accurately reflects the staff's belief about its intended state;
2. A sense of urgency about meeting the need of high performance for all students.
3. A commitment by the Board of Education to an instructional plan that is annually reviewed but enduring over time to meet the goal of high performance for all students;
4. A written set of norms that will guide the professional interactions in the district in all its work;
5. A written mechanism to assess the effectiveness of the staff functioning as a team at both the district and school level;
6. A written District/School/Department Growth Plan that is data driven and based on agreed upon best practice strategies for reaching specific learning objectives;
7. School leaders who are focused on improving instruction and student performance;
8. A written curriculum that is aligned with standards and tied to the State assessments;
9. A recognition that State tests are not the exclusive, nor the best, means for determining student performance;
10. A continued focus and dialogue about the work of the classroom and the instructional tasks that students are given.

The success that Norwalk has experienced could not have been realized without the dedication and commitment of Norwalk's teachers and school administrators. This cannot be minimized. They are the most valuable resource. The dialogue is continuous and sometimes contentious. While a District can develop a road map it intends to follow and, indeed, needs it to guide its path, it would be naïve to assume that the construction of a plan is all that is needed. The focus has to be on the instructional core (what students need to do in each classroom.) If you change the content to demand rigorous work, you must change the work of teachers and if you change the work of teachers, you must change the work of students. This change involves curriculum and has to be guided by a theory of action. Too often, practitioners will reject the idea that they are. (I-1 Curriculum Focus) The elements of change are interconnected operating from a theory of action. Some view it as too academic and not practical. In many cases the conversation may be filled with, "But in my school, we're different…" We know this is not so. If a Theory of Action leads the District's work, which may initially only be the theory of the superintendent, over time it begins to be uncovered and made visible to all. As the culture matures to one of a true learning community, the focus on the work becomes the mainstay of the culture and, as Lao Tse notes:

> The people will say,
> We did this ourselves.

REFLECTION

In support of curriculum development, Superintendent Corda had three problems dealing mainly with implementation and infrastructure: 1). He had to rebuild the personnel so there would be enough people to do curriculum development 2). He had to create a story supporting curriculum development and the additional personnel 3). He had to hone the use of plans to point in a consistent direction, that of curriculum development needs.

Rebuild Personnel

Given that the previous superintendent and board had cut central office staff, Superintendent Corda, needed to reverse direction in order to get enough staff on board to do the curriculum development work. His plan put in place supervisors for major areas of concern, as well as an assistant superintendent position designed to be a support for curriculum development. (I-3 Resources) Next came the trade at the school level for full-time assistant principals specifically to enhance the curriculum effort, against eliminating Reading Recovery teachers at the school level. All of this rebuilding of personnel can be categorized in the "infrastructure " area.

Justify Curriculum Development

Superintendent Corda had to also build a rationale for justifying curriculum development. He began with the board helping them to generate goals to support curriculum development. That was followed by rebuilding personnel through hiring of additional staff. Lastly, he used school and district plans to support the curriculum development processes. (I-1 Curriculum Focus)

Hone Plans

Superintendent Corda kept a close eye on the development of school and district plans so that they supported the district sponsored curriculum development efforts. Once these efforts were in place, Superintendent Corda was able to turn the details of curriculum development, dealing with alignment, structure of the curriculum and assessment over to his curriculum supervisors. Without this infrastructure in place, it would have been impossible to succeed in a curriculum development effort, at any level. Clearly, the superintendent saw that providing the infrastructure (I-3 Resources) to do the work was clearly work that he had to do before curriculum development could get off the ground. And, in reality, no one else in the district had the overview to put these significant changes into place.

Stability

Superintendent Corda needed three years to develop the infrastructure of the district so that curriculum development would be successful. He was able to maintain a working relationship with the Board of Education because he knew that the coming "improved achievement" could be years away. He came to the district in 2000 and there was not significant achievement growth until after 2006 (See the next chapter for details.) (Stab-1 Stability) The fact that it took over seven years for significant improvement to be made shows one of the downsides of focusing on curriculum. But it appears that the improvements were well worth it in the end. The fact that Superintendent Corda remained in Norwalk suggests the importance of stability at the top of the organization, especially if the goal is improved achievement through curriculum development.

REFERENCES

Ainsworth, L., (2003) *Power standards: Identifying the standards that matter the most.* Englewood, CO: Lead and Learn Press.

Argyris, C. and Schön, D. (1974) *Theory in practice: Increasing professional effectiveness.* San Francisco: Jossey-Bass.

Argyris, C. and Schön, D. (1978) *Organizational learning: A theory of action perspective.* Reading, MA: Addison-Wesley.

City, Elizabeth A., Elmore Richard F., Fiarman, Sarah E., & Teitel, L. (2009) *Instructional rounds in education: A network approach to improving teaching and learning.* Cambridge: Harvard Education Press.

Danielson, Charlotte, (1996) *Enhancing professional practice, A framework for teaching,* Alexandria, VA: Association for Supervision and Curriculum Development.

Danielson, Charlotte, (2002) *Teacher evaluation to enhance professional practice,* Alexandria, VA: Association for Supervision and Curriculum Development.

Elmore, Richard. (2000) *Building a New Structure for School Leadership.* Washington, DC: The Albert Shanker Institute.

Elmore, R., (2002) "Leverage Points and Improvement Strategies", unpublished notes, prepared for the Connecticut Center for School Change Superintendents' Network.

Fullan, M., (1993) *Change Forces,* London: The Falmer Press.

Katzenbach, J. and Smith, D. (1993) "The discipline of teams " Harvard Business Review, March-April.

Marzano, R. (2003) *What works in school s.* Alexandria, VA: ASCD.

Morrissey, M.S. (2000) Professional Learning Communities: An Ongoing Exploration, Southwest Education Department Laboratory (http://www.sedl.org/pubs/change45/)

Popham, James (2006) "Defining and Enhancing Formative Assessment", paper prepared for presentation at the October 10-13, 2006 meeting of the Formative Assessment for Students and Teachers subgroup of CCSSO's State Collaborative on Assessment and Student Standards held in Austin, Texas.

Reeves, D., (2002) *Making standards work,* Denver, CO: Advanced Learning Press.

Smith, M. K. (2001)'Chris Argyris: theories of action, double-loop learning and organizational learning', the encyclopedia of informal education, www.infed.org/thinkers/argyris.htm. Last update: July 02, 2008.

Stiggens, Rick, "Assessment *for* Learning: A Key to Motivation and Achievement" *EDge Magazine,* November/December 2006 (Vol. 2, #2, p. 3-19).

Tuckman, B. "Developmental sequence in small groups." *Psychological Bulletin,* 63, 1965. 384-99.

In: Curriculum
Editor: David A. Squires

ISBN: 978-1-62948-673-4
© 2014 Nova Science Publishers, Inc.

Chapter 10

DOING CURRICULUM FOR IMPROVED ACHIEVEMENT IN NORWALK, CT

Salvatore J. Corda, Ph.D[1] and John Keogh[2]

[1]Previous Superintendent in Norwalk School District, Norwalk, CT, US
[2]Previous Math Supervisor of in Norwalk School District, Norwalk, CT, US

INTRODUCTION

The curriculum story begins three years into Superintendent Corda's tenure with the reorganization of staff at the elementary school s to provide for district curriculum leadership, the ensuing refocusing of the high school and middle school program, and the melding of programs at the elementary level to form consistent curriculum expectations. The chapter details how different strategies were used to develop a single curriculum across the district. Key strategies focused on alignment (Al-1 Included, Str-4-Alignment) and assessment (A-1 Uniform Assessment, Str-5-Assessment) as tools for standardizing a curriculum among diverse schools. (References to Appendix A – Summary of the ASIA Criteria for Refining or Designing Curriculum Process and Product are given after important criteria are mentioned.)

SETTING UP CURRICULUM DEVELOPMENT

Dr. Corda, Superintendent of Norwalk, at the beginning of his tenure, knew that Norwalk could not move forward in its desire to improve student achievement without a strong curriculum *(I-1-Curriculum Focus)*. Dr. Karen Lang, the assistant superintendent for curriculum and instruction, began an extensive curriculum review process as her first major initiative. Since the district did not have at that time a curriculum specialist devoted solely to mathematics, she had to contract with an outside consultant to lead this review. Dr. Louise Herot, who had been a distinguished mathematics leader in the Easton/Redding district and was at that time working for the Connecticut Academy for Education, Math, Science and Technology, was chosen to conduct an extensive review of Norwalk's middle and high school mathematics program. While she found that Norwalk had a strong teaching staff, she also found that the curriculum was repetitive, that the implementation of the curriculum was highly inconsistent, and that teachers had not received any professional development to assist in curriculum implementation. *(Str-1-Content, Str-2-Time Parameters, Str-3-Instructional Process).*

The next step Corda took to improve student achievement was to begin adding staff to the department of curriculum and instruction. *(I-3-Resources)* By the 2004-5 school year, three years into his tenure, he had created the position of "Instructional Specialist" in Language Arts, Mathematics, Social Studies and Education for Gifted Students, Science, English Language Learning, and Early Childhood Education. Each instructional specialist would bear responsibility for the entire K-12 program in a particular curriculum area. Lang was responsible for filling these positions with people capable of making a significant impact in student achievement. Her first hire was a person who had already spent over thirty years in the district, the last seven as mathematics department chairperson at one of the district's high school s. John Keogh had essentially led the rewriting of the high school curriculum under the guidance of Dr. Herot. While highly respected by the teachers and administrators who had worked with him, Keogh lacked any experience teaching in or working with elementary school s and teachers. Nevertheless, both Corda and Lang believed that he was the right choice for this position.

ANALYZING TEST RESULTS

A review of the district 2002-2004 Connecticut Mastery Test (CMT) results confirmed the perception that student achievement in mathematics had declined significantly in recent years. The CMT at that time was administered annually in September to all public school students in grades four, six, and eight. In 2004, based on the percentage of students at or above the proficient level and at or above the state goal, Norwalk's fourth graders ranked eighth of the thirteen districts in its district reference group (DRG H). Norwalk's middle school students ranked even lower, twelfth in grade six and eleventh in grade eight. These results were consistent with those in 2003 and contributed substantiatlly to the common perception that the middle school mathematics program needed the most immediate attention. The district's high school data, based on the tenth grade Connecticut Academic Performance Test (CAPT), were not so dismal, as Norwalk ranked fourth in the DRG. *(A-1-Uniform Assessment, Str-5-Assessment)*

DEVELOPING A PLAN FOR CURRICULUM DEVELOPMENT: ASSESSMENTS

Under the guidance of Lang, Keogh developed a program growth plan. The primary goal for this first year (2004) was to ensure implementation of the new secondary mathematics curriculum. He wasted no time revealing his first initiative to secondary teachers on the professional development day held the day before school opened for students – all middle school grade levels and high school core subject areas would have uniform quarterly assessments aligned completely with the new curriculum.

(A-1-Uniform Assessments, Str-5-Assessments) The assessments would help ensure that the new curriculum was implemented and that pacing guides were followed. Keogh would collect raw data by school from each of the assessments and provide teachers with a complete item analysis to determine which curriculum objectives proved problematic for the students *(A-3-Monitor and Evaluate)*. This data would provide the raw material for his next initiative: quarterly district level workshops by grade level (middle school) or by core subject area (high school).

Herot was contracted to lead the middle school work shops and Keogh would lead the high school workshops. One purpose of the workshops was to get teacher input into the development of the assessments, which became a professional development opportunity as well as contributing to teacher buy-in of this initiative.*(I-4-Group Support)* In addition, assessment data would be reviewed with a central question to be addressed at each workshop related to the aforementioned problematic objectives – Was poor student performance due to a weakness in the assessment, a gap in the curriculum, or a need for better instructional strategies? *(I-2-Teacher Involvement)*

In the first year, teachers were provided substitutes by the district for four full days spread out over the four quarters of the school year. Since the process of developing the assessments would be time-consuming, Keogh wanted to be sure there was time in the workshops to address issues in curriculum implementation.

In subsequent years workshops were reduced to half-days for a number of logistical reasons. Consistent with the emphasis on the instructional core, *(Str-1-Content)* these workshops became more focused on reviewing student work and on discussions of instructional strategies while still providing time for improving assessment tools and reviewing student achievement data.

All middle school teachers received extensive professional development in activity-based learning and the use of manipulatives to support concept development, and many of them shared activities they had used successfully with other teachers across the district through these workshops *(I-4-Group Support)*.

In the spring of 2008 the state rolled out a new model curriculum for grades six through eight, which necessitated another review of the middle school curriculum to check for alignment to this new state document. At the same time, the district provided curriculum leaders with professional development centered on the work of Doug Reeves (2002) and Larry Ainsworth (2003) on priority standards with the intent that all core curriculum areas begin the identification of priority standards at the secondary level. Keogh decided to assemble small committees of teachers to identify and "unwrap" priority standards in grades six to eight as well as in high school algebra and geometry beginning in the summer of 2008 *(I-4-Group Support)*.

He also conducted informational sessions for all secondary teachers on the entire process and the criteria used in the identification of the priority standards and indicated that only items related to these standards would be measured in the district assessments *(A-1-Uniform Assessment, Str-5-Assessment)*. Beginning in the summer of 2009, the same committees that were engaged in the work on the standards shifted their attention to the revision of the district's pacing guides to ensure that sufficient time was allotted to the teaching of these standards.

CHANGE OF EMPHASIS IN MIDDLE SCHOOL AND HIGH SCHOOL

Keogh also changed the nature of the district's middle school assessments *(A-1-Uniform Assessments, Str-5-Assessment)*. In school years 2006/7 to 2009/9, Keogh, with input from a handful of middle school teachers, identified five strands in need of special focus (which are revised annually) based largely on trends in student achievement data on the various CMT strands. All middle school teachers administer district assessments in early October, mid-January, and late May that measure student learning in these five areas alone and report the results on a common spreadsheet created by Keogh. This data is then compiled, organized, and reported three times per year to the teachers and to the middle school principals and is used by each school's building data team *(A-3-Monitor and Evaluate)*. Teachers are expected to use their own student data from these assessments to inform their instruction as well as identify and support students that require intervention in a particular area *(I-4-Group Support)*. Norwalk's middle school students (both whole group and in key subgroups) have made significant progress in mathematics achievement in the past five years, as partially documented in tables 10.1 and 10.2.

Table 10.1. Middle School CMT scores 2004-2009

	CMT: % at/above proficient			CMT: % at/above goal		
Grade level	2004 (gen 3)	2006 (gen 4)	2009 (gen 4)	2004 (gen 3)	2006 (gen 4)	2009 (gen 4)
6	66%	72%	78%	43 %	47%	55%
7	-	68%	81%	-	40%	51%
8	62%	67%	82%	39%	42%	57%

Table 10.2. CMT scores 2006-2009 by subgroup - % proficient/better

	GR 6 2006→2009	GR 7 2006→2009	GR 8 2006→2009
Black	55%→57%	49%→65%	48%→65%
Hispanic	64%→74%	62%→77%	60%→77%
F/R lunch	55%→67%	48%→69%	50%→69%

At the high school level, Keogh believed that the highest priority should be to provide all students with access to a rigorous college preparatory curriculum *(Str-1-Content)*. With the complete support of both high school principals, the district now required that all ninth grade students, who had not yet done so, complete a full year of algebra and that in addition by the end of the tenth grade all students complete a full year of high school geometry. To provide students who would need more time to meet the algebra standards, Corda was able to convince the Norwalk Board of Education of the need for the addition of a "mathematics enhancement" course to provide regular ongoing support within the school day. Currently, all ninth graders identified as needing this support have a double period of mathematics every other day with all classes scheduled into a computer lab where they are able to use the Carnegie Learning on-line program as well as receive small group instruction from their algebra teacher. The non-honors geometry curriculum was revised to integrate the three other

Connecticut curriculum domains (algebraic reasoning, numerical and proportional reasoning, and working with data) *(Al-2-Standard Way)*. While Keogh has devoted less and less time each year to addressing the high school mathematics program, the district's two comprehensive high schools currently rank first and second in virtually every measure of student mathematics achievement of all high schools in Norwalk's current District Reference Group (DRG). Norwalk's tenth graders outperform students in Connecticut as a whole in most subgroups as illustrated in the Table 10.3 below:

Table 10.3. Percent proficient or better by subgroup, 2009 CAPT (HS Test)

	Black	Hispanic	F/R Lunch	ELL
State	46.3	54.3	51.9	35.8
Brien McMahon HS	55.9	73.0	58.5	51.5
Norwalk HS	49.4	66.0	57.3	39.3

COMPREHENSIVE EVALUATION OF ELEMENTARY MATHEMATICS IN NORWALK

The other major goal for Keogh's first year was to perform a comprehensive evaluation of the elementary mathematics program through dialogues with administrators and teachers, classroom observations, and analyses of elementary curriculum documents and materials *(A-3-Monitor and Evaluate)*.

Keogh found that the underachievement of Norwalk's students was largely rooted in its elementary mathematics program in spite of the fact that the district's elementary school s were properly focused on teaching and learning and were largely staffed by teachers who worked very hard and cared deeply about their students.

Any significant improvement in mathematics achievement in Norwalk would require addressing needs in the three major areas of curriculum, assessment, and instruction. Norwalk had a very comprehensive curriculum document for its K-5 program, but for a number of reasons the taught curriculum did not match the written curriculum *(Al-1-Included, Str-4-Alignment)*.

First of all, the amount of content the teachers were expected to cover in a given year was overwhelming *(Str-1-Content)*. There was no pacing expectation to guide the written curriculum *(Str-2-Time Parameters)*. Mathematics instruction at the elementary level was overly focused on developing computational skills *(Al-3-State Standards; Al-4-Assessment Specifications)*, while the Connecticut Curriculum Framework and the CMT blueprint focused on conceptual learning over computation. This focus on computation was in part due to an over reliance on the very traditional program that had recently been adopted, which was not well aligned with the local or the state curriculum. By all accounts, the limited professional development that had been provided to support curriculum implementation was provided by the textbook company and was lacking in quality. Understandably, the textbook had become the *de facto* curriculum.

ASSESSMENTS AND TIME USE IN CLASSROOM ON MASTERY

Also, the use of the publisher's assessments as the primary means by which teachers assessed student learning was not suitable primarily because of the lack of alignment of the assessments to the new curriculum *(Str-5-Assessment, A-1-Uniform Assessment)*. Furthermore, most teachers expected student mastery of everything they had taught, whereas in the Connecticut Framework it was expected that many concepts and skills would be introduced in one year through exploratory activities with mastery not expected until the following year. As a result of this misunderstanding, teachers ended up spending extra time re-teaching everything they covered that students failed to master, thus creating a situation where students had no exposure to significant chunks of the curriculum in a given year. Thus, students at a particular grade level did not have the background to master certain concepts that they should have explored in the previous year, a result that compounded itself as students advanced in grade level. It was no wonder that students in grades 6 and 8 had performed so poorly in the geometry strands of the CMT and that high school teachers complained that students had almost no background knowledge of geometry, as the geometry portion of the curriculum was often sacrificed to the extraordinary amount of time devoted to teaching computation *(Str-4-Alignment)*.

ALIGNMENT

Immediately after releasing his evaluation report of the elementary mathematics program in early 2005, Keogh began to address the issue of alignment of the elementary curriculum, knowing that a complete curriculum rewrite was not scheduled to take place until the next decade *(Al-1-Included, Str-4-Alignment)*. In the spring of 2005 he produced a document for each of grades two to five that simply listed by content domain the essential objectives that students were expected to master at that particular grade level as distinguished from the content objectives that students would be expected to master at a later date, according to the State Standards *(Al-3-State Standards)*. This created a more focused curriculum and was intended to prevent teachers from dwelling too long on a particular topic because they were re-teaching every objective in that topic regardless of whether the objective was intended to be mastered or merely explored for future mastery *(Str-2-Time Parameters)*. Interestingly enough, while most teachers embraced this document, some felt that this negated the need to overhaul the entire mathematics program, which Keogh felt was an essential piece in the overall plan to significantly improve student achievement.

PILOT PROGRAMS FOR ELEMENTARY SCHOOLS

Keogh had no difficulty convincing Lang and Corda that the District's current program was not aligned with either the state standards or the state assessment (CMT) *(Al-3 State Standards; Al-4-Aseessment Specs)*. In the meantime, Kendall Elementary School under the leadership of Principal Anthony Ditrio, a former math teacher and math curriculum leader, had independently arrived at the same conclusion and was piloting in a kindergarten and a first grade classroom a brand new program, *Connecticut Voyages*. Keogh, Lang, and Corda decided to conduct a Kindergarten to grade two pilot of Voyages in four school s, including Kendall, for the 2005-6 school year. *(A-3-Monitor and Evaluate)* Although this limited pilot met with mixed results (as well as strong resistance in several schools) due in large part to some acknowledged errors Keogh made in the pilot's implementation, the district leadership saw some positive results from the trial.*(A-3-Monitor and Evaluate)*.

In the meantime, Keogh had been researching four other standards-based mathematics programs utilized in various Connecticut districts and decided that *Growing With Mathematics*, with its strong basis in applying best practices in literacy to teach mathematics, could be a good fit. Corda decided to fund an expanded pilot for the 2006-7 year in which all twelve elementary school s would use either *Growing With Mathematics* (GWM) or *Voyages*. After presentations on both programs, the principals would have the option of which program they wished to pilot in their K-two classrooms with the understanding that one of these two mathematics programs would be used in all grade levels in all school s in 2007-8 *(A-3-Monitor and Evaluate)*.

The majority of school s chose to pilot GWM, with a couple of schools joining Kendall School in using *Voyages*. Keogh would lead the pilot in the GWM schools, while Ditrio, who already was convinced the *Voyages* was making a difference in his school but was aware that there was considerable dissatisfaction with this new program in two other schools, volunteered to provide the professional development for the *Voyages* schools. Ditrio acknowledged that the previous year's professional development, provided by presenters from outside the district, did not come close to adequately supporting Norwalk's teachers. Keogh would be responsible for getting regular feedback from teachers and administrators *(Str-6-Managed)* and taking appropriate measures to address any issues as they arose. Keogh also visited eighty-five classrooms in Kindergarten, first, and second grade during the year, met with grade level teams, and spoke to parent groups. At the same time he provided professional development to teachers in the upper elementary grades in such areas as teaching fractions conceptually and developing estimation and number sense in order to prepare them for teaching a standards-based mathematics program the following year *(I-4-Group Support)*.

The expanded pilot went much more smoothly the second time around largely due, in Keogh's opinion, to the diligence, openness, and hard work of Norwalk's teachers. For the following year, Ditrio and two other principals wanted to continue using *Voyages*, while the principals of the nine other elementary school s (including two school s that had been part of the original *Voyages* pilot) wished to use GWM. While ideally all schools would use the same program, Keogh felt that it would be an unfair imposition on teachers to force them to teach what essentially would be a third different program in three or four years (depending upon the school), and the agreement had been that the teachers and principals in any given school would have the final word on which program they would use *(I-2-Teacher Involvement)*. Consistent with the belief articulated in the Systems Thinking element of the Research Based Planning model that some strategies had to be identical and some could be different, the decision was made to allow the schools to use the program they had elected since the programs were both standards-based and the curriculum in all schools would be the same.

Ensuring Uniformity of Approach while Using Different Programs: The Importance of Assessment. Keogh then needed to ensure the uniformity of the curriculum objectives being taught in all district school s regardless of the mathematics program being used. At the same time, he needed to make adjustments to ensure the curriculum was aligned to the new grade level expectations (GLEs) and curriculum framework documents *(Al-3-State Standards)*.

Based on the axiom that teachers will teach what is assessed, Keogh chose the district's progress report as the vehicle most likely to impact classroom instruction. Indicators based on the Connecticut GLEs were developed for each of the approximately fifteen objectives on the district's uniform progress report (the latest revisions of these documents are available online on the district's website) and some uniform assessments were developed to be used in all school s regardless of which program they were using *(A-1-Uniform Assessments, Str-5-Assessment)*.

Keogh would monitor achievement data from both the CMTs and the district assessments to see if one program was serving Norwalk students better than the other – ultimately data would drive decision-making in regard to future decisions about which program to use *(A-3-Monitor and Evaluate)*. To this date the dramatic gains in student achievement have occurred across the board, regardless of which program a school was using. From the beginning the whole implementation of standards-based mathematics has been a central piece of the district's improvement plan. Since the initial implementation, Keogh has continued to provide regular professional development by grade level to the elementary teaching staff although 2009/10 budget cuts scaled back the number of sessions with each grade from four to two.*(I-2 Teacher Involvement)*

PACING GUIDES PROVIDE DISTRICT GUIDANCE FOR HOW TO USE TIME IN THE CLASSROOM

Each summer Keogh meets with committees of math teachers from each grade level to review and revise the GWM pacing guides *(Str-2-Time Parameters; 1-2-Teacher Involvement)*. Ditrio developed pacing guides for the *Voyages* program. These pacing guides include a pacing calendar and in grades three through five "topic notes" that include suggested activities for each lesson as well as a suggested performance task for each of the mini-units (called topics in GWM). Connecticut's Growing With Mathematics Consortium adopted Norwalk's format for these topic notes for use in other GWM districts. The district also added two numeracy coaches to work with individual teachers, as well as forming grade level teams. One primary responsibility of the coaches is to support all teachers new to the district in teaching the mathematics program used in their school. *(I-3-Resources)*

STUDENT ACHIEVEMENT IMPROVED

The impact of these actions at the elementary level on student achievement in Norwalk's elementary school s has been dramatic, particularly in grades three and four. The 2008/2009 third graders were the first cohort to have had a standards-based mathematics program in grades one to three, while the 2008/2009 fourth graders had such a program in grades two to four. In contrast, 2008/2009 fifth graders only had a standards-based mathematics program in grades four and five. The overall increase in students achieving at the goal level or better as well as at the proficient level or better is documented in Table 10.4 *(A-3-Monitor and Evaluate).*

Table 10.4. CMT scores 2006-2009 % at/above proficient % at/above goal

Grade level	2006 (gen 4)	2009 (gen 4)		2006 (gen 4)	2009 (gen 4)
3	72%	84%		47%	65%
4	70%	83%		44%	61%
5	75%	83%		51%	58%

Even more impressive is the narrowing of the achievement gap (Table 10.5). In 2009, almost eighty percent of Hispanic students achieved at the proficient level or better.

Table 10.5. CMT scores 2006-2009 by subgroup - % proficient/better

	GR 3 2006→2009	GR 4 2006→2009	GR 5 2006→2009
Black	47%→71%	50%→65%	55%→68%
Hispanic	66%→79%	66%→79%	71%→80%
F/R lunch	57%→74%	55%→71%	59%→75%

From 2006 to 2009, there was a fifty-nine percent increase in black students achieving at the goal level or better in grade three and a forty-six percent increase in grade four. The percentage increase in the percentage of Hispanic students achieving at the goal level or better in grades three and four was similar (fifty-six percent and fifty-eight percent respectively). Some feared that the emphasis on language development in the new mathematics curriculum would hurt students at the lowest level, but Norwalk has reduced the percentage of students achieving below the basic (the lowest level) from almost fifteen percent to about seven percent. Third graders in 2008/2009 slightly outperformed students in the state as a whole for the first time *without controlling for demographics.*

The measures taken to improve mathematics achievement in Norwalk contain many elements of the ASIA framework. The careful alignment of the curriculum to state assessments and curriculum documents, the use of pacing guides to outline time-bound units, the use of curriculum-embedded assessments to measure student progress, the regular revision of curriculum documents and the use of data to inform this process, and a management system to collect and report student achievement data serve as key components of the ASIA framework are clearly evident in the work Norwalk has done in its mathematics curriculum.

CONCLUSION

The measures taken to improve mathematics achievement in Norwalk contain all elements of the ASIA framework. The top priority in all of the curriculum work done was the careful alignment of the curriculum to state standards. For example, the elementary benchmarks developed for the progress reports were based on the newly-defined grade level expectations (GLEs) and the district testing program was aligned with Connecticut's assessment specifications. Alignment was also highlighted in the effort to consolidate elementary programs toward one set of curriculum expectations, as well as being used to redirect teacher effort toward mastery of only those skills required at that grade level. Priority standards taken from the state's curriculum framework were identified and unwrapped.

Many of the ASIA structural elements are present in Norwalk's mathematics curriculum. In particular, extensive time and resources was and is devoted to establishing time parameters for the teaching of important content through the development of pacing guides at each grade level (and at the high school level, for all core subjects) that are revisited annually with teacher input to ensure that the allotment of time for a particular unit is realistic to achieve student mastery of all prioritized objectives. Also, the mathematics program improvement plan specifies who is responsible for managing each aspect of the plan.

The implementation of the mathematics curriculum meets most of the ASIA criteria. Teachers play a specifically defined and significant role in all curriculum development. The implementation plan is clearly defined annually through the mathematics program improvement plan. Regular released time for teachers was provided by the district – grade level professional development days at the elementary level and quarterly grade level or subject level professional development or committee meeting days at the middle and high school levels. Resources are also allocated annually for summer curriculum work by grade level or subject areas committees in conjunction with the mathematics instructional specialist.

Last but not least, the thoughtful use of district assessments has contributed greatly to Norwalk's success in improving student achievement. Uniform assessments are employed across the curriculum. Not only are the assessment standards aligned to state standards, the actual test items themselves are constructed to mirror the items in state assessments. Both individual student and school grade/subject level performances are reported to teachers and administrators in a manner similar to the state reporting of assessment results. All schools have established data teams in which teachers use district assessment data to collaborate on instructional improvement.

In: Curriculum   ISBN: 978-1-62948-673-4
Editor: David A. Squires   © 2014 Nova Science Publishers, Inc.

Chapter 11

BRISTOL PUBLIC SCHOOLS IMPROVE STUDENT ACHIEVEMENT

Michael Wasta, Ph.D.

Former Superintendent of Bristol Public School District, Bristol, CT, US

The Bristol Public School System serves the city of Bristol Connecticut. Bristol is a small city (pop. 60,000) located in central Connecticut. Never a wealthy city, Bristol has seen a dramatic change in the population of students attending the local public schools over the past two decades. Students qualifying for free or reduced lunch, the common indicator of poverty levels in school s, has more than doubled during this period from approximately 18% to more that 36%. This increase in students living in poverty is usually associated with a parallel decrease in student performance as measured by State assessments. In Bristol's case however, in spite of this dramatic increase in students living in poverty, student achievement has actually increased equally dramatically. Some examples:

- The proficiency level of 4th grade students on the Reading subtest of the Connecticut Mastery Test (CMT) overall increased by 15.6% from 2000 to 2009.
- The proficiency level of 6th grade students on the Reading subtest of the CMT increased by 11.4% during the same period and in Math the 6th grade scores increased by 11.6%.
- In grade 8 the proficiency level increased by 13.4% in math and 11.8% in Reading on the CMT.
- At the 10th grade level the proficiency levels on the CAPT increased by 12.1% in Math and by 9.6% in Reading during the same period.
- At the same time that overall test scores were rising, the gap in performance between subgroups was closing and the percentage of students graduating and going on to college was increasing.

Although the Bristol Public Schools still have a long way to go, this kind of improvement has made them the highest performing urban school district in the State of Connecticut. To explain this achievement one must look back over ten years when dramatic changes began in the Bristol Public Schools. (References to Appendix A – Summary of the ASIA Criteria for Refining or Designing Curriculum Process and Product are given after important criteria are mentioned.)

In 1997 achievement in the Bristol Public Schools by all measures could best be described as "flat". Test scores would go up a little one year, down a little another year with no long term systemic change. In spite of this stagnation, there was no outcry to improve things. Everyone seemed to accept that this was Bristol and this was the way Bristol students performed and that was that.

As the State, and especially Federal governments began to take a more active role in challenging districts like Bristol to raise achievement it became apparent to the leadership in Bristol that something dramatic would need to be done to get the "line of student achievement moving upward".

Bristol needed a "theory of action" in which to anchor a dramatic change initiative. As the Superintendent and Assistant Superintendent studied the literature and the current'best thinking' on systemic school turnarounds they settled on the work of Dr. Douglas Reeves and the Center for Performance Assessment, now the Leadership and Learning Center. They selected Dr. Reeves as a guide due to the fact that he both challenged very strongly the widely accepted notion that student achievement was predetermined by their socioeconomic status and that schools could do little to overcome this status and because he presented a comprehensive model for holistic system improvement (Reeves, 1995).

Dr. Reeves' model involved changing virtually every aspect of the system by focusing on the following strategies:

1. Developing a common vision among key stakeholders both within and outside the system about what the community desired as outcomes for their children. This Holistic Accountability System would be the long term guidance system for the district.

2. Creating a series of Data Teams at all levels of the system – District, School and classroom that would move all professional staff from a model of isolated practice to a model of collaborative practice and move decision-making from one based upon intuitive models to data-based decision-making. (**I-4-Group Support**)

3. Focusing teacher's attention on the effectiveness of their instruction by making them more aware of the literature on effective teaching practices and having them study the relationship between how they taught and the performance of their students. It was no longer acceptable for a teacher to say, "I taught it. If the students didn't get it it is their fault." Now, a teacher didn't teach it until all students demonstrated that they "got it."

4. Totally revising the curriculum throughout the district. The curriculum documents in the district were really meaningless. Even though some had been revised no one was paying any attention to them. Teachers were largely teaching what they wanted, when they wanted for as much as they wanted. The curricula were not aligned well with the high-stakes tests, they were not focused, and they were not scaffoled well between grade levels. (**I-1-Curriculum Focus**)

Although Bristol did many, many things during this systemic change process, the remainder of this chapter will focus on this last issue of redoing the curriculum. Before going on however it is important to emphasize that Bristol learned during the 13 years of moving this reform forward *(Stab-1-Stability)* that you have to do it all. If you revise your curriculum but teachers use ineffective teaching practices you will not improve. Likewise if you improve your instructional practice s but your climate is toxic or your curriculum is misaligned you will not succeed. So while a well articulated, viable, aligned curriculum is essential to improving student outcomes, by itself it is not sufficient. *(I-1-Curriculum Focus)*

REVISING THE CURRICULUM

As stated earlier, Bristol had extensive curriculum in all academic areas. Unfortunately, these curriculum documents had little to do with what was actually being taught in the classrooms throughout the district. This may have been just as well since an analysis revealed that the curriculum in most areas was very poorly aligned with the high stakes tests used in Connecticut *(AL-4-Assessment Specs)* to measure student progress the Connecticut Mastery Test and the Connecticut Academic Performance Test.

The challenge facing the leadership of the district was to change the behavior of 700 teachers in regard to curriculum. These teachers were used to teaching pretty much whatever they wanted in their classrooms after the door was closed. How could we convince them that they had to make a significant change in their behavior? The approach that the leadership decided upon was to involve all 700 teachers directly in the process of developing an understanding of the necessity of making this change to a more shared practice when it came to curriculum and abandoning the personal practice they had embraced for so long *(I-2-Teacher Involvement)*. This direct approach was taken for two reasons; first, teachers are professionals and as such need to be approached with a degree of respect for that status. They needed to understand the problem and develop their own thinking around the change being advocated. Simply telling them was not going to work. The consequences of the current system needed to be explained clearly and thoroughly and the possibilities of a new way needed to be demonstrated. Secondly, once teachers generally accepted the need to change they would embrace the change more fully if they each had a direct part in shaping the new way of doing things.

To accomplish the first issue of developing an understanding of the consequences of the current system the leadership developed a presentation that was delivered to each faculty throughout the district. This presentation was designed to accomplish several things:

– Explain to teachers that the rules have changed, that it was no longer sufficient that some of the students succeed but that now *all* students needed to succeed. And in order to accomplish this new mission, we would have to change our practice.
– By virtue of a data based presentation, describe the current flat performance across the district and the status of Bristol students compared to surrounding districts and comparable districts throughout the state.
– Graphically demonstrate to each teacher the status of the current curricula and the obvious misalignment. **(Al-1-Included, Str-4-Alignment)**

This latter point was made by virtue of a simple exercise. A 3X5 index card was given to each teacher at a staff meeting. Each teacher was asked to write on the index card the five most important things they were going to teach their students this year in their subject. Elementary teachers were asked to focus on mathematics. Teachers were to then turn over the card and write the 5 most important things the students should know coming into their class in order for them to be successful in accomplishing the stated priorities on the other side of the card. All of this work was done individually by the teachers. When they were done the teachers were then asked to compare their answers with colleagues teaching the same course (secondary level) or same grade (elementary level). As was expected, in each case there was virtually no agreement with what was on the cards. This simple exercise, that involved all 700 teachers made it clear to them in their own words that the curriculum was woefully misaligned and lacking focus.

Now that we had their attention and had demonstrated to each of them the problem that the current state of the curriculum was causing, it was time to involve each of them in designing a better curriculum. *(I-2-Teacher Involvement, I-1-Curriculum Focus)*

At the time the Connecticut State Department of Education had done a better than average job of aligning the various State curricula documents with the State's high stakes assessments (CMT and CAPT) *(AL-1-Included,Str-4-Alignment, Al-3-State Standards, Al-4-Assessment Specs)*. However the standards that the state had produced for each grade level in each content area were overwhelming in number. For example, the 2nd grade mathematics curriculum had over 150 standards. The first step therefore in the reconstruction of curriculum was to prioritize the standards that were to be covered in each curriculum in each grade level *(Al-2-Standard Way)*. Again, the idea was to involve all 700 teachers in this activity. In an extraordinary example of logistics planning the district leadership under the direction of Mrs. Denise Carabetta, Director of the Office of Teaching and Learning, prepared material for all 700 teachers to be trained by their building leadership teams in a process to prioritize the standards in their area of instruction (elementary teachers chose either literacy or numeracy). Throughout two consecutive days of work, each teacher participated in a process of reviewing the state standards in their area of instruction, (for many of them this was the first time they had seen the state standards) and prioritizing the standards according to three criteria: 1. Is it tested on the State assessment, 2. Is it necessary for the next level of instruction, 3. Is it important in life *(Str 4 – Alignment, Al-1-Included, Al-2-Standard Way)*. This prioritizing approach was one developed by the Leadership and Learning Center. It was called "Making Standards Work" and had been taught to the leadership team from each school by Larry Ainsworth from the Center the previous June.

After each curriculum area was reconstructed using the above process, grade levels of teachers met to align the standards with the grade levels both below and above them *(AL-2-Standard Way, AL-3-State Standards)*. These were very intense discussions as teachers parceled out standards primary ownership to specific grade levels, while building in appropriate scaffolding and review. There were long discussions about where a particular standard should be introduced, if and how much a standard would be revisited both within and across grade levels and which grade level would have what piece of this continuum. The emphasis throughout all of this work was that this curriculum that the teachers themselves were building would not only be the official curricula for the district, but in a change from the past would be the curricula that would actually be taught and that each student would be expected to master *(Str-1-Content)*. Teachers understood that the documents that were going to be produce would be subject to review as the curricula were introduced and real students started to work through the material. Teachers were essentially making their "best guesses" at this point based upon their experiences.

Following this huge process that involved all teachers, the products that each group had produced were turned over to a smaller group of curriculum writers composed of teachers and leaders *(I-2-Teacher involvement, I-4-Group Support).* This group was responsible for polishing the curriculum and sending it back to all effected teachers for comment. This "accordion" process was repeated several times until the group felt the curriculum was aligned to the standards and contained the appropriate balance with no standards being over or under emphasized. *(I-2-Teacher Involvement)*

So now we had a curriculum that was aligned with state standards and assessments, *(AL-4-Assessment Specs, Al-3-State Standards)* aligned between grade levels and prioritized. The next challenge was to think of ways in which we could ensure that the designed curriculum became the taught curriculum. We did this through three strategies. *(Str-6-Managed)*

The first strategy was to require each teacher to post in their classroom the standard or standards from their curriculum that they were focusing on during that unit of instruction. For example, in a high school physics class one teacher had an small white board on which he wrote, " By the end of this unit you will be able to …." and here he listed the three standards he was addressing. In an elementary classroom each teacher was asked to do the same but only for literacy and numeracy. And rather than stating the standard in the formal language, the teachers were asked to translate each standard into "student friendly" language. Again this activity required teachers to think about the standard. This posting activity was closely monitored in the beginning by building and district leaders. Eventually over time the posting of standards was replaced by essential questions that the mastery of the standards would lead to since these were more engaging for students. *(I-5-Written Plan)*

The second strategy was to create common assessments. *(Str-5 –Assessment, A-1-Uniform Assessment)* This was very powerful in ensuring that teachers remained focused on the priority standards in the curriculum. The commons assessments were created by the teachers themselves. *(I-2-Teacher Involvement, A-4-Course Teachers Work Together)* They had to focus on the priority standards that were expected to be taught during the timeframe covered by the assessment. Some flexibility was allowed in the testing window in recognition that each class may move in a somewhat different pace. Since the results of these assessments were shared within the department and school, it was obvious if someone had "birdwalked" off of the curriculum. *(A-1 –Uniform assessment, Str-5-Assessment)* These assessments reinforced the notion that was repeated over and over again by leadership in staff meetings, *(I-4-Group Support)*

> "As a teacher, you do not have the right to decide what to teach your students. That is a group decision called a curriculum. You have to right to decide how to teach the material but not what or when."

As the assessments began to be administered and the results shared, administrators were asked to speak to teachers whose results seemed to indicate that they had not followed the curriculum to ascertain the reasons and to assist teachers who were struggling to abandon individual decision-making in this area for group decision-making. *(Str-6-Managed)* The attitude was that we know change like this is hard and we are willing to be patient and provide assistance, to a point. With only 3 or 4 exceptions teachers were able to make the change and move to a more collaborative practice.

The third strategy was to work with all teachers but particularly secondary teachers to move them away from the strong reliance they had acquired on the textbook. *(I-4-Group Support, I-2-Teacher Involvement)* A graphic example is the work of the math departments at the high school s. With the assistance of a highly skilled and knowledgeable math consultant, Raymond McGivney, the mathematics department was led through a process of focusing on the curriculum standards in an aligned manner that differed from the sequence and emphasis presented in the textbook. Although it may seem obvious that if the sequence of skills in the curriculum that was designed by the teachers differed from the textbook, we should use the textbook only as a tool, this was not the case *(I-3-Resources)*. The math teachers found it very difficult to accept the notion that you did not simply start on page one and proceed through the book in order. The idea of starting on chapter nine and then moving to chapter three etc. was very difficult for them. And even though the teachers realized that the textbook did not always offer the most appropriate kinds of examples for their students or enough, they also found the idea of identifying and sharing their own ideas to supplement the text difficult. With dogged persistence and even some destruction and recreation of textbooks they succeeded in aligning the text with the standards and assessments *(AL-3-State Standards, AL-4-Assessment Specs)*. Moving from isolated practice to shared practice is not painless. *(I-4-Group Support)* The mathematics teachers at the high school s were rewarded for their efforts however when they saw the number of students who were successful in their classes and on state assessments steadily rise.

This example of the mathematics department was repeated in all other departments. Each teacher had to participate in the experience of redesigning the curriculum they were going to teach. *(I-4-Group Support, I-2-Teacher Involvement)* How effective would this process have been if a small group of teachers or consultants had done this work and handed it to the teachers? Without their deep involvement and experiencing the difficulty involved the teachers could not have developed the understanding they needed to maintain and implement the needed changes.

THE KEYS TO SUCCESS

What does Bristol's experience tell us with regard to the successful implementation of curriculum? Frankly, designing a well aligned and focused curriculum is not that difficult. Curriculum specialists can do this in fairly short order *(Al-1-Included, Str-4-Alignment)*. In Bristol's case it would have been much easier and quicker to have a group of specialists sit in a room and design a well aligned, clear, focused curriculum. We would have had very nice curricula in virtually all areas in a year or two instead of the five years our process took. And that curriculum would have sat on the bookcase in teachers classrooms as countless predecessors had. The key was to involve virtually each and every teacher in the process in order to develop their *shared understanding* of the curriculum and its' importance in advancing student achievement. *(I-2-Teacher Involvement)*

By having large numbers of teachers grapple with all of the problems, they developed a deeper understanding of the curriculum process and the importance of transitioning from a practice based upon isolation to one based upon collaboration. *(I-4-Group Support)* This involved a movement from independent action, which they had been very comfortable with, to sacrificing individual decision-making for the judgment of the group and group decision-making. The difficulty of this transition cannot be overestimated. Leaders need to spend time on assisting teachers to make this transition through a variety of strategies as cited above. *(Str-6-Managed)*

Bristol's success in this area as well as others was based upon a deep respect for teachers as professionals. Simply telling teachers what to do does not work. When teachers are approached as the professionals they are and are shown compelling evidence to change their practice they will. And when it comes to designing a more effective practice it is essential that as professionals, the teachers are involved deeply in creating the new ways of working. *(I-2-Teacher Involvement)*

After all of the curricula had been revised and student achievement had begun to move dramatically upward, the senior teacher in the district with more than forty years service addressed the entire staff. He said that he had been completely re-energized by this experience. As he moved from an isolated practice in which he was firmly imbedded, to a collaborative practice *(I-4-Group Support)* where he created new and more exciting curriculum and lessons, he had experienced the greatest success in his long career. He only regretted that he had not done it sooner.

REFERENCES

Reeves, D., (2002) *Making standards work*, Denver, CO: Advanced Learning Press.

In: Curriculum

Editor: David A. Squires

ISBN: 978-1-62948-673-4

© 2014 Nova Science Publishers, Inc.

Chapter 12

FARMINGTON, CT (HIGH SES)

Eileen S. Howley, Ed.D.

Former Assistant Superintendent in Farmington School District, Farmington CT, US

FARMINGTON OVERVIEW

The Farmington Public Schools service approximately 4200 students and include a comprehensive 9-12 high school, 7-8 middle school, a 5-6 upper elementary school and four K-4 schools. Farmington is located in Hartford County and the overall town population is approximately 24,000. The 2007-2008 District Strategic School Profile indicates that approximately 5.4% of students are eligible for free/reduced lunch while 1.5% are not fluent in English. Approximately 9.3% of PK-12 students receive special education services in the district. Farmington belongs to the District Reference Group (DRG) B, which represents a classification of districts whose students' families are similar in education, income, occupation, and needs. DRGs range from A to I with A as the highest income ranking and I the lowest. (References to Appendix A – Summary of the ASIA Criteria for Refining or Designing Curriculum Process and Product are given after important criteria are mentioned.)

The following charts summarize recent achievement results based on state testing performance indicator s. A variety of indicators are used to measure student achievement related to central office goals. A selection of corporate indicators is listed below.

	2003	2004	2005-2006 administered in March 2006	2006-2007 administered in March 2007	2007-2008 administered in March 2008
Grade 3			81.3%	76.2%	77.0%
Grade 4	79%	79%	79.4%	84.2%	80.1%
Grade 5			82.4%	82.1%	87.4%
Grade 6	82%	82%	89.2%	86.8%	84.9%
Grade 7			88.6%	84.5%	88.8%
Grade 8	89%	88%	87.7%	89.4%	83.5%

Figure. Connecticut Mastery Test (CMT): Reading % at Goal Standard or Above.

Connecticut Academic Performance Test (CAPT) % at goal and above: Reading Across the Disciplines (Response to Literature and Reading for Information)

	2004	2005	2006 March	2007 March	2008 March
Grade 10	66.7%	80.2%	74%	73.9%	71.7%

Connecticut Mastery Test (CMT) Writing % at goal

	2003	2004	2005-2006 administered March 2006	2006-2007 administered March 2007	2007-2008 administered March 2008
Grade 3			78%	81.9%	85.2%
Grade 4	85%	69%	76.6%	87.8%	84.8%
Grade 5			91.0%	87.5%	88.6%
Grade 6	86%	82%	81.2%	84.7%	77.7%
Grade 7			81.4%	81.1%	80.9%
Grade 8	86%	83%	86.9%	89.6%	86.9%

CAPT - % at Goal: Writing Across the Disciplines (Interdisciplinary and Editing and Revising)

	2004	2005	2006 March	2007 March	2008 March
Grade 10	69.8%	82.9%	69%	79%	85.4%

Connecticut Mastery Test (CMT) – Mathematics % at goal

	2003	2004	2005-2006 administered in March	2006-2007 administered in March	2007-2008 administered in March
Grade 3			74.8%	78.9%	79.0%
Grade 4	81%	77%	78.8%	86.6%	78.9%
Grade 5			79%	78.6%	88.6%
Grade 6	82%	86%	79.6%	83.8%	86.0%
Grade 7			80.7%	81.7%	84.2%
Grade 8	83%	83%	80.9%	82.2%	83.4%

Connecticut Academic Performance Test CAPT - % at or above Goal in Mathematics

	2004	2005	2006 March	2007 March	2008 March
Grade 10	65.2%	70.1%	73.5%	76.4%	74.1%

Farmington prides itself on being a "standards-led" school system. To achieve this mission, curriculum alignment, structures and supports for implementation were all critical factors in becoming "standards-led." Upon my entrance to the school system in 2001, as Assistant Superintendent, it was clear that an expectation of "standards-based curriculum" had been launched, but the infrastructure to support this change had not been fully built. Curriculum work did not exist in a vacuum, but rather, was structured as part of the larger district theory of action for large scale instructional improvement.

THE FARMINGTON DISTRICT THEORY OF ACTION

The curriculum work in Farmington resides in a community that has a clearly defined theory of action regarding continuous improvement. It is through this lens that the work of curriculum was nested. City, Elmore, et al. (2009) have contextualized the notion of a theory of action into school and district level improvement. They note that in a solid theory of action, we are looking for specific causal connection from the actions of superintendents, central office and building-level administrators, to instructional practice. In other words, it represents an if/then statement that is driving what we are doing and why we are doing it. Using this definition, the superintendent constructed a written district theory of action to guide, focus and drive our collective efforts at improvement. (*I-5-Plan Written*) While he published this theory to the leadership team in 2006, the tacit theory of action was one that was commonly known by staff and cultivated over years. It is described below.

Farmington's district theory of action, under the leadership of the superintendent, was one of continuous improvement, that if we continuously monitor our progress, use data and aim toward high and rigorous standards, students will achieve (*A-3-Monitor and Evaluate*). This continuous and strategic improvement model was shared widely in the district and with the board and larger community and was heartily embraced by the administration and faculty. It is available on the website (www.fpsct.org,) and district reports, see 2007-2008.) This coherent system was the backdrop for developing the infrastructure of curriculum.

Together with the superintendent of school s, we developed, shared and refined both our district and personal theories of action. Our theory is driven by a nested-layer approach to school and district improvement. Figure 1 illustrates this nested layer approach.

The theory of action became the blueprint for how to accomplish this strategic approach to large scale instructional improvement. The nested layer approach was the driving force behind the theory of action. If we "nest" each effort in a system (as illustrated in the figure) or in the systems that drive the total organization, we harness the collective energy and move the organization forward in a collective capacity (*I-4-Group Support*). When all of our shared energies are focused on the same goals, the trajectory toward the goal is catapulted forward. This figure illustrates that the board of education and superintendent of school s set the vision and the focus on the organization. These parameters create boundaries for the work and help to focus our collective energies. The second ring illustrates how the mission, vision and goals of the organization boundary the work and drive the energy inward.

The program development plan of the central office attempts to define the plan and action that will foster the mission. The school development plans are then nested into the larger program development plan, again, in the service of the mission, vision and goals.(*Str-6-Managed*) The vertical teams and curriculum coordinating council help to foster the work of the district and support the school and district plans.(*I-2-Teacher Involvement, I-4-Group Support*) Then the specific teacher evaluation (EEPD) teams and grade and course level teams concentrate their energies on working toward the district mission and goals as they are translated into the schools. Ultimately all of the work is nested to support the instructional core, the work of the intersection of the teacher, the students and the standards driven content.(*Str-1-Content, Str-3-Instructional Process*) The key priorities are: standards and essential understandings for student achievement, efficacy as a belief system to promote achievement, collaboration as an environment to focus on learning, and data as a vehicle for examining progress. *(Al-3-State Standards)*

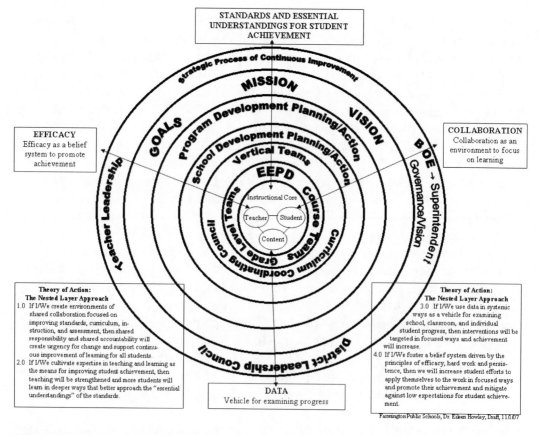

Figure 1. Nested Approach to Improvement.

This blueprint both for how we will do business as well as what we will aim to accomplish became a "driver" of the structures and processes to support curriculum development and implementation. *(I-1-Curriculum Focus)* The theory also became a tool for accountability for the office of the assistant superintendent. At the mid year and end of year, we examined progress toward the goals and priorities as defined in the school and program development plans.

DISTRICT PROGRAM DEVELOPMENT PLAN

The district level program development plan was the means by which we articulated expectations for improvement in standards, curriculum, instruction and assessment (*I-5-Plan Written*). The plan helped to focus the work and concentrate the energy in a coherent and focused direction. The plans and theory also served as a means for personal and public reflection of the extent to which we are meeting or not meeting our expectations, for the extent to which the theory has translated into measurable action and outcomes (*A-3-Monitor and Evaluate*). Annually, a public summary of results and outcomes for every school and the larger program development plan were published at a Board of Education meeting and are placed on the website for public viewing. The curriculum work is an integral part of this overall plan of continuous improvement (*I-1-Curriculum Focus*).

As with school development plans that often rely upon a school improvement committee, this plan was strengthened by the input of a Curriculum Coordinating Committee (CCC) (*I-4-Group Support*). This committee primarily shaped and informed the district wide coordination and monitoring of curriculum within and across school levels. The council included school administrators, faculty and the chair person of the board of education curriculum committee. The committee met to ensure that there are opportunities for long range and systemic curriculum renewal. The council monitored the development and implementation of the K-12 subject areas' standards across grades and subjects and provided feedback to the assistant superintendent regarding the structures that support curriculum implementation. The CCC represented the "think tank" of the office of the assistant superintendent and provided the deep and truthful discussion about the state of the state of curriculum and issues across the district related to curriculum and instruction.

Each year, the committee was asked to "take stock" of the "state of the state" of curriculum and essentially to evaluate the existing systems and whether or not there was a need to modify those systems or strengthen particular areas (*I-6-Curriculum Revision*). It was not uncommon to use this committee to float emerging ideas, to seek input on whether the ideas have merit or to discern what is happening to keep our existing systems from changing (*I-2-Teacher Involvement*). The team was instrumental in shaping the program development plan in powerful ways and for determining areas in need of improvement.

DEFINING STANDARDS-BASED CURRICULUM

The process of becoming a standards-led school system began with the articulation of district standards, (*A1-6-Other Categories*) with a full faculty training on what it meant to be standards led. Small groups of discipline specific committees then drafted a set of expectations for what we wanted our students to know, be able to do, and understand (*I-1-Curriculum Focus*). Our local standards were derived over time through teacher and administrator teams that carefully examined their fields, national and state standards in their disciplines, and then derived a set of local expectations that reflect the mission and vision of the school community (*AL-6-Other Categories*). The work of central office was to deepen those expectations into the systems of the organization, to foster the movement from a vision of a standards-based system to creating systems and processes that supported being and continuously improving as a standards-based system.

A key task was to define what each of the key terms in being standards-led meant in practice. Simplifying the key elements of a standards led system was a means to begin shared discussions about the values in the respective disciplines and the aims or goals for what we want our students to achieve that cut across all areas and all levels. (figure 12.2)

STANDARDS	Answer the question....
Essential Understandings	**Why** should we study the discipline? Why is this essential to learn?
Content Standards	**What** content, knowledge or skills do students need in order to develop their essential understandings of the discipline?
Performance Standards	**How** well do students demonstrate their understanding? How does it look?
Assessments	**How** will students demonstrate what they know, understand, and can do?

Figure 2. Standards and the Essential Questions That They Help to Answer: (AL-1-Included, Str-4-Alignment, AL-3-State Standards, AL-5-Local Testing Aligned).

This work on developing a common language helped to ground abstract concepts in concrete principles of practice and helped teachers to connect between the familiar and the slightly less familiar. These definitions were used repeatedly at the Board of Education table, in teacher and principal meetings, and at every available opportunity to reinforce these concepts.

In the early development stage of standards based curriculum, much time was spent on unit development; however, it was clear that the level of specificity in instructional design was not viewed positively, but rather, seemed to hamper teacher commitment to the unit design. Consequently, we moved to the construction of maps that defined the essential understandings, content standards, length of units, as well as the assessments and assured learning experiences for each unit. (*Str-1-Content, Str-4 –Alignment, Al-1-Included, Str-5 – Assessment, A-1-Uniform Assessment*) These maps then became the means by which we could better balance the curriculum as well as enable teams to design instruction based on their particular students needs. These maps became vital curriculum documents that teachers had on the table for each planning meeting. It was a key move at the secondary level to ensure that individual courses were purposeful and had balance. This shift to map development, from developing individual units also allowed for balancing between and among courses or the pathways that students would experience over a sequence of courses. The maps made for useable and useful curriculum documents that were purposefully part of teachers planning.

This continuous distillation of the components in a standards-led system began to create a shared vocabulary and shared set of expectations between and among the disciplines. In short, the common vocabulary and constant reinforcement of the language helped to make the standards-based expectations accessible and understandable.

STRUCTURES THAT WORK: VERTICAL TEAMS

Moving to a standards-based curriculum required a new structure to monitor curriculum effectively. We established the concept of "vertical teams " as the means to monitor curriculum design, development and implementation. (*I-2-Teacher Involvement, I-4-Group Support*) "Vertical Teams" were defined as the means of K-12 program examination. The vertical teams were designed to accomplish town wide curriculum coordination and articulation. They were structured to ensure that all school s and key leadership roles were represented and that teachers and administrators alike had a role in making curriculum decisions for their various disciplines. For example, the teams include principals, town-wide staff, such as the Director of Literacy, resource teachers—designated teacher leaders who have one release period for per day for curriculum based needs, department leaders and building representatives from elementary school s when there is no specific discipline based leadership position—such as a representative for the science team. The key concept is that those who are closest to the work were empowered to make decisions about the work. The teams engaged in the following work.

- **Analysis of issues** in curriculum implementation: the teams' primary function is to analyze the effectiveness of the implementation of standards-based curriculum (**A-3-Monitor and Evaluate**). Their job was to identify key issues and curriculum needs across the grade levels. The teams then prioritized issues and determined whether action needed to be taken or projects initiated. The teams could recommend that ad hoc committees be established to accomplish particular tasks. The teams engaged in problem solving to address critical needs and issues in their disciplines across grade levels and school s. Teams regularly analyzed the standards, worked to better align standards and curriculum, and assessed the implementation.
- **Ad hoc committees** were established by the vertical teams to address the issues, challenges, or needs that were identified. (**I-4-Group Support**) This enabled the appropriate and key individuals to be involved. Ad hoc committees had shorter, more targeted agendas, such as developing a particular grade level assessments, or longer term work, such as an in depth analysis of a particular portion of a program. The purpose was to have a clear focus for the committee's work and for the committee to accomplish a specific identified task. Ad hoc committees also allowed for broader teacher participation depending upon the nature of the issue at hand.
- Curriculum Vertical Teams also identify and develop **long range plans** for curriculum implementation. (**I-5-Plan Written**) Teams evaluated the standards, examined curriculum alignment issues, balanced the standards across grades and levels, suggested revisions to curriculum documents, identified the need for writing new curriculum, and suggested professional development. These long range plans provided the template for continued re-visitation of the strength of the standards

themselves. The teams monitored the status of curriculum design and development and considered action steps to better strengthen the standards.

To support this continuous process of program examination and monitoring, *(I-6-Curriculum Revision, Stab-1-Stability)* the teams were required to document their progress against a set of criteria of effective curriculum. This analysis served as a means of both accountability for the work and a means for gauging progress over time.*(A-3-Monitor and Evaluate)* At the start of the school year, annually, the vertical teams analyzed their progress in the indicators of development, including evidence and data related to standards, unit or resource guide development, curriculum alignment, curriculum implementation, assessments, data collection, and instructional design. They then used this analysis to shape both short term and long term goals, to recommend ad hoc committee work, and to guide their own work and progress throughout the school year. Each fall, Central Office staff reported to the Board of Education regarding the progress in standards-based curriculum design and development. The results of the vertical teams' analysis formed the foundation of the Program Development Plan for the Central Office.

Year	Key Activities
1999-2001	Launch a "standards -led" approach with faculty; establish standards by discipline; establish a set of criteria regarding what it means to be standards led; articulate a "white paper" explaining standards-led
2001-2002	Develop units of study with teachers l eading teachers; begin implementing standards led curriculum; establish vertical teams; Develop District Program Development plan that reflects curricular expectations
2002-2003	Continue to refine curriculum unit design; continue vertical teams; refine rubric of how to evaluate curriculum through the vertical teams
2003-2004	Continuous monitoring of vertical team work
2004-2005	Continuous monitoring of vertical team work
2005-2006	Beginning to pilot curriculum maps versus units Make Theory of Action Explicit
2006-2009	Continued refinement of "map" expectations

Figure 3. Timeline of Key Activities.

DESIGNING STANDARDS-BASED CURRICULUM

To promote teacher ownership of curriculum, Farmington had a long standing practice of teachers helping teachers to write and critique their curriculum units against a set of criteria, based on the work of Wiggins and McTighe *(I-2-Teacher Involvement)*. We derived our own set of criteria that included a checklist related to each of the three stages of curriculum design.

For example, in Stage one, reviewers would determine if the following characteristics were adequate or inadequate:

–   Unit summary appropriately frames the unit.
–   Essential understandings clearly state the "big ideas" or concepts of the unit in the form of generalizations.
–   Content standards are clearly articulated and tied to student performance. (**Al-3-State Standards)**
–   Unit outcome statement provides clear learning goals.
–   Essential questions are provocative and will foster inquiry, transfer of knowledge, and new understandings.
–   Knowledge and skills listed are essential to attainment of the content standards. (**Str-1-Content)**

This practice of teachers helping teachers to write curriculum had established a foundation upon which we could raise the expectations for the curriculum design process. To align the curriculum to the standards, reviewers would analyze the text to locate the standards and analyze the assessments to ensure alignment between and among that identified standards, assessments and instructional design (*A-1 –Uniform assessment, Str-4-Alignment, AL-1-Included, Str-5-Assessment, Str-3-Instructional Process*). Designers were required (over time) to code their assessments to particular standards as an additional means for aligning the curriculum to standards. (*Str-5 –Assessment, A-1-Uniform Assessment, Al-5-Local Testing Aligned*) The four day institute design provided time for teams of teachers to work together in an academy setting to write curriculum, with some teacher oversight and peer-review of the final product (*I-2-Teacher Involvement*). The institute, for new writers, included a review of each stage of design, a shared analysis of a unit, to illustrate the design principles in action, followed by direct instruction on each stage, time for designers to write and time for feedback on each stage of design. We also differentiated the design for more experienced writers, using a presentation that included the pitfalls for each of the three stages of design, such as big ideas that are too many or not really covered in full. The design standards drove the curriculum academy design. The teacher team derived a "checklist" for completion of units and teacher leaders provided feedback to writers whereby designers had to meet these standards to achieve "completion (and payment) for the units. A sample is listed above.

This peer review process of curriculum design (*I-2-Teacher Involvement*) ensured particular design standards were met (i.e., standards are aligned with content standards); *(Al-6-Other Categories, Al-3-State Standards)* however, these coaches were less comfortable providing feedback to peers that was both potentially more critical and that questioned their colleagues decision making on the issue of quality. Therefore, one more level of review was added, in addition to peer review, to ensure that curriculum met not only design standards, but also served to foster our standards and promote student achievement of those standards (*AL-1-Included, Str-4-Alignment*). Over time, the Office of the Assistant Superintendent required reviews of the documents to ensure that the curriculum documents were of the highest quality and met all design standards. This rigorous review raised teacher expectations for curriculum design and promoted high standards for curriculum that would be used by others. The review was narrative, versus a checklist and was more directive in its approach. For example, to one team, selected parts of the feedback include:

> Dear Design Team,
>
> It was a pleasure to review your grade 11 unit: US Foreign Policy During the Cold War. The unit meets or exceeds UBD standards as reviewed by your trainer/coach. The stage one design is well conceptualized and clearly articulates the purposes of the unit and focus of the learning. The addition of the "topical" essential questions helps to clarify your main course essential question, but in some ways makes it more of a challenge to ensure that the over arching essential question is attained. It is a minor suggestion, but the main essential question might be revised slightly to better capture the more open ended nature of the question. For example, "How successful..." might suggest one right answer. Perhaps another phraseology might be, "to what extent has the American government been successful in fulfilling democratic principles over time?... It is only a language nuance, but "how" questions can easily be interpreted to simply they were or were not successful...the direct reference to your essential questions in the performance task promotes greater alignment. Nicely done. When you combine the smaller assessments, they appear to answer the essential question through the more topical questions. I will be curious to see if the student work that is generated is able to fully answer whether students understand the extent to which the US has been successful in fulfilling democratic principles over time....your analytic scoring rubric is powerful. As you use the rubric, I encourage you to consider trying to more fully define what the work looks like when it is "advanced", "appropriate, "inadequate." Can you be even more descriptive of what the work looks like when it is at the level? What attributes does the work reveal? For example, does an advanced argument include multiple sources? Nuanced interpretations across multiple texts? Do the lower performances rely upon single course or illustrate connections that are not substantiated by evidence? I think those conversations, based on student work, will be useful conversations in your team meetings and could help to more fully define your expectations. I look forward to seeing this implemented in the fall. Congratulations on a job well done.

This excerpted set of emailed feedback is intended not only to provide feedback on the particular map but also to serve as a "teaching" means, to help to teach and facilitate the design team to think deeply about their teaching practices that move beyond the written curriculum document (*Str-3-Instructional Process*). The intent of the feedback is both to provide directed editorial feedback on the quality of the curriculum draft itself and to utilize every opportunity that can to lead district staff toward the vision of teaching and learning that we promulgate. *(Str-6-Managed)* To reinforce team work, reinforce the use of student work as a means for evaluating teaching, and to stress that curriculum implementation is an ongoing process that leads to better standards based teaching is all integral to the feedback. Even for the highest quality submissions, we consistently reinforce the district expectations that have been articulated in the larger program development plan and fabric of each of the systems of the school system—from teaching standards to learning standards, to expectations for collaboration and broad sense of efficacy beliefs about students. Curriculum is the means, not the end, for fostering those expectations. *(I-1-Curriculum Focus)*

As the curriculum design work evolved, the unit design was taking too long to accomplish for secondary coursework, in particular. So, the design team, using the principles of Understanding by Design, derived a "map" design for a full course. This map design allowed the articulation of both stage one and state two design across the entire year and included some minor guidance on stage three or instructional design. The expectations was that teacher teams would design the instruction to support the stage one and two design and lead all students to be successful on the assessments as defined. These maps paralleled the unit design process, but clarified year long expectations. (*Str-3-Instructional Process, Str-6-Managed*) This was primarily a practical decision as the time to write units in detail would not allow us to set clear expectations across courses (as some units were developed and many were not) or ensure that the course was balanced (many units took on a life of their own and became too large to be fully taught.) The maps provided boundaries for the work and became living, used documents by teacher teams on a regular basis. The maps then went through a parallel process of review as the units. In essence, at the secondary level, the maps replaced individual unit design. At the elementary level, the map design was applied to reading and writing curriculum as well.

In summary, the two levels of review allowed for a broader view, across multiple grades or courses, that promoted greater curriculum alignment and balancing. *(Str-6-Managed)* These newly written maps and units were then returned to the vertical teams for their review and to determine the process for dissemination.

COMMUNICATING RESULTS

To facilitate communication with all staff about the progress that the vertical teams were making, a "Curriculum Bulletin" was used as another tool for supporting the work of the district. (*Str-6-Managed*) The Bulletin summarized the work and progress of each of the teams approximately every six weeks. Since this document is sent to all faculties, it also became a means for teaching staff about key initiatives, district programs, and reinforcing district beliefs. To this end, each issue began with a brief editorial that addressed those key themes, followed by summaries of the work in progress for each of the teams.

The staff bulletins served as a means to reinforce the principles of curriculum design as well as to provide and reinforce key district themes or to address issues that arose across the teams. The bulletins were designed as a means to keep faculty informed, to respond to staff issues and needs as well as to hold the teams accountable for their work and progress over time.

IMPLICATIONS FOR TEACHERS

Developing curriculum that is standards driven and that teachers use and are held accountable for is heavily dependent upon teacher collaboration and teacher participation in the work (*I-2-Teacher Involvement*). The processes described above are contingent upon a faculty that is willing to work in teams at the classroom and course levels to make the written documents come alive through development of daily lessons and through careful analysis of results to drive instruction. The guiding beliefs that undergird this work call upon teachers to be full partners in the design of instruction and full participants in the collaborative process (*I-2-Teacher Involvement*).

At the broader district level, this model also relies upon teams of teachers who are willing to commit to design curriculum, who are open to feedback to improve their work and who are willing to lead others in this work. It is a shared effort and requires a shared set of beliefs about teaching and learning, Being willing partners in the design and development of curriculum, and committing to collaboration, also extends to the district level work of the various committees.

In these capacities, teachers need to see themselves as decision makers and leaders in curriculum design and implementation. The processes are successful when teachers see their work and ideas reflected in the documents themselves and when they can share their learning and understanding with others (*A-4-Course Teachers Work Together*).

IMPLICATIONS FOR PRINCIPALS

In a parallel fashion, principals are also essential to making the curriculum framework successful. They are required to help lead the curriculum teams, participate in the district level team work and then are held accountable for how they translate the district wide initiatives into their buildings and school improvement plans (*I-4-Group Support*). In parallel ways with faculty, principals become key participants and leaders in the curriculum work. The work of school improvement needs to be connected to the curriculum efforts as well. The school development process needs to include issues of curriculum and instruction in its improvement efforts.

Principals also need to consider professional development for staff to embrace and work with any new curriculum documents or information (*I-3—Resources*). Time needs to be allocated for teachers to work together in teams to use the curriculum documents and monitor the implementation. Principals need to both structure time for, support and supervise teams to support these curriculum based efforts at instructional improvement. This structural need is one that principals need to attend to ensure that the work will happen. It needs to be built into the overall system. Moreover, principals need to commit to observing and providing feedback to teams about their work in progress. The work of curricular and instructional improvement cannot be done in isolation.

IMPLICATIONS FOR CENTRAL OFFICE

The work of central office is about building coherence and alignment across the systems of the overall school system (*AL-1-Included, Str-4-Alignment*). The work of curricular improvement needs to be aligned and integrated with the other systems. Attention must be paid to how the curriculum systems align with the other systems, such as teacher evaluation. For example, if we have curricular expectations, are they aligned with our teacher standards and competencies of performance? If teachers are expected to work in teams, then how is that reflected in our agreed upon definitions of good teaching in our teacher evaluation systems? If teachers are expected to engage in professional development related to curriculum, instruction and assessment, then how are they held accountable for implementing the expectations (*Str-6-Managed*)? The structure, implementation and infrastructure for curriculum needs to be both coherent and aligned with other systems in the organization. If the organization relies on a continuous model of improvement, then how do we ensure that curriculum is also continuously monitored, aligned and that there is an adequate infrastructure to support the implementation?

REFERENCES

(1999). Wiggins, Grant and McTighe, Jay. *Understanding by Design: Professional Development Workbook*, ASCD.

(2005). Wiggins, Grant and McTighe, Jay. *Understanding by Design 2nd Edition*. ASCD.

(2006) Wagner T., Kegan R., et al. Change *Leadership: A Practical Guide to Transforming our Schools*. John Wiley & Sons, Jossey-Bass.

(2009) City, E., Elmore, R., Fiarman, S., and Teitel, L. *Instructional Rounds in Education*. Harvard Education Press.

INTRODUCTION TO PART FOUR:
CHAPTERS 13, 14 AND 15

The last section of the book has three chapters: the first chapter (13) delineates the commonalities of the districts who used curriculum to improve student achievement. The second chapter (14) examines other popular improvement strategies through the ASIA framework and suggests areas that potential adopters might want to consider if their goal is improving student achievement. The third chapter (15) suggests steps in planning to implement the ASIA framework with your schools and district.

In: Curriculum
Editor: David A. Squires

ISBN: 978-1-62948-673-4
© 2014 Nova Science Publishers, Inc.

Chapter 13

COMMONALITIES AND DIFFERENCES OF DISTRICT STORIES OF USING CURRICULUM TO IMPROVE ACHIEVEMENT

David A. Squires, Ph.D.

Southern Connecticut State University, New Haven, CT, US

This chapter highlights the commonalities and differences in district stories of using curriculum to improve achievement according to the categories developed from the district stories for Appendix A: Summary of the ASIA Criteria for Refining or Designing Curriculum Process and Product. It will also include a brief summary of those chapters' findings. You will recall that Appendix A listed the sub-areas for the ASIA framework: Alignment, Structure of the Curriculum and Stability, Implementation and Infrastructure, and Assessment

I had developed the ASIA framework as I listened to the stories from the districts which were told to me verbally before the writing on the book began. One of the reasons for writing the book was that the ASIA framework was so consistent within the district stories. At the beginning of the writing, the authors were given directions to write about their districts using the ASIA framework.

Not surprisingly, all districts reported on the four components of the ASIA framework, except the Norwalk superintendent, who asked that the math curriculum director's story be introduced, so that the complete story would be told. (The combination of both stories together addressed the ASIA frameworks.)

After the district stories were written, I completed two tasks. First, I examined the research around each ASIA area and listed the major ideas in each area. Secondly, I returned to the stories and compared the major ideas from the research against the stories, with the idea that I needed at least two of the stories to mention a sub-area to include it as a part of Appendix A. (Only one area had only two – Al-5-Local Testing Aligned- the rest had many more.)

So, the sub-areas are a result of a compilation of research in each of the ASIA frameworks, confirmed by stories from the field. The sub-areas are useful if a district wishes to replicate the success of these districts in placing curriculum front-and-center in an effort to raise student achievement. These sub-areas are listed below from Appendix A.

Table 13.1. Sub-areas of the ASIA framework (from Appendix A)

From Figure 3.2 Alignment:

AL-1-Included Is alignment included as a piece of the curriculum design?

AL-2-Standard Way Has a standard way to construct alignment been designed? (For example, from the balanced curriculum, are significant tasks aligned with standards and assessment specifications in a standard way?)

AL-3-State Standards Does the alignment include aligning to state standards?

AL-4-Assessment Specs Does the alignment include aligning to state assessment specifications?

AL-5-Local Testing Aligned Is the local testing aligned with the State assessment specifications?

AL-6-Other Categories Does the alignment include other categories such as Bloom's Taxonomy and/or national standards, or the recently constructed national standards for Reading, Math, Social Studies and Science?

From Figure 4.1 Structures of Curriculum and Stability:

Str-1-Content Does the curriculum specify the Content (subject matter) of the curriculum?

Str-2-Time Parameters Are Time parameters used so teachers know how much time should be devoted to particular content?

Str-3-Instructional Process Does the curriculum specify the Instructional Process used to teach the curriculum content?

Str-4 –Alignment Is Alignment included in the curriculum design? (See the Alignment section.)

Str-5 –Assessment Does the curriculum specify the parameters for Assessment? (see the Assessment section)

Str-6-Managed Does the written curriculum design specify how the curriculum will be Managed? (Who is responsible for seeing the curriculum is being completed?)

From Figure 4.2 Stability

Stab-1-Stability Does the district have stability at the upper levels of administration so that a 3 to 5 year curriculum development process can be conceptualized and completed?

From Figure 7.5 Implementation and Infrastructure:

I-1-Curriculum Focus Has the district established a common focus on curriculum?

I-2-Teacher Involvement Have teachers been involved in the designing and refining the curriculum design or development strategy?

I-3—Resources Have appropriate resources been allocated to the curriculum plan? (specifically funding for teacher release time, professional development for teachers and principals, and support staff to assist in and monitor classrooms)

I-4-Group Support Has an individualized and team support for teachers and principals on the process of curriculum improvement planning as well as the strategies that are expected to be implemented? Do parents have a role in the process?

I-5-Plan Written Is the plan for implementation written down, with processes for evaluating the implementation done on a regular basis?

I-6 Curriculum Revision The curriculum is revised and modified on a frequent basis, based on the results of testing.

From Figure 7. 5 Assessment Criteria:

A-1 –Uniform assessment Are uniform assessments employed across the curriculum? (Uniform assessments means that everyone who teaches a course gives the same assessments.)

A-2-Time in Schedule Is additional time built into the yearly schedule for teachers to use the results of the assessments to re-teach or enrich the curriculum? (Is time provided for reteaching and/or enrichment after, for example, each unit?)

A-3-Monitor and Evaluate Is there a way to monitor and evaluate whether the extra time is producing anticipated results?

A-4-Course Teachers Work Together Do teachers teaching the same course collaborate on using the test results to improve instruction?

To summarize how the stories supported theses sub-areas and were supported by the research, we listed the sub-area in the district story by the author's words in the chapters describing the district curriculum development initiative.

Finally we summarized the sub-areas on the chart that follows by the school districts described, to see if there were commonalities and differences among the districts on the sub-areas of the ASIA framework. (Each "x" represents one mention of the area in the district stories.)

The sub-areas are listed in the first column with each of the districts and the Balanced Curriculum listed in the following columns along the top of the chart.

One caveat – the structure of the curriculum section has two repeated categories from other sections: Str-4 Alignment and Str-5 Assessment are repeats of Al-1 Included and A-1 Uniform assessment. The structure of the curriculum included alignment and assessment and overlapped with the sub-areas of alignment – Al-1 Included, and assessment – A-1 Uniform Assessment. Otherwise the sub-areas are mutually exclusive.

We would once again emphasize that all districts contained the four areas of the ASIA framework: Alignment, Structure of the Curriculum and Stability, Implementation and Infrastructure, and finally, Assessment. But not all districts mentioned all areas from the four research area.

We believe that districts can use the research as a guide, but not as a mandate. We believe that districts can use curriculum as a way to improve student achievement, if they pay attention to the ASIA framework and its sub-areas.

The chart is used to highlight the major findings both within each district and across districts. We begin by discussing each district separately.

Alignment	Aldine, TX	Garden Grove, CA	Norfolk, VA	Norwalk, CT -Corda	Norwalk, CT - Curr	Berlin, CT	Farmington, CT	Bal Cur
AL-1-Included	x,x	x,x,x	x,x		x,x,x	x,x,x,x	x,x,x,x	x,x
AL-2-Standard Way	x				x,x	x,x,x		x,x
AL-3-State Standards		x	x	x	x,x,x	x,x,x	x,x,x	x,x
AL-4-Assessment Specs				x	x,x,x	x,x,x		x,x
AL-5-Local Testing Aligned							x,x	x,x,x
AL-6-Other Categories	x,x	x,x	x				x,x,x	x
Structure of the Curriculum								
Str-1-Content	x,x	x	x,x,x	x,x	x,x,x,x	x	x,x	x,x
Str-2-Time Parameters	x,x,x	x,x,x	x,x,x		x,x,x,x			x
Str-3-Instructional Process					x		x,x,x	x,x
Str-4-Alignment	x,x	x,x,x	x,x		x,x,x	x,x,x,x	x,x,x,x	x,x
Str-5-Assessment	x,x	x,x,x,x	x,x,x,x	x,x	x,x,x,x,x	x,x	x,x	x
Stab-1-Stability	x,x	x,x	x,x,x	x,x	x	x	x,x,x	x,x,x,x,x
Implementation and Infrastructure								
I-1-Curriculum Focus	x	x	x	x,x,x,x,x,x		x,x,x	x	x
I-2-Teacher Involvement	x,x	x,x,x	x,x	x,x	x,x,x	x,x,x,x,x,x,x,x	x,x,x,x,x,x	x,x
I-3-Resources	x,x	x,x	x,x	x,x,x,x	x,x	x	x	x
I-4-Group Support	x,x,x,x	x,x,x,x	x,x,x,x,x,	x,x,x,x,x,x,x	x,x,x,x,x,x	x,x,x,x,x,x,x,x,x	x,x,x,x,x	x
I-5-Plan Written	x,x			x,x,x,x		x	x,x,x	x,x
I-6 Curriculum Revision	x,x	x	x,x			x		x,x,x,x
Assessment								
A-1-Uniform assessment	x,x	x,x,x	x,x,x,x	x,x	x,x,x,x,x,x	x,x	x,x	x,x,x,x
A-2-Time in Schedule			x,x		x			x,x
A-3-Monitor and Evaluate	x		x		x,x,x,x,x,x	x,x	x,x	x,x,x
A-4-Course Teachers Work Together						x	x	x

MAJOR FINDINGS BY DISTRICT

Three Booker Prize Districts

These districts were extensively studied when applying for the Booker Prize, and the district stories represent hours of interviews, observations and document reviews. As a result, the descriptions are more broadly based than the others in the book which generally represent one person's opinion of what transpired. So, we might conclude that the findings from the winners of the Booker Prize are more "objective" than the other stories. At the same time they are a composite of many people's impressions, structured by the criteria of the Booker Prize. And these large districts were able to improve student achievement through focusing on curriculum. However, these districts, because of their involvement with the Booker Prize, were not necessarily paying attention to the sub-categories of the ASIA framework, as these sub-categories were not part of the criteria for the Booker Prize. Although all four districts addressed the ASIA framework, they did not specifically pay attention to all the variables the research suggested. Through viewing the chart (Table 13.1) you will notice that most areas suggested by the research have been addressed by at least one of the districts. There were a few areas in each of the ASIA sub-frameworks that were not addressed by any of the Booker districts:

Table 13.2. Areas from the research not addressed by the Booker Prize winners

Alignment
    Al-5 Local Testing Aligned

Structure of the Curriculum
    Str-3 Instructional Process

Implementation and Infrastructure
    I-5 Plan Written

Assessment
    A-4 Course Teachers Work Together

Assessment, Alignment, Teacher Involvement and Group Support were areas that were strongly emphasized by each of the Booker districts. (See p.3-8-23 through 3-8-25 for a summary of ASIA elements addressed across the Booker Prize districts.)

Norwalk, CT

There were two stories for Norwalk, one from the superintendent's point of view, and the other from the Mathematics curriculum director point of view, although both authored both chapters. The superintendent's chapter was concerned mainly about creating a cogent framework (story) for his staff and the school board. AYP had to fit with No Child Left

Behind, had to fit with state frameworks, and local and state assessment strategies, and had to fit with various plans (district, school, personnel, and achievement). As was amply illustrated in the chapter, putting together this story was no small feat, especially as the district had had a contentious superintendent previously. Many patterns had to be broken successfully in order to pull off improving curriculum. For me, the take away conclusion is that superintendents must create a plan that will make sense to many different audiences (school board, staff, parents, community). The fact that the curriculum improvement plan yielded improved achievement is no small feat. More detail is given on p.3-9-32 through 3-9-33 which summarizes his accomplishments as rebuilding personnel, justify curriculum, hone plans, and stability within the district.

The math supervisor's story involved the entire ASIA framework, where the superintendent's did not, partially, I suspect, because the Math Supervisor's story was about the "nuts and bolts" of the curriculum development process. For me it was fascinating how the superintendent determined that curriculum would be the strategy, and then found people who knew enough about the curriculum development process to design a system that resulted in improved student achievement. Although the math supervisor did mention alignment and assessment, he was very focused on teacher involvement, resources, and group support in the Implementation and Infrastructure area of the ASIA framework, a familiar refrain in many of the stories of curriculum. The structure of the curriculum, particularly the content and the time parameters were also important. The Math supervisor talked the most about the importance of assessment in the scheme of curriculum and gave descriptions of why various strategies were used. More summary detail is given on p.3-10-15 through 3-10-16 of this book.

Berlin, CT

The areas from the research mentioned most often in Berlin, CT., were Teacher Involvement and Group Support. The superintendent had to change the "traditional way things were done" and he did this with extensive work to involve staff in the curriculum development process. The fact that all teachers participated in staff development focused on the rationale for why curriculum is important, the specification of the curriculum including alignment, and the development of assessments, is the main point the superintendent was making.

He also focused on the purpose of the state standards and the importance of aligning state standards and assessments to the curriculum. This alignment process took place with involvement from all the teaching staff, so they would further understand the rationale for why things were changing.

He used a very powerful example, that all teachers participated in, that demonstrated the importance of having an aligned curriculum.

The fact that all teachers participated and that there were few reported "problems" after indicate the power this example demonstrated. He chose the example carefully, because he knew the entire process of curriculum development rested on the example's success. On p.3-11-10 through 3-11-11, there is an expanded summary of important points.

Farmington, CT

Farmington, CT, a high SES district, was not under the pressure the other districts reported about improving achievement so that they could "pass" the requirements of "No Child Left Behind." Their scores were high before curriculum implementation and would probably continue without curriculum implementation.

The superintendent, before the associate superintendent came on board, had begun a district-wide initiative to have the district be "standards-led". While the "standards-led" headline was in place, there was not much infrastructure that supported the "standards-led" effort. The story told by the Associate Superintendent was about how she put flesh on the bones of the "standards-led" man tra.

Dr. Howley, the associate superintendent, described her process. Not surprisingly she emphasized, as others have, the importance of teacher involvement and group support. There was clarity at each step along the way that teachers would be involved. However, when the direction emphasizing unit plan s did not work out, she was able to change directions emphasizing instead a curriculum map as a way to develop and reach consensus on units. So teachers had input along the way, but the system was flexible enough to change when things didn't work.

More emphasis was placed on describing how the system would be managed, than had been present in the descriptions of other districts. The curriculum development process had to fit into the district's improvement work.

The district didn't contain their alignment process only to state standards and state assessments but insured addressing local concerns by developing their own standards. This can also be seen as part of helping teachers to buy into the process of curriculum development involving standards.

The district provides a good example of how curriculum work can be structured in a high SES district.

Balanced Curriculum

Balanced Curriculum addressed all areas pointed out by the research, except Stability. However, stability has been a factor in implementing the Balanced Curriculum. In a large district in Michigan, the Balanced Curriculum was brought in by the Superintendent, who retired three years after beginning writing the curriculum. The curriculum was never implemented, despite the fact that it was written to be aligned with state standards and assessment, because the new superintendent did not support anything that the old superintendent had accomplished.

Management and curriculum revision are two areas that are emphasized in Balanced Curriculum. There is a management system that allows teachers to record their progress on the website and allows administrators to generate preformed reports for their school or for the district as a whole. As a result of teachers entering comments on the website, and the use of the results of state tests, curriculum revision can take place on a yearly basis based on the comments and test scores. These two features allow a "user friendly" interface with the website.

The fact that all districts that have used the Balanced Curriculum as a framework for curriculum development, and that have done a good job of tracking curriculum implementation across the district, these districts have seen student achievement improve in every case. It is gratifying to see that these districts that followed the ASIA framework and focused on curriculum development got gains in student achievement in all cases. This was true over the large range of districts served from inner-city (District 13 in Brooklyn, NY) to rich districts (Englewood Cliffs, NJ).

MAJOR FINDINGS ACROSS DISTRICTS

Districts that addressed curriculum directly, and who followed the ASIA framework (Alignment, Structure of the Curriculum and Stability, Implementation and Infrastructure, and Assessment), made gains in student achievement. These included low, medium and high SES districts as well as urban districts who won the Booker Prize. We believe that focusing on curriculum while employing the ASIA framework, is a way that others might improve student achievement in a significant way.

The major finding across districts was that all addressed the ASIA frameworks of Alignment, Structure of the Curriculum and Stability, Implementation and Infrastructure, and Assessment. The take-away message for me is that curriculum can be used as a framework for improving student achievement as long as the ASIA framework is addressed in the curriculum development and implementation work. These districts accomplished the task of curriculum development by addressing the ASIA framework so their student achievement improved.

Districts tended to emphasize Implementation and Infrastructure, and Structure of Curriculum over the other two areas of Assessment and Alignment. This is understandable as these were summaries of districts' efforts and I think that district folks thought most about Implementation and curriculum structure over alignment and assessment, which are only two things that need to be considered. The Booker Prize districts had fewer references for each category than the CT districts because there was smaller amount of space devoted to the Booker Prize districts (The three Booker Prize districts were covered in one chapter versus the Connecticut districts which each had a chapter or two apiece.) The Balanced Curriculum model had the most even coverage with the exception of the Management and Curriculum Revision categories, which were highly emphasized.

The next section of the book Part IV: Using the ASIA Framework as a tool for analyzing and producing district plans for increasing achievement, contains two chapters. The first uses the ASIA framework to show how popular change strategies can be integrated into curriculum development. The second chapter shows how a fictitious district used the ASIA framework to plan their curriculum development initiative.

In: Curriculum
Editor: David A. Squires

ISBN: 978-1-62948-673-4
© 2014 Nova Science Publishers, Inc.

Chapter 14

OTHER POPULAR AVENUES FOR DISTRICT IMPROVEMENT: USING ASIA TO ASSESS THEIR POWER

David A. Squires, Ph.D.
Southern Connecticut State University, New Haven, CT, US

ABSTRACT

In reading through the district stories about using curriculum as a framework for improvement, many innovations were interwoven into ancillary efforts for curriculum development. As these are part of the stories of district curriculum development, we thought that discussions of these "ancillary efforts" were important. The innovations considered in this chapter are: Power standards, Professional learning communities, Common assessments, Data-driven decision making, and Walk-through's. We will consider these as if they were being implemented alone, and assess their power to produce student achievement gains using the ASIA framework. References to the district stories will be given.

POWER STANDARDS

Power standards developed as a reaction to the number of standards and benchmarks required at each grade level. The analysis indicated (Marzano, 2003, p. 24-25) that there were too many standards to teach during the instructional time available in classrooms for the year. According to Marzano, it was impossible to cover all the standards (individually) in the existing time available to a classroom teacher. Scherer (Scherer, 2001, p. 15) comments, "By my reckoning, we would have to cut content by about *two-thirds*." Rather than "cut content", the identification of power standards (an important subset of the standards) was a way to identify the most important of the standards and highlight those as central to cover. There would be time to cover a reduced number of standards.

Garden Grove, CA; Norwalk, CT; and Bristol, CT, used the ideas of Reeves (1996-2004) and Ainsworth (2003) to identify the Power Standards for their district from the state standards. The strategy worked in these cases, as student achievement improved. However, student achievement improved in those districts using and implementing the "Balanced Curriculum" approach, which aligned the curriculum to *all* the state standards; the result was also improved achievement. Why did both approaches work?

Balanced Curriculum did not align to one standard at a time as they did in identifying power standards, but said that an instructional significant task could align up to five standards at a time. This assumes that more standards can be covered in an instructional activity (significant task). Therefore it was possible to cover all the standards with the 40 to 60 significant tasks that made up the yearly curriculum. Some standards are covered more than once as they are addressed in more than one significant task. Therefore both approaches identified priority standards. And each district had a way to insure that they were actually taught by all teachers. So both strategies produced improved achievement. This highlights the importance of alignment, whether to Power Standards or all the standards, to produce improved achievement.

The down side of Power Standards is this: when the standards were developed, they addressed everything that students needed to know and be able to do for the year in that subject area. Choosing the most important does not address all of the areas that are important. For example, many English-Language Arts standards address the four areas of reading, writing, speaking and listening. But speaking and listening is rarely the subject of the tests. So, if I had to prioritize the "power standards" I would choose reading and writing because they are covered heavily in the test. This ignores the important role of speaking and listening in English/Language Arts has an important role in the scope and sequence of a curriculum. One could counter with the argument that when reading and writing get better, there will be room in the curriculum for speaking and listening. But the districts in our sample, never talked about establishing areas that were not initially emphasized, in subsequent curriculum development efforts.

PROFESSIONAL LEARNING COMMUNITIES

Professional Learning Communities is one way that staff development for teachers is delivered. It was mentioned in Norwalk, CT specifically while all the districts used teams to develop and implement their curriculum. Speck (1999) defines Professional Learning Communities this way:

> A school learning community is one that promotes and values learning as an ongoing, active collaborative process with dynamic dialogue by teachers, students, staff, principal, parents and the school community to improve the quality of learning and life within the school. Developing schools where every aspect of the community nourishes learning and helping everyone who comes into contact with the school to contribute to the learning community are important concepts. (p. 8)

This model views learning by the staff as ongoing, collaborative and reflective with the goal of discerning what the next best step is for the organization. So, staff development isn't just teachers attending a workshop, but it focuses on the interaction among the teachers during and after the workshop as a way to enhance what is being learned. (An excellent resource is: Schools as professional learning communities: Collaborative activities and strategies for professional development by Sylvia M. Roberts and Eunice Z. Pruitt. 2003).

Thessin & Starr (2011, p. 48-54) caution against just putting teachers in groups and expecting a learning community to result. Consequently, they developed a model for implementing learning communities that includes the steps of: Inquiring, Analyzing Data, Looking at Student Work, Examining Instruction, Assessing Student Progress and finally, Reflecting on the Results. Stamford, CT (the school district where the work was accomplished) recommends, "Lead PLC work with clear expectations and proved differentiated supports in the first year " (Thessin & Starr, 2011, p.53).

If used alone to improve student achievement, we would suggest spelling out the steps, like the ones above, to define the exact process used in getting to a professional learning community. The idea of a professional learning community does not specify what needs to be addressed in the group, rather the group focuses on "improving the quality of learning and life within the school." The extent to which the PLCs focus on the ASIA framework may delineate the degree to which student achievement will improve. For example, if the PLC focused on alignment issues, or implementation of the curriculum, this would bode well for improved achievement. If the PLCs choose to focus on school climate, they may not be as successful, as school climate is not part of the ASIA framework.

Beginning teaming or PLCs is an implementation problem in itself and districts considering this direction, should carefully assess whether they have the capacity to implement both curriculum development and PLCs. Curriculum development as a group process, lends itself to supporting true PLCs. The stories from Garden Grove, CA and Bristol, CT, show how subgroups can be effective in working on curriculum development. But such success yields a word of caution; while there are a small number of "right" ways of proceeding, there are many traps for the unwary of processes that do not produce the desired results, as was pointed out in the Thessin & Starr article quoted earlier. Carefully thinking though implementation issues is critical for success of these efforts (see Chapter 6 Implementation: A Model for Making Implementation Plans). Districts in this book were well planned for their curriculum development efforts, some of whom used PLCs and groups of teachers to their advantage. A series of highly structured activities led up to the process for developing the curriculum, and PLCs or teacher groups can be an important area for leveraging curriculum development.

COMMON ASSESSMENTS

Early on in the standards movement, Betty Steffey linked the development of standards with the importance of linking standards to assessment, as a way to know whether the standards were being obtained (Steffey, B., 1995). Authentic assessment and curriculum alignment: Meeting the challenge of national standards. Rockport, MA: Pro>Active Publications.) All of the districts in this book developed assessments on a district-wide basis. The logic is irrefutable: students are required to take high stakes tests from the state once a year. It is both possible and logical to give assessments during the year that cover the same ground as the standardized test. In this way, students can "prove" that they know about the standards addressed on the yearly assessment.

This is a change from how assessments were traditionally done. Traditionally, teachers assessed their classes based on tests that they designed. There was little concern about whether teachers were testing the same information, so the tests were not comparable.

The purpose of common testing is for teachers to collaborate (perhaps as a PLC) and design a common test for a certain amount of content. Districts in this book designed common assessments for a semester, a quarter, a month, or a unit, or, in the case of the Balanced Curriculum, a significant task. Then results of these tests could be used to "prove" that students were mastering the standards contained in the time period used. The assessments could also help teachers to know where remediation would be needed. Chapter 7 of this book describes an assessment system, implemented in two districts, that required additional time for remediation/enrichment on the unit objectives, so that the tests were used to provide teachers with direction for re-teaching or enrichment. There is a hierarchy here.

- Tests are developed individually by teachers to assess the content taught.
- Tests are standardized across teachers teaching the same course.
- Time is built into the schedule for re-teaching and enrichment to take place.
- Tests are designed to provide data for re-teaching and enrichment decisions.

No district in this book, developed this type of assessment system, but it is probably a direction which will become popular in the next few years. There is already a good deal of research to support this as a way to improve student achievement through the research done around Mastery Learning (Squires, D.A., (2009). p. 89 - 101).

As the districts in this book point out, a system of assessment coupled with an aligned and implemented curriculum, is prerequisite for using common assessments and curriculum to improve student achievement. And the districts incorporated assessment in many different ways into their curriculum development plans. So, we conclude that the model works in the real world of school s.

What if we only developed assessments and ignored the other facets of the ASIA rationale. Unfortunately, we were unable to find any descriptions of programs that just used assessments to improve results. Most used assessments in conjunction with the standards. An example is the work of Ainsworth, L and Viegut, D, 2006, Common formative assessments: How to connect standards-based instruction and assessment. Thousand Oaks, CA: Corwin Press. Their process begins by identifying power standards, and then using this information to develop rubrics and common formative assessments. (See Ainswrokth, L. & Viegut, D., 2006. P. 14) Unfortunately, there is little information provided by way of examples, of how power standards get divided into Conceptual Units and what the structure of the conceptual units entail. What is important, though, is that the identification of the power standards insures alignment of the assessments with important state standards. This model is assessment driven, not curriculum driven, as it uses assessments as the most important piece of the improvement scheme, aligning the assessments to standards, while ignoring the process of converting the power standards to conceptual units (more of a curriculum piece.)

This model ignores the Curriculum Structure piece of the ASIA model. Specifically, in concentrating on assessments, ignored are:

- Content
- Time Parameters
- Instructional Process
- Management

But, districts that used this assessment model, because of the alignment to power standards, still got improved achievement, although they did not have a structured curriculum, just structured assessments as a stand in for a structured curriculum. We conclude that alignment and assessments are the two most powerful elements of the ASIA framework.

DATA-DRIVEN DECISION MAKING

"To be effective, data-based decision making cannot be seen as a fad that is here today and gone tomorrow; it needs to be routinely adopted as a pedagogical way of life in the school's culture (Kowalski, T.J, Lasley, T.J., and Mahoney, J.W., 2008)

We are surrounded by data. Teachers make hundreds of decisions each day in the classroom backed up in one form or another by data. Groups of teachers in grade-level or course-level groups by school, make more decisions based on data. Administrators also make lots of decisions based on data. Data-based decision making is often used in conjunction with curriculum to focus on the results of common assessments. All of the districts reported in this book used data-base decision making on the common assessment results. This at once restricts the data to be used in the data-based decision making process, while also giving a focus to the data-based decision making process. Because assessments are given on a regular basis, the process is repeated so it is likely to affect a school's or district's culture. Without a link to curriculum and common assessments, data-based decision making can lack focus and therefore have its power reduced.

It is important to establish a standard structure for looking at test results on a regular basis, so teachers don't have to reinvent the process each time they go through it. Kowalski et al. (2008) provides one structure that can be used that has four parts: collecting, connecting, creating and confirming.

Collecting data, in this case means collecting the results of common assessments. It would be important for teachers and administrators to decide before this process is in use the format that the data will take. Will the results show each students score? Will the scores be ranked from the best results to the poorest results? Will the average and standard deviation be given for each class? Will there be an indication of how students did on this unit last year? Next, how will it be delivered to the teaching staff? Will assessment results be given individually to teachers, with them deciding what is appropriate to share? Or will the data for the grade level be given to the groups to encourage sharing and analyzing the results?

The second phase is connecting the data, to other data. For example, a teacher might connect the test data to what she did in the classroom on that topic. Ways of connecting data need to be decided before the process starts. For example, let's suppose that when teachers analyze their scores, they come up with different ways to connect the data. Will everyone just do their own thing, or will there be a process in place to help them reach a common decision. One way to handle this is to have teachers explain areas they would like to explore, using their data, and then come to a consensus on one or two areas on which the group as a whole will focus. Running through different scenarios and having a way to handle each as it comes up is important to help the process be easily adopted by different teacher groups.

The third phase is creating, or doing something with the data. Let's imagine that teachers were focusing on one set of outcomes that were tied to a specific series of lessons. However, each teacher approached the lesson series with a different focus. The teachers may decide to collaborate on a series of lessons that can be used next year that will address each of their specific issues. It will take time out of this year, but the curriculum will be better for next year.

The last step is confirming the findings. Did the change work out to have the desired effect? For example, if the teachers decided to adopt a single lesson plan for all, did the lesson plans have the desired effects on the test results next year? This question provides a more specific framework to look at the assessment results from next year? If this way works, it could be proposed for the district to adopt the series of lessons for other school s to use, so they also could get more consistent results.

Confirming that there are findings, that the findings are agreed upon, and that positive results are spread further, are three sub-steps in confirming the findings.

Data-base decision making can impact student achievement, but there needs to be processes in place to focus the data collection, proved ways to connect the data to other areas that might affect the outcomes, creating ways to do something with the data, and confirm that what was done had the desired result. The more districts can create processes to cover common problems, the more likely that data-based decision making will be used consistently to improve achievement. But just saying that you are using data-based decision making won't make the grade.

WALK-THROUGHS

Walk-throughs is a process whereby an administrator and teachers, either individually or in groups, walk through a classroom in a relatively short period of time (3-10 minutes) while recording notes on things they notice. Done over an extended period of time, patterns in the data across classroom walk-throughs can be recognized and shared with the teacher. This has the potential to change the model for teacher supervision. Previous models, such as clinical supervision, focused on intensely observing one lesson, and providing teachers with feedback based on the individual observation of one lesson. Walk-thoughs bring more people and more observations into the teacher supervision process, although the process is consolidated in a shorter period of time (Downey, C.J., Steffy, B.E., English, F.W., Frase, L.E., Poston, W.K., 2004). If walk-throughs are not focused on curriculum implementation, walk-throughs probably will not be powerful enough to change the culture of the district, as the process will have too many foci.

Walk-throughs have been used to reinforce curriculum implementation. For example, if a standard curriculum has been developed for a district, we would expect to see lessons in Math focused on re-grouping, as this was the time the district had set aside for teaching second graders about regrouping. If a walk-through indicated that a teacher was working on a different topic, then the administrator could question the teacher's rationale for addressing the other issue at this time.

Walk-thoughs could also be more specifically focused. For example, let's suppose that a group of second grade teachers in one school were having difficulty teaching the concept behind multiplication. They had asked the administrator in the school (or another teacher outside the grade level) to do a walk-through of their lessons to see where things were working in individual classrooms, and point out anonymously where things were not working. The observer was asked to focus on patterns across classrooms, while not specifying individual needs. One or two teachers seemed to have a good way of approaching this area, that was identified by the observer. They were asked to sit down and develop a way to develop lesson plan s that would work for everyone, with one or two other teachers on the grade level. This collaborative planning did indeed produce a better and more consistent way to teach the idea of multiplication, based on the results of the assessment in the next year.

Part of the success of this process was not only the walk-through process, but the fact that they had a way of recording what they intended to do, and were able to carry that out when the time came to evaluate the process next year. In reflecting on their success, the ability of the grade level to focus on the process over multiple years was important. The grade-level's note taking appeared as one of the key determiners of the results.

CONCLUSION

The process of Power Standards, Professional Learning Communities, Common Assessments, Data-driven Decision Making and Walk-Throughs all can help in the problem of developing and implementing a curriculum which meets the ASIA frameworks. Without curriculum as a central focus, each has a good possibility of losing the unifying punch that they receive when paired with curriculum implementation. Putting each within the context of curriculum development helps to focus the processes while strengthening curriculum implementation. But each will "cost " the district time, effort, and training time in order to get everyone able to implement these processes fluidly which will help to improve student achievement. Not all districts chose to use all of these processes, which probably means they may have been helpful, but were not necessities.

The "take-away" for teachers and administrators who want to use curriculum as a vehicle to improve student achievement is one of caution.

- Don't overload your system.

Curriculum development, done well, is difficult enough. It is important to thoughtfully consider the amount of time curriculum development as well as the other processes will take to plan and deliver the curriculum well. If the time is too much, then the system has a good chance of not being implemented at all, or implementation will result in problems.

- Planning well is the key.

Using a planning model, such as the one shown in Chapter Six, is essential to knowing that the plan will work. Planning should help to surface a wide range of problems. If the system doesn't confront these problems, there may be a deficit in the planning model being used. Planning is a relatively "cost free" way of tying out your best ideas to see if they have a possibility of working before implementing them in the "real world".

- Use innovations that have previous success to couple with curriculum implementation.

Success breeds success. Choose innovations carefully to couple with curriculum, based on their proven functionality in previous settings. You won't have time to develop and implement a curriculum and review processes and procedures for Professional Learning Communities and Walk-throughs too. Choosing what and how much to focus on is a critical planning decision usually made at the Central Office level. If you are a building administrator in this scenario, it is important that you are very conservative in recommending or commenting on what the district puts on its plate.

- If these processes are not focused on curriculum implementation, it will be difficult to use the power of the processes to improve student achievement.

Districts in this book have used these processes to supplement curriculum development and implementation. The good news is that these processes work when supporting district curriculum implementation. Using these processes alone may not have the power of using them with curriculum implementation. Districts must move judiciously in deciding how much to "pile on" in implementing the curriculum.

REFERENCES

Ainsworth, L. (2003). "Unwrapping" the standards: A simple process to make standards manageable. Englewood, CO: *Advanced Learning Press.*

Ainsworth, L. and Viegut, D. (2006). Common formative assessments: How to connect standards-based instruction and assessment. *Thousand Oaks,* CA: Corwin Press.

Downey, C.J., Steffy, B.E., English, F.W., Frase, L.E., Poston, W.K. (2004). The three minutes classroom walk-through: Changing school supervisory practice one teacher at a time. Thousand Oaks, CA: *Corwin Press.*

Kowalski, T.J., Lasley, T.J., Mahoney, J.W. (2008). *Data-driven decisions and school leadership: best practices for school improvement.* Boston: Pearson/A and B.

Marzzano, R.J. (2003), *What works in school s.* Alexandria, VA: Association for Supervision and Curriculum Development.

Reeves, D.B. (1996-2004). Making standards work: How to implement standards-based assessments in the classroom, school, and district, 3rd edition, Englewood, CO: *Advanced Learning Press.*

Roberts, S.M., and Pruitt E.Z. (2003). Schools as professional learning communities: Collaborative activities and strategies for professional development. Thousand Oaks, CA: *Corwin Press.*

Scherer, M. (2001). How and why standards can improve student achievement: A conversation with Robert J. Marzano. *Educational Leadership,* (Volume 59, Number 1. pp. 14-15).

Speck, M. (1999). The principalship: Building a learning community. *Upper Saddle River,* NJ: Prentice Hall.

Squires, D.A. (2009). Curriculum alignment: Research-based strategies for increasing student achievement. *Thousand Oaks,* CA: Corwin Press.

Steffy, B.E. (1995). Authentic assessment and curriculum alignment: Meeting the challenge of national standards. Rockport, MA: Pro>Active Publications.

Thessin, R.A. and Starr, J.P. (2011). Supporting growth of effective professional learning communities. *Phi Delta Kappan* (Volume 91, Number 6. pp. 49-54).

In: Curriculum
Editor: David A. Squires

ISBN: 978-1-62948-673-4
© 2014 Nova Science Publishers, Inc.

Chapter 15

PLANNING CURRICULUM DEVELOPMENT AND IMPLEMENTATION

David A. Squires, Ph.D.
Southern Connecticut State University, New Haven, CT, US

ABSTRACT

Working with districts over the past 15 years to write and implement a balanced curriculum has been a wonderful experience; especially as so many of the districts that I worked with saw their student achievement improve (Squires, 2013). Now, thousands of students are getting better results because the curriculum was developed and well implemented using the Balanced Curriculum model. As is evident by the chapters about other school districts, the balanced curriculum is not the only way to get improvement, as the districts highlighted in this book also used curriculum as a framework for improving achievement.

In this chapter I will highlight lessons learned along the way about developing and implementing curriculum. Using ideas described in chapter 6, we will highlight what major roles need to know and be able to do in planning, developing and implementing curriculum. For those with experience of working within a district, this will give one model to compare your district's curriculum writing and implementation efforts.

We begin by dividing the effort into three areas: planning, writing, and implementing curriculum. To plan, we create a planning team to guide the process of writing and implementing curriculum. We don't separate curriculum writing from curriculum implementation because how the curriculum is implemented will, in part, depend on how the curriculum was written. We believe that such curriculum development and implementation has the potential to last over several years, and we believe that such an effort needs people who can stay the course over those years, so the effort is not wasted.

THE PLANNING TEAM

Ideally, the planning team should consist of 5-10 people who represent different perspectives on the district, such as teachers, principals, central office officials, and the superintendent. (Larger districts may want more people on the planning team.) The superintendent will want to choose these people carefully. They should have the ability to see the big picture, conceptualize the scope of the work, and see beyond the plan to problems that might arise. These need to be the vision people who believe that curriculum can be a way to boost achievement. But they also need some folks who can work with the details to put such a plan in place. Hopefully, they will also have experience in implementing large projects on a district-wide basis. (When I began this work, I assumed that most central office staff had experience in developing and implementing projects of this scope. I was wrong. Most central office staff had experience starting up projects affecting one or two grade levels, but not something as comprehensive as curriculum development on a K-12 basis.)

As part of constructing a planning team, the leadership will have to decide whether they want a consultant as part of a team. Consultants have:

- Experience in curriculum development in many districts
- Encountered issues which may be new to district folks
- A model of how curriculum should be developed and implemented
- Save time by guiding the district to adopt a proven model
- Recommend procedures and processes that are outside the district's experience, but would improve the district's experience in writing and implementing curriculum

Districts might also decide to go it alone which would be appropriate if the district has lots of experience in developing and implementing curriculum. The districts examined in this book used a combination of consultants to assist the district initially, and a "go it alone" process as they became more experienced. Decisions about using a consultant depend on the openness and honesty of the planning team and their leaders in realistically assessing the district to determine if a consultant is needed. At times, it may be difficult for a curriculum director, with little experience in developing and implementing curriculum on a K-12 basis to admit he/she needs help. The district needs to choose the consultant carefully so the consultant knows his/her boundaries defined by what the district is looking to do.

The planning team will need to spend time conceptualizing what they want to accomplish over a number of years. One strategy to get the conversation started is to develop a purpose statement which summarizes what you want to accomplish in a few sentences. The purpose statement will be useful in helping others in the district understand the district's direction. Below is a purpose statement from Newburg, NY for the Balanced Curriculum.

1. To improve student opportunity and achievement:
   Align and balance curriculum, instruction and assessment for all students at all levels in all subjects, beginning with English Language Arts (K-12). The ELA curriculum will be aligned with NYS Learning Standards and Assessments, the TerraNova CTB/McGraw Hill tests and the National Council of Teachers of English/International Reading Association (NCTE/IRA) English Language Arts Standards.
2. The Newburgh Enlarged City School District and the Newburgh Enlarged City School District Board of Education will:
   adopt, implement and work for continuous improvement of the process of aligning and balancing the curriculum.

3. The curriculum Alignment Project will:
   - build the capacity to improve student opportunity and achievement;
   - produce documents that
     (1) describe the curriculum (units, timelines, significant tasks with objectives),
     (2) indicate alignment and balance of units and significant tasks with the NYS Learning Standards and standardized assessments, and
     (3) contain the internal unit assessments that are aligned with the units.
   - implement and institutionalize the process and the aligned and balanced curriculum
4. The curriculum Alignment Project will:
   partner students, parents and community members to create an awareness of the Learning Standards and their value, and the importance of an aligned and balanced curriculum.

This document was one page in length so it served as a good handout when staffs in the thirteen school s in the district were informed about the purpose of the project. If representatives of the Planning Team conducted the overview session, they would have to know what the structure of the curriculum model would be.

When a planning team begins, they do not have knowledge of the structure of the Balanced Curriculum. To rectify this, the planning team came together for 3 hours to learn about the Balanced Curriculum model by dividing the planning team up into two groups who developed a fictitious unit suited to their collective backgrounds. They also briefly discussed with the consultant a tentative schedule for two weeks of curriculum development workshop, so the planning team could talk knowledgeably about what would happen over the summer in curriculum development. An outline of what the planning team had to do follows:

- Learn about the Balanced Curriculum model through simulating developing one unit
- Decide a process for informing all teachers in the district that curriculum development would occur in the summer, and ask them to think about volunteering.
- Develop a script to be used as the basis of the presentation to teachers, so all would hear the same message.
- Check the resources to make sure the plan for curriculum development was doable fiscally.
- Schedule the curriculum development time during the summer.
- Coordinate with the teachers' union and inform the school board.
- Place the information on the district web -site, with a contact person to answer questions.
- Decide on an application process for teachers to apply for curriculum development. (We wanted all 13 school s represented with approximately 5 people assigned to a specific grade level. We also wanted to make sure we had representative teachers from Special Education and the ESL program represented at each grade level.)
- Prepare presenters for the summer curriculum development work, on parts that folks would feel comfortable presenting. (This district used a manual of the Balanced Curriculum process, to help guide presenters, as the district wanted to develop local capability as quickly as possible so local teachers and administrators could conduct future workshops.)

- Set up the daily schedule. (We recommend 5 hours/day for two weeks to develop units, significant tasks, alignments and assessments. We started at 8am and went until 1pm., with no break for lunch, but teachers volunteering to bring in snacks. Five hours a day proved sufficient as the teacher's productivity would suffer if the day went longer.)
- Place applicants into teams. Teams were divided by grade level on a K-12 basis with representatives from Special Education and ESL placed on the teams.
- Decide on a place to hold the curriculum development work. The team decided that there should be a copier available to the teams, and that each team needed a separate room to work in when they weren't together as a group. (An elementary school was chosen, with the total group meeting in the cafeteria, and individual teams meeting in classrooms. This meant rescheduling the school clean up during the summer to a later time.)
- Decide on roles and responsibilities of providing the staff an overview of the new curriculum at the beginning of school after the summer. Decide how to organize district staff for the day or two of presentations and trial use.
- Decide on the roles and responsibilities of principals, teachers and others staff members in implementing the curriculum in the fall. (What should they know and be able to do?)
- Decide on how to use the management component of the Balanced Curriculum software so teachers could record that they had completed significant tasks
- Appoint a "point person" who will answer questions the staff might have about logging onto the web site, recording completion information, and getting copies of the curriculum from the web site. Decide how this will be publicized in the district.
- Decide how the district and school data teams will use the data generated by the web site to incorporate into their work during the next school year. (This may mean a meeting between the planning team and the district and school data teams before the summer curriculum work begins. All agreements should be written down and widely shared. Think through what the training needs of the data teams will be and when that will take place.)
- Generate roles for principals in helping to implement the process. Principals should meet with grade levels to assess their comfort in using the curriculum and encourage teachers to log on, make comments and record completions. Principals should run a completion report for their school (they only have access to their individual school's data) and follow up with teachers who have not yet recorded their completions or made comments.
- The district will need to have a way to monitor whether teachers at individual school s are implementing the curriculum. The district person will need to run a completion report for the district which shows how many significant tasks each individual teacher (listed by schools) have completed. The district person will need to follow up with principals who do not have teachers who are recording their significant task completions or entering comments for their units and significant tasks.
- The planning team needs to set expectations and training opportunities so that staff have the necessary skills to fully implement the Balanced Curriculum.
- We recommend the planning team meet of a weekly basis in September as the curriculum is being rolled out, and once a month after that to focus on problem areas

in implementing the curriculum. These meetings need to be scheduled well in advance of the school year, so the time is freed up for this necessary process.

- Teachers design lesson plan s based on the significant task descriptions.

January – March

- During this time frame, the planning team will need to concentrate on what will happen during the summer, as well as on implementation issues that have arisen. We strongly recommend that the curriculum be "tweaked" on the basis of teacher completions of units and significant tasks, test scores and item analysis from the spring testing, and teacher comments on the web site. Such "tweaking" takes two to three days during the summer, involving two or three of the original authors who know the curriculum well. They need to examine the completion reports for their grade level to determine if most people got through the curriculum and what units or significant tasks were left out. Teacher comments will also point to areas that need to be revised. The item analysis from the test scores will indicate where more time and/or content is needed. If the scores of students indicate a great need, units or significant tasks can be revised for the following year.
- If many teachers did not complete the curriculum, that indicates that more time may be needed. The planning team, if there is a problem across grade levels, may decide to revise the time available for teaching a particular subject by reducing the time devoted to other subjects.
- It is important to publicize that curriculum revision doesn't happen on a five or seven year cycle, but the curriculum is updated on a yearly basis.
- Plan an update for the school board
- Schedule curriculum work for the summer. Again a subject area's units, significant tasks, and alignments can be completed in a two week, five hour per day, period. Curriculum revision needs to be scheduled so it doesn't interfere with other curriculum development or summer school.
- Plan how the new curriculum will be introduced in the school s.
- Confirm the roles and responsibilities of teachers and principals in the process.
- Appoint people to lead the roll out of the new curriculum.

The role of the planning team is to have a small number of people leading the project across a number of years so as to be responsible for curriculum development for the district.

CURRICULUM DEVELOPMENT

Although we have done curriculum development in many ways with school districts, the way that has worked the best over the largest number of school districts has been to take two weeks during the summer and work 5 hours a day from 8-1 with no break for lunch. This way, everyone has a half day to do other activities. We have also released teachers in small groups during the year on a monthly or regular basis, but this means that teachers are missing classes and subs need to be hired. Teachers don't seem to concentrate as well during the year, so the process takes longer. This way also requires more supervision, because it is not usually possible to release all grade levels on the same day due to the shortage of substitute teachers. A supervisor (or a trained teacher or consultant) would have to deliver the training.

For the curriculum development, teachers would have to know and be able to do:

- Know the components of the curriculum design (For Balanced Curriculum that would mean that they would need to know the function of units, significant tasks, alignments, and assessments, and know how to enter them on the websites)
- Develop a scope and sequence for the training for 10 days, 5 hours a day. See example below:

Overview of Workshops

Day 1
Overview of Model
Good R/LA program
Ranking Standards
Develop Unit Titles

Day 2
Develop Unit Begin and End Dates
Unit Introductions and Rubrics
Placing unit intros on web -site
Gallery Walk of Unit Titles
Meet with Grade Levels above and below, do deals
Review State Test Gr 3-8

Day 3
Overview of Significant Tasks with Rubric
Print State Standards and Assessments for your grade level
Review Standards and Tests for implications for significant tasks
Placing significant tasks on Web Site, getting standards from web site

Day 4
Continue working on Significant Tasks
End of day meet with grade levels above and below – work on sequence

Day 5
Finish working on Significant Tasks
Role of Validators in validating significant tasks using rubrics

Day 6
Deliver significant tasks to Grade Levels above and below. Share work.
Assignments for proof reading

Day 7
Alignments

Day 8
Continue alignments
Adjust curriculum once it is aligned and the team reviewed the reports.

Day 9
Continue Adjustments
Final check list of checking the curriculum

Day 10
Final Check of curriculum completed
Suggestions for Ramp Up of curriculum in the Fall
Role of Grade Level Teams for Fall
Making comments on the curriculum

- Know how to get reports from the website.
- Provide a generic log on so that those teachers, who are not curriculum authors, can see the progress of curriculum implementation and make comments. (If this option is used, teachers will need training on accessing the website and making comments, which will be completed before the summer work.)
- Assessment can be also be scheduled if time is available. Otherwise, assessments are done during the next year on released time. (The curriculum can go into implementation without common assessments being completed.)
- Teachers working on the curriculum will know about comments and completions.
- Teachers who developed the curriculum are great candidates for leading the in-service activities in the fall when the curriculum is introduced to the rest of the staff. Teachers have felt most comfortable if a script is developed for their presentation to their grade level group. This helps to insure that everyone is hearing approximately the same thing. (The script may be developed by the planning committee, or by volunteers from the curriculum authors.)

IMPLEMENTING THE CURRICULUM – AN INTRODUCTION FOR THE WHOLE DISTRICT

In a large district, the whole staff can meet at a central place (the high school auditorium) to receive an overview, usually delivered by the Superintendent or Curriculum Director. After that grade levels can be assigned to classrooms in the high school or other schools in a district, where the grade level authors of the curriculum can meet with teachers at that grade level and introduce the curriculum and tell how the implementation will be managed and reported to the Planning Committee. Time is set aside for grade level teachers to explore in concert, the curriculum using available computer labs. Lastly, teachers will practice translating significant tasks into lesson plan s, a key skill that all teachers will have to know and be able to do. What classroom teacher s should know and be able to do as a result of this session.

- Roles of the principals in monitoring curriculum implementation will be reviewed as well as additional help that may be available from English/Language Arts Resource personnel.
- Grade level meeting expectations will be reviewed so that all will know how grade level meetings can support curriculum implementation.
- The role of data teams will also be reviewed as they will play a role in monitoring the curriculum implementation.
- Finally, the role of Central Office Staff, such as the curriculum director, special education and ESL supervisor, will be given in support of teachers implementing the curriculum.
- Roles for the Special Education Teachers and ESL Teachers will define how they will use and adapt the curriculum in coordination with the classroom teacher s of Special Education and ESL students. (It is expected that Special Education and ESL students follow the same curriculum with minor modifications).

IMPLEMENTING THE CURRICULUM – ONGOING PROCESSES

Classroom teachers will also be informed about the role of principals in monitoring the curriculum, and using grade level meetings as a way to support curriculum implementation. Principals or English/Language Arts Specialists can help grade levels develop a format for reviewing curriculum progress. One format might be teachers meet at the conclusion of the unit to review what went well and what needs to be improved. Then comments are placed on the web site to let the curriculum authors know about the recommended changes in this particular unit. Or, teachers can meet before the unit to develop plans for addressing the unit. Not everyone needs to address the unit in the same way; at the conclusion of the unit the grade level will come together and discuss their experience in teaching the unit in different ways. If there are meetings among grade level leaders, a calendar can be developed that will specify what units of the curriculum will be addressed.

IMPLEMENTING THE CURRICULUM – PLANNING FOR NEXT SUMMER

Somewhere between January and March, the planning team will want to begin planning for next summer. A look back on the successes and failures of the previous year will help the team capitalize on those things that were done well and those things which need to be improved. They will need to look at whether

- whether the curriculum embedded tests were developed over the school year,
- whether the implementation is having the desired effects,
- recruiting talented authors for the next area of curriculum development,
- determining when authors will meet to revise the next year's curriculum,

- Describing what changes in the summer routine established last year could be improved.

Hopefully, the district feels confident enough so that they can handle the stand up staff development of the summer work themselves. (Districts that have done this, sometimes hire the consultant to assist them in their planning tasks.) Districts will also have to decide whether the manuals provided for the first summer, would be useful in helping to guide curriculum development for the new subject area. Districts may want to consider whether they have enough resources to complete more subject areas, but that also involves hiring more teachers, another resource issue.

CONCLUSION

This chapter has dealt with the complex role of curriculum implementation and further curriculum development. Districts may want to use a consultant to help them through "new" territory with an experienced consultant who can provide a model for developing the curriculum during the first year and helping to plan the second year as the district takes more responsibility for the process.

The book as a whole presents various district led models of curriculum development that have resulted in improved student achievement in Connecticut and across the country. By carefully attending to the ASIA framework (Alignment, the Structure of the Curriculum, Implementation and Assessment) a school district can be assured of making gains in producing student achievement. This can be done with existing teachers and administrators who know best what the needs of the district are, and can incorporate those needs into a district's curriculum, which is, after all, a plan for fulfilling what students know and should be able to do.

REFERENCE

Squires, D.A. (2013). The balanced curriculum model: Description and results. SAGE Open, January-March 2013; vol. 3, 1: 2158244013478012, first published on February 27, 2013.

APPENDIX

SUMMARY OF THE ASIA CRITERIA FOR REFINING OR DESIGNING CURRICULUM PROCESS AND PRODUCT

From Figure 3.2 Alignments

AL-1-Included Is alignment included as a piece of the curriculum design?

AL-2-Standard Way Has a standard way to construct alignment been designed? (For example, from the balanced curriculum, are significant tasks aligned with standards and assessment specifications in a standard way?)

AL-3-State Standards Does the alignment include aligning to state standards?

AL-4-Assessment Specs Does the alignment include aligning to state assessment specifications?

AL-5-Local Testing Aligned Is the local testing aligned with the State assessment specifications?

AL-6-Other Categories Does the alignment include other categories such as Bloom's Taxonomy and/or national standards, or the recently constructed national standards for Reading, Math, Social Studies and Science?

From Figure 4.1 Structures of Curriculum and Stability

Str-1-Content Does the curriculum specify the Content (subject matter) of the curriculum?

Str-2-Time Parameters Are Time parameters used so teachers know how much time should be devoted to particular content?

Str-3-Instructional Process Does the curriculum specify the Instructional Process used to teach the curriculum content?

Str-4 –Alignment Is Alignment included in the curriculum design? (See the Alignment section.)

Str-5 –Assessment Does the curriculum specify the parameters for Assessment? (see the Assessment section)

Str-6-Managed Does the written curriculum design specify how the curriculum will be Managed? (Who is responsible for seeing the curriculum is being completed?)

From Figure 4.2 Stability

> *Stab-1-Stability* Does the district have stability at the upper levels of administration so that a 3 to 5 year curriculum development process can be conceptualized and completed?

From Figure 7.5 Implementation and Infrastructure

> *I-1-Curriculum Focus* Has the district established a common focus on curriculum?
>
> *I-2-Teacher Involvement* Have teachers been involved in the designing and refining the curriculum design or development strategy?
>
> *I-3—Resources* Have appropriate resources been allocated to the curriculum plan? (specifically funding for teacher release time, professional development for teachers and principals, and support staff to assist in and monitor classrooms)
>
> *I-4-Group Support* Has an individualized and team support for teachers and principals on the process of curriculum improvement planning as well as the strategies that are expected to be implemented? Do parents have a role in the process?
>
> *I-5-Plan Written* Is the plan for implementation written down, with processes for evaluating the implementation done on a regular basis?
>
> *I-6 Curriculum Revision* The curriculum is revised and modified on a frequent basis, based on the results of testing.

From Figure 7. 5 Assessment Criteria

> *A-1 –Uniform assessment* Are uniform assessments employed across the curriculum? (Uniform assessments means that everyone who teaches a course gives the same assessments.)
>
> *A-2-Time in Schedule* Is additional time built into the yearly schedule for teachers to use the results of the assessments to re-teach or enrich the curriculum? (Is time provided for reteaching and/or enrichment after, for example, each unit?)
>
> *A-3-Monitor and Evaluate* Is there a way to monitor and evaluate whether the extra time is producing anticipated results?
>
> *A-4-Course Teachers Work Together* Do teachers teaching the same course collaborate on using the test results to improve instruction?

ABOUT THE AUTHORS

David A. Squires, Ph.D.

David A. Squires is a professor at Southern Connecticut State University in the Educational Leadership Department. This is his fourth book. *Effective schools and classrooms: A research-based perspespective* published by Association of Supervision and Curriculum Development in 1982 sold over 80,000 copies. *Aligning and balancing the standards-based curriculum* and *Curriculum Alignment: Research-based Strategies for Improving Student Achievement* in 2005 and in 2009 are published by Corwin Press. He is CEO of ABC Education Consultants, LLC which hosts the Balanced Curriculum, a web based curriculum development tool that focuses on alignment of the curriculum to standards and assessments. Every district that has used and implemented the curriculum using the Balanced Curriculum has seen dramatic improvements in student achievement (see www.balancedcurriculum.com for more information.)

Heather Zavadsky, Ph.D.

Dr. Heather Zavadsky is the director of Ed Practice Connect, an organization created to improve education systems through practice-based actionable research and evaluation. She has over twenty years of experience in education, and her research expertise includes systemic district reform and turnaround, effective human capital strategies, district data and accountability systems, and special education. She recently published her second book on district reform for Harvard Education Press (HEP) entitled "School Turnarounds: The Essential Role of Districts. Prior to her research career, Zavadsky taught for six years in the area of special education, and tutored students with autism. In addition to teaching, she is trained and certified as a principal and superintendent.

Meghan Matins, Ed. D.

Meghan G. Martins is an administrator in the Danbury Public Schools, where she oversees the instructional program for secondary schools. During her time in Danbury, the high school has shown tremendous gains in closing the achievement gap and was recognized by the College Board as a School of Distinction. Before joining Danbury, she taught middle school and adult education in Bridgeport, CT and served as a consultant for the Connecticut State Department of Education where she worked extensively with struggling, urban districts.

Eileen S. Howley, Ed. D.

Dr. Eileen S. Howley is currently the Executive Director of LEARN, a regional educational service center in Old Lyme, CT. Prior to her arrival in December 2012, she served as Assistant Superintendent for Instruction and Curriculum in the West Hartford Public Schools, Interim Superintendent of Schools and Assistant Superintendent in the Farmington Public Schools, Farmington, CT. She also served as the Bureau Chief of Curriculum at the Connecticut State Department of Education (CSDE), a teacher and staff development specialist with Area Cooperative Educational Services, and as a teacher of English in Avon, Connecticut. She has consulted with districts across the state and the country on best practices in instructional improvement and teacher development. She earned her doctorate at the University of Hartford and focused her research on expert teacher development. She earned her Master's degree in Educational Leadership from Central Connecticut State University and her Bachelor's degree from St. Michael's College, Winooski, Vermont.

Sal Corda, Ph.D

Salvatore J. Corda is a former associate professor at Southern Connecticut State University. Prior to that, he was a superintendent of schools in two urban school districts for twenty years. In both instances, student achievement increased in all groups, including a noticeable decreasing in the achievement gap between African American and Hispanic students and their white student counterparts. A member of the Superintendents' Network of the Connecticut Center for School Change for nine years, he was an active participant in the development of instructional rounds chronicled in *Instructional Rounds in Education* (City, E.A., Elmore, R. F., Fiarman, S.E. and Teitel, Lee. 2009.) Dr. Corda is currently an independent consultant working with school districts and schools focusing on creating the capacity for systemic improvement for all students, and does Executive consulting for superintendents and other district and school leaders.

John Keogh

John J. Keogh is a former mathematics teacher and K-12 mathematics curriculum leader for Norwalk Public Schools, Connecticut's sixth largest school district. He is currently working as an educational consultant specializing in providing professional development and developing curriculum in mathematics for all grade levels, and is the lead writer for a new mathematics program aligned with the Common Core State Standards. He also specializes in high school reform, and chairs accreditation teams for the Commission on Public Secondary Schools, a division of the New England Association of Secondary Schools and Colleges. I am currently self-employed after 40 years with Norwalk Public Schools, although I am in the 4th year of a work agreement with Fairfield Public Schools (my biggest job by far in my roll as educational consultant), am employed parttime by Cooperaative Educational Services in Trumbull, and am in the second year of a work agreement with Stamford Public Schools.

Michael J. Wasta, Ph.D.

Michael J. Wasta is a consultant in private practice. Previously Dr. Wasta served as Supetintendent of the Bristol Public Schools in Bristol CT. During his tenure in Bristol, Dr.Wasta led the district through a transformational change process. This comprehensive reform effort resulted in a dramatic improvement in student achievement at the systemic level. Since leaving Bristol, Dr. Wasta has served as a Professional Development Associate for the Leadership and Learning Center providing leadership training thourhgout the country and abroad. Dr. Wasta recently completed a long-term consultation association with the Connecticut State Department of Education. Currently Dr. Wasta provides consultation to districts interested in putting teachers at the forefront of reform.

ABOUT THE WEB SITE

The Balanced Curriculum web site is found at www.balancedcurriculum.com and is used to store curriculum information from participating districts. Use the buttons and the blued hyper links to learn more about the Balanced Curriculum process, services, results, articles and the staff at ABC Curriculum Consultants. Sample courses can be accessed by typing in DEMO as your user name and DEMO as your password. Then choose a course by clicking on "Select Course." To descend to the next level, click on any of the blue hyper links. Click on "Main Menu" to return to the home page.

INDEX

D

F

G

H

I

K

L

M

N